D1263428

DATE DUE

DEC 2 3 1988	
DEC 2 1 1990	DEC 1 1 1989
DEC 2 0 1991	MAR 3 1 1992
	DEC 0 4 2006
MAY 2 8 1996	
DEC 2 3 1999	
APR 1 0 2000	
OCT 1 4 2002	

| UPI 261-2505 | PRINTED IN U.S.A. |

Laboratory Animal Husbandry

Laboratory Animal Husbandry

Ethology, Welfare
and Experimental Variables

by

MICHAEL · W · FOX

State University of New York Press

Framingham State College
Framingham, Massachusetts

Published by
State University of New York Press, Albany
© 1986 State University of New York
All rights reserved
Printed in the United States of America

No part of this book may be used or reproduced in any manner whatsoever
without written permission except in the case of brief quotations embodied in
critical articles and reviews.

For information, address State University of New York Press, State University
Plaza, Albany, N.Y., 12246

Library of Congress Cataloging in Publication Data

Fox, Michael W., 1937
    Laboratory animal husbandry.

    Includes bibliographies and index.
    1. Laboratory animals. 2. Laboratory animals — Behavior. 3. Animals,
Treatment of. 4. Animal experimentation. I. Title.
SF406.F69   1986   636.08'85   85-9766
ISBN 0-88706-137-0
ISBN 0-88706-138-9 (pbk.)

SF
706
F69
1986

About the Author

M ichael W. Fox is a veterinarian and ethologist. His earlier research was on the behavior and development of wolves, dogs, and related canids, and he has served on committees for the Institute for Laboratory Animal Resources and was chairman for the Subcommittee on Laboratory Animal Ethology. He holds degrees in veterinary medicine and doctorates in medicine and ethology from London University. He is currently Scientific Director of the Humane Society of the United States and Director of the Institute for the Study of Animal Problems, Washington, DC.

Table of Contents

Introduction

L aboratory animal husbandry is expanding today beyond the narrow framework of disease control and nutritional problems. Concerns over the physical environment, such as optimal lighting, ventilation, and cage size, were until recently addressed only in relation to disease control. One area of major concern, namely the behavioral and psychological well-being of the laboratory animals, is beginning to receive increasing attention. This is necessary for two reasons. First, on humane grounds: we have ethical responsibilities towards the animals that we use in research. Second, on scientific grounds: *bad* animals — i.e., animals whose physiological and psychological states are not known or are abnormally stressed — mean poor research and, conceivably, poor medical applications.

The effects of captivity on the behavior of wild animals and the stress effects of cage rearing, social and environmental deprivation, or crowding on domesticated and laboratory animals are of particular importance, especially in terms of the development of abnormal behavior (Hediger 1950; Fox 1968). This complex area is of concern to veterinarians in whose care and jurisdiction lies the health and well-being of laboratory animals and to the scientist whose research may be influenced by such effects.

The time is ripe for the application of ethology to laboratory animal care since the basic principles of this new integrative science have been already published (Fox 1975).

Social and environmental experiences early in life can influence development and later behavior, physiology, and disease resistance in all the animal species commonly used in research (Fox 1971). No less profound consequences of domestication and, by analogy, "laboratorification" over several generations must also be understood (Fox 1978); otherwise, the behavioral phenotype of the animal remains as unknown and,

ix

Figure I-1

Standardization of cages, diet, etc. is only the first step towards optimal animal care of good research. These socially isolated cats in barren cages may be behaviorally and physiologically abnormal.

as such, constitutes a significant source of experimental confounding. It is just as important, therefore, to ensure that each animal has an optimal, known, and standardized life history prior to experimentation, as it is important to know that it is healthy and of a particular genetic stock, breed, or species. Otherwise, one may not know what kind of animal one is working with (see Fig. I-1). The issue of *normality* awaits analysis.

This monograph details many influences of the laboratory environment on animal behavior, physiology, and responses to induced diseases, drug tests, and the like. Even routine laboratory procedures may affect the animal adversely in relation to a given experiment and, if not identified and controlled, could either invalidate the findings or lead to erroneous inferences.

Laboratory Animal Science is one of the major journals in the world on laboratory animal care that reflects accurately the current "state of the art," the conceptual orientation, and major priorities of interest and concern. Over 1300 articles that were published in this journal over a period of 10 years (from 1966-1975) were categorized into various subjects. Of these articles, the most frequent papers were on disease diagnosis and control, laboratory animal facility design and ventilation, basic husbandry including nutrition and breeding, basic physiological and biochemical measurements, anesthesia and experimental surgery, animal restraint and animal *models* of certain diseases.

Only a little over one percent of all papers published during this 10 year period had anything to do with applied ethology and psychophysical pathology. A few authors addressed such problems as emotional stress, effects of cage size on behavior and physiology, and other environmental influences on behavioral response to drugs and physiological measurements.

Perhaps such a paucity of studies reflects an underlying lack of training or interest in the behavior and psychology of laboratory animals on the part of scientists. How widespread is the attitude that laboratory animals are unfeeling automata, or the notion that animal care need only address physical well-being since the animals' psychological well-being cannot be objectively determined? Such a *Cartesian* or mechanistic view may be more prevalent among some scientists than others; for example, at an address to the National Council of the National Society for Medical Research, Dr. Dale Schwindaman of the Animal and Plant Health Inspection Service staff emphasized that caged dogs that had formerly run free often develop psychological problems related to the stress of being confined: abnormal stereotyped behavior (repetitive pacing or circling), depression, anorexia, coprophagia (eating feces), self-inflicted injuries, and refusal to eliminate body wastes. Following Dr. Schwindaman's paper, Dr. Bernard Trum, Chief of the New England Primate Center, echoed the Cartesian view, according to Dr. Dallas Pratt (1976), as follows:

> Dr. Trum said that if there were psychological aspects, they were not the animals' but those of the "welfare people . . . ; because the psychological aspects of the animal cannot be measured as well as the physiological." He then continued with the remarkable observation: "You accept the stereotypic action of an animal as being wrong, bad, or something. This is to accept something that is not acceptable. This may be the normal action of that particular animal under the condition which he is kept. It doesn't mean he is unhappy. In fact, he may be the happiest animal in there . . ."

Such a remark may not only be Cartesian in origin but may also stem from ignorance of or indifference toward the sophisticated and objective measures that can be made on an animal's behavior and emotion-correlated physiological reactions. Stereotypic actions are generally regarded by ethologists as a sign of frustration, boredom, or other emotional distress.

Modern innovations with sensors, biotelemetry, and automatic behavioral recording devices have direct application to the field of laboratory animal care, together with the techniques of objective behavioral analysis afforded by advances in ethology (Lehman 1975). Lehman states:

> While it is true that there is a dearth of studies on animals, such a scarcity may not be due entirely to scientists' "Cartesian mechanistic view." It should be emphasized that among the lay public there has been a developing attitude (which manifests itself in some political views) that any research that will not directly aid mankind should not be funded. Researchers applying for grants — to study drinking behavior in rats, or preference in nesting materials, etc., have been turned down for more "relevant" research such as cures for cancer. Thus a re-education of the public as well as some scientists is necessary to emphasize the importance of studying animals so that better use can be made of them, and their general care enhanced through a better understanding of their basic needs, an understanding which will not be forthcoming if the essential and much needed ethological research is not funded or encouraged.

The relevance of ethology to laboratory animal care will be shown in this monograph. For too long, the behavioral-psychological aspects of animal care have been neglected, and it is hoped that this book will stimulate not only interest and concern but also more applied research to improve the care and quality of animals used in biomedical research. This research should reduce the number of animals needed, as well as enhance the validity of research findings derived from them.

I must emphasize that this monograph is not intended to be an exhaustive survey on laboratory animal care, ethology, and welfare. It is a highly selective survey designed to raise more questions than answers concerning the routine care and behavioral needs of laboratory animals and those experimental procedures that may have adverse effects upon either the animal, the research design, or both. Some critics may contend that many of the references cited are biased in favor of the thesis that laboratory animals may suffer physically or psychologically under certain husbandry regimens and that this monograph is so much on the side of the animals that proposed humane reforms, such as endeavoring to make the laboratory environment more "natural" for them, are impractical, naively idealistic, too costly, or simply not necessary. It will be demonstrated, however, that in order to do good research on live animals, the scientist, veterinarian, and laboratory animal technician must all be on the side of the animal and that the many variables adversely affecting both the animal and the experiment must be addressed. Good science and humane ethics are consonant and complimentary.

Acceptance of this view will do much to revolutionize the treatment and husbandry of laboratory animals since it is, in the final analysis, holistic, or integrative, and ethical. Nonholistic or Cartesian (mechanistic and reductionistic) treatment and husbandry, in ignoring the animal's psychological state and environmental and social needs, does not contribute to the real advancement of science and medicine. Regardless of the ethics of subjecting laboratory animals to all forms of physical suffering and psychological distress for the benefit of humanity, Cartesianism undermines the relevance of laboratory animal research, as well as the validity and safety of its applicability to human subjects.

As will be shown in this book, animal research has generally overemphasized the physical aspects of disease and, in the process, has reinforced the kind of medical science and practice that ignores the social, emotional, and environmental aspects of health and "dis-ease". This reductionistic research paradigm is mirrored in the way laboratory animals are cared for: social, emotional, and environmental aspects of their overall well-being are generally ignored. If this were not the case, then all animal research laboratories, research protocols (including toxicity and other safety tests), grant applications, animal models, and research publications would address such questions as: how many animals were kept together; how were they housed, what kind of food were they fed, and how frequently did they receive human contact.

The Institute of Laboratory Animal Resources (*Animal Resources News,* July 16, 1973:3) published the results of a survey of 12 American journals reporting psychological, biochemical, and physiological studies on animals, conducted to assess the adequacy of the environmental history of animals used for research. A total of 191 reports were selected on a random basis from 1968 and 1969 issues of these journals. Seventeen items believed to be either essential or helpful in the description of experimental procedures were selected:

> The frequency of description of each item was: species, 100%; strain, 80%; sex, 61%; weight, 38%; age, 51%; source, 19%; pre-experimental treatment, 6%; method of selection, 6%; type of housing, 15%; number of subjects per cage, 21%; cleaning schedule, 4%; feeding schedule, 4%; type of diet, 36%; frequency of handling, 0.5%; type of bedding, 7%; environmental temperature, 21%; and lighting conditions, 8%. It was concluded that many investigators do not realize the influence of these and other environmental variables on experimental results or at least do not adequately describe the environmental history of animals used for experimentation.

A similar analysis of over 4000 scientific articles published between 1972 and 1974 on psychological, nutritional, physiological, and biochemical studies in which animals were used as subjects was done by Lang and Vesell (1976). There were insufficient details of species and strains used; less than 20 percent of reports mentioned physical factors such as conditioning prior to study, amount of handling, and method of selection for experimental groupings. Some 30 percent mentioned the type of food given and/or frequency of feeding, while less than 10 percent described housing conditions such as the type of bedding, method of cage cleaning, type and size of cage, and population density. Details about other environmental variables such as photoperiod, humidity, ventilation, and ambient temperature were even more sparse. The authors found that investigators generally ignore the impact on experimental results caused by the many variables that can affect their animals, and they observed:

> The omissions . . . suggest that many investigators do not fully recognize the influence of environmental and genetic variables on experimental results, or the fact that failure to give an adequate description of these variables makes it difficult, if not impossible, to duplicate an experiment in other laboratories.

Lang and Vesell (1976) concluded:

> At present we know too little about the normal requirements of most species of animals to recommend a standard or uniform environment or genotype for all experiments of a particular kind. This lack of standards makes it even more important for investigators to be aware of the role that slight variations in the environment or genetic constitution may play in the interpretation of data.

The intention of this book is in part to demonstrate the critical importance of the influence these and other variables have on the quality and validity of animal research, as well as the need to consider these variables in the design of experiments and in the general care of laboratory animals. This book is, therefore, a timely critique of current standards of laboratory animal care and methods of husbandry.

REFERENCES

Fox, M.W., ed. 1968. *Abnormal Behavior in Animals*. Philadelphia: W.B. Saunders.

Fox, M.W. 1971. *Integrative Development of Brain and Behavior in the Dog*. Chicago, IL: Univ. Chicago Press.

Fox, M.W. 1975. *Concepts in Ethology: Animal and Human Behavior.* Minneapolis, MN: Univ. Minnesota Press.

Fox, M.W. 1978. *The Dog: Behavior and Domestication.* New York: Garland Press.

Hediger, H. 1950. *The Psychology of Animals in Zoos.* London: Butterworths.

Pratt, D. 1976. *Painful Animal Experimentation.* New York: Argus Archives.

Lehner, P. 1979. *Handbook of Ethological Methods.* New York: Garland Press.

Chapter 1

The Laboratory Animal Environment: Room for Concern

C oncern over the welfare of laboratory animals used in biomedical and industrial research comes from two different sources. First, since the *animal's welfare* is vital no valid research can be conducted on a sick or stressed animal (unless such variables are deliberately introduced and controlled). Second, inadequate *animal facilities* mean bad research or, at least, questionable conclusions that might be invalidated by or contradicted by similar studies conducted under optimal conditions. Environmental factors affect an animal's functioning at virtually all levels, from endocrine secretion to overt behavior.

Most of the scientific emphasis to date has been upon the physical well-being of the animals, but, the more we learn about behavior and psychology, the more we find that abnormal behavior and psychological stresses do affect the animal physically. The Cartesian mind-body dichotomy and the underlying view that animals are simply physiological machines are still with us; for better science and better research animals, these concepts must be changed.

In spite of environmental and physical standards (cage size, temperature, nutrition, and disease control) and genetic standardization set by national scientific advisory committees, many factors in the realm of behavior and psychology have been totally neglected. Existing standards will be reviewed critically in this monograph, and the concept and feasibility of creating a standardized laboratory animal "model" for biomedical research will be explored.

It is not suprising that, with highly sophisticated and continuously evolving research technology and the development of more advanced and specialized fields of research, the development and sophistication in our knowledge and care of laboratory animals has been hard pressed to keep pace. This may well be attributed to a lack of interest in and funding of

1

research in the field of laboratory animal care and applied ethology. Although clean, some laboratory animal facilities today are in other respects still in the Dark Ages.

Many of the factors that may affect the behavior and physiology of laboratory animals and that, if uncontrolled and unrecognized, may cause doubt to be cast on any research conclusions derived from such animals will be detailed in this monograph. This is not meant to imply that, even though their complexity and variability is of a magnitude hitherto not widely recognized or controlled, it is virtually impossible to do any but the crudest research on animals. The researcher may, for example, decide to introduce certain variables in the experimental design and, by so doing, gain some control and insight over organism-environment interactions. But without squarely confronting these issues, biomedical research with animals may well continue to proliferate and spawn further volumes of questionable data derived from even more questionable animal subjects. This would be an enormous waste of resources, talent, public funds, and animal life.

The life history and environment of each laboratory animal must be known and understood if the research derived from it is to be of any benefit to humanity.

Standardized laboratory animal research models are in vogue today, but their validity is illusory if the husbandry system is not conducive to the animals' physical and behavioral well-being or sufficiently controlled to correct for extraneous stress variables. Consider, for example, a recently terminated chronic lung pollution study: the beagles (the "model" species or "tool") were grossly overcrowded, hyperaggressive, stressed with many years of confinement, and under constant pulmonary irritation caused by their own evaporating urine. Housed for years in small "environmentally controlled" chambers into which known amounts of air pollutants were circulated, the beagles were introduced to so many physical and psychological stresses that the effects of the pollutants on the lungs could not be determined.

This is an extreme example of crude, costly, and ethically questionable research. There are many more in which subtleties in the laboratory animal's psychology and physiology, if ignored or not recognized, will invalidate some or all research conclusions concerning various experimental treatment effects.

Some critics may say that this monograph is too fine grained in its analysis and that the subtle factors described in subsequent chapters that can change an animal so as to influence the results are (a) irrelevant to the studies (b) too complex to control.

In answer to (a), the studies are probably extremely crude and poorly designed, for example, those determining the LD_{50} of a new drug or nonessential commercial product. This type of testing is *not* research; it is product testing or development. There are many factors that can influence the validity of such studies, and to ignore them because the protocols are *standardized* is scientifically and ethically reprehensible. Some of the factors discussed in this monograph must be recognized if any improvements are to be made in such routine use of laboratory animals, as well as in pure or basic research.

In answer to (b), it will be shown that a higher degree of sophistication and standardization in animal care and in the laboratory animal environment is possible. Deliberately including certain natural variables, such as an enriched environment and social groupings, will also enhance validity in several research areas (see Fig. 1-1). But in view of the complexity of interrelated variables, the use of animals in biomedical research, when such variables are not considered, must become a thing of the past. More refined experimental techniques need to be developed and, where possible, alternatives to the use of live animals must be found. There is also a wealth of unanswered questions concerning the husbandry of and behavior of laboratory animals that awaits appropriation of funds to support essential detailed investigation.

The humane concern over the use of animals in research splinters into many factions and ethical points of view. While some condemn all research as unnecessary vivisection, others accept the need for use of animals in biomedical research. Some who speak for animal rights and teach reverence for life are also realists; they do not condemn scientific research outright, but seek to work constructively to improve it for the ultimate well-being of both animals and people. The passage of the Animal Welfare Act in 1966 and subsequent amendments represent major steps toward more sound scientific and humane standards of laboratory animal care. It should be emphasized that concern over the care of laboratory animals also involves effective internal communication between research people and good public relations. In many laboratories, for example, the animal care staff are quite separate from and not involved in the research. This can lead to communication problems. If some variable in the environment is changed — i.e., a new bedding is used or a light is changed — and the investigator is not informed, he may find results in his work for which he cannot account. The animal care staff, not knowing what type of research is being conducted, cannot know what variables might be important and may inadvertently do things that lead to problems with the research. If the investigator cannot

Figure 1-1A

Figure 1-1B

These foxhounds show marked behavioral differences if caged in groups than if caged alone. Differences in blood coagulation are now suspected as being due to such differences in social grouping.

be in complete control of his experimental animals' environment, a method of communicating with the animal care staff must be established and a working protocol agreed upon.

Similarly, animal care staff should advise the investigator if they feel he or she is doing things to the animals that may be inhumane or not in the best interests of good research. It may be less stressful to the animals for the investigator to conduct certain tests in the animal room rather than take the animals to his laboratory, which might even be in another building. Such attention to detail can help reduce extraneous experimental variables.

Laboratory animal veterinarians in the United States have told me about researchers who have allowed a monkey to die from dehydration because it did not learn to drink from a dispenser; not noticed decubiti on a monkey's leg after it was kept in a restraining chair for weeks — the limb eventually had to be amputated; not bothered to monitor body temperature in a baboon anesthetized for over six hours, during which time extremely sophisticated equipment was being used to study its brain activity.

One of the best examples of the often profound ignorance researchers show about the animals they study is provided by Moore and Stuttard (1979). They tell how two behavioral or *Skinnerian* psychologists misinterpreted the greeting behavior of cats under observation as some special, learned, stereotyped behavior that was mystically linked with something called "superstitious" operant conditioning. The observing scientists did not realize this was a natural, spontaneous and species-typical innate behavior elicited by human presence. Scientific paradigms that so distort reality can likewise distort understanding of the animals involved, and they can thus impair empathy and limit the ability and motivation of researchers to provide the animals with appropriate care during and after experimentation. I am not over generalizing or resorting to hyperbole in expressing my concern for laboratory animal welfare and my belief in animals' rights. Dr. Randall Lockwood informs me in a personal communication of a neuropsychologist colleague of his who thought one of his cats had an upper respiratory infection. Dr. Lockwood examined the cat and found that the cat was purring. When he told his colleague that the cat was just purring, his American colleague asked "What is purring?"

Obviously those responsible for animal care cannot also be expected to supervise ongoing experiments by research scientists. Rigorous protocols need to be established, and researchers and students need to be trained in the basic principles of laboratory animal care. Professor Stephen Clark, in his book *The Moral Status of Animals,* observes that, "The religion of science has helped to create the cultural ideal which I have christened the pseudopsychopath, to deaden or to render unrespectable the normal affections and sympathies which we feel as mammals. . . ." That a moral philosopher should speak so vehemently against the scientific establishment and what he feels are the prevailing attitudes towards animals need not be dismissed as entirely antivivisectionist hysteria. There are valid ethical grounds for concern over the uses and treatment of laboratory animals just as there are scientific grounds for concern over their husbandry. The major part of this book will deal with the latter, and in the final chapters the subject of ethics and animal rights will be explored.

That today, laboratory animal care specialists are talking about providing single-caged primates with objects to manipulate, music to listen to, and mirrors and television to watch is a sign of a growing recognition of ethical and scientific concerns from an animal welfare point of view. That such attention and concern for the welfare of laboratory animals has been lacking in the past is a historical fact. That in the past, emphasis has been almost exclusively upon nutrition, reproduction, and diseases may not be so much a reflection of the indifference of scientists, but rather of their immediate priorities. Today, more than ever before, scientists, veterinarians, and others are beginning to recognize the need for more knowledge in the applied, multidisciplinary science of animal welfare. Now that such good progress has been made in nutrition, reproduction, and disease diagnosis, treatment, and prevention, the next priority is the welfare of laboratory animals from an ethological as well as ethical perspective. We are ready now to explore further avenues of improvement for the ultimate benefit of science and humanity and for the immediate benefit of the animals we keep in our animal laboratory facilities for biomedical research purposes.

Chapter 2

Present Standards and Questionable Conditions

How many animals should be placed in the same cage, and how large should the cage be? Should animals of the same or different sex be caged together? How much lighting should they have since some species, like the laboratory rat, are nocturnal? What is the best age to wean offspring, and what is the best litter size for optimal growth and normal development?

These and many other questions that will be subsequently raised have received little objective — i.e., scientific — investigation. Most standards of laboratory animal care, housing, and routine procedures such as cage cleaning and handling the animals seem to have evolved on the basis of intuition and tradition, coupled with economic considerations and convenience to the caretakers.

Spatial Needs

A brief survey of recommended cage sizes for various laboratory species (see Tab. 2-1) reveals a subjective cultural difference in standards, rather than differences according to a sound scientific rationale. The fact that the recommended cage sizes for cats, dogs, and primates in England are double the dimensions suggested by American authorities would logically seem to imply the English and American animals are in some way different. From what we know of these animals, such an interpretation is illogical. This therefore leads one to the obvious conclusion that the entire process whereby cage size requirements are determined is illogical and unscientific. Cage size is probably determined more by

Table 2-1   Cage Size Recommendations

		AGENCIES	
SPECIES	USDA	NIH	UKHO
Mice	—	15 sq. in.	10 sq. in.
Rats	—	—	40 sq. in.
Guinea Pigs	60 sq. in.	60 sq. in.	73 sq. in.
Rabbits	3 sq. ft.	3 sq. ft.	6 sq. ft.
Cats	2½-3 sq. ft.	2½-3 sq. ft.	5½ sq. ft.
Dogs (medium size)	12 sq. ft. according to (to body length)	12 sq. ft.	20 sq. ft.
Monkeys (medium size)	—	4.3 sq. ft. (2½ ft. high cage)	7 sq. ft. (4 ft. high cage)

KEY: U.S.D.A.   United States Department of Agriculture

         N.I.H.   National Institutes of Health

         U.K.H.O.   United Kingdom Health Organization

tradition, economics, and some vague subjective impression about the animal's space requirements.*

Unfortunately, traditions can be changed more easily than can economically dictated constraints. The contruction costs of an animal

---

* *Boot, et al. (Lab. Anim. 19:42-47, 1985) in a study entitled Influence of housing conditions on pregnancy outcome in cynomolgus monkeys, found that those kept alone in larger cages (70 × 70 × 100 cm) had fewer losses of offspring than those housed in pairs in cages of this same size or alone in smaller cages (45 × 45 × 60).*

cage do not, however, increase in proportion to the size of the cage; manufacturing cages may cost more than the materials. So economic constraints, to some extent, are illusory. When cages are machine-made or moulded, the costs of modifying the mass-production assembly line to make larger cages may be prohibitive to the manufacturer unless the increased costs can be passed on to the researcher.

One reason for using small cages is so that more animals can be kept separately or in small groups in a limited amount of space. This may be a false economy since crowding and other social factors may be psychophysiologically stressful, lead to increased aggression, disrupt sexual behavior, and cause other phenotypic changes (see Chapt. 4).

Unfortunately, the cage size tradition is perpetuated by the mass-production system, (as well as by the economics of housing as many animals as possible in a given space) and it may seem unreasonable to discard relatively new and serviceable cages for new and larger ones.* Even so, a radical reformation is needed in the standards of cage size recommended for the various laboratory species on humane grounds. An arboreal or active terrestrial animal should have room in which to swing, leap, or run; in other words, it should be able to satisfy its basic activity drive not its need for "exercise," which is an anthropomorphic view. It should have sufficient space to permit its normal instinctual motor actions to be discharged (see Fig. 2-1).

In the absence of adequate freedom, this activity drive may be discharged in abnormal motor patterns, including the rocking, pacing, weaving, and whirling in carnivores (Fox 1965; Thompson and Heron 1954) and primates (Berkson 1967, 1968; Berkson et al. 1963). Abnormal compulsory regimes may also develop in rodents (Kavanau 1967) and birds (Keiper 1969) as an adaptation to confinement. Such behavior patterns tend to develop their own autonomy (Morris 1966) like an obssesive-compulsive neurosis, and they can lead to physical deterioration and even self-mutilation (Meyer Holzapfel 1968; Tinklepaugh 1928).

Not surprisingly, restricted cage rearing has been shown to have a demonstrable effect on joint mobility. Turnquist (1983) found that caging affects joint mobility in patas monkeys; the earlier in life the confinement, the greater is the effect. In free-range patas, joint mobility stabilizes around 18 months while, in cage-raised animals, it remains high and unstable and continues to vary significantly among more

---

* In some animal facilities, cages for primates have been enlarged by welding two cages together and removing the center panel. This way, the animals have more room, and young ones can be kept in small groups together.

Figure 2-1

Rhesus monkeys in a government research facility with clean but impoverished cage environments.

mature animals. That identical cage confinement greatly increased the variability of joint mobility and, thus, affected animals differently is a paradox only further study can solve.

Cage size per se may not be the only factor responsible for the development of stress and abnormal behavior. Social isolation (see Chapt. 5) and lack of an enriched or varied environment (see Chapt. 7) can also contribute significantly.

TOILET NEEDS

Some animals in small cages, especially dogs and monkeys, cannot satisfy their normal elimination behavior patterns and are forced to defecate and urinate where they live and sleep. This is quite *contranaturem* and a two-compartment cage or a cage with a run is the humane option. Those species with the natural toilet behavior of not eliminating in or near their den or sleeping area should not be forced to do so. Even slatted wood or wire floors allowing feces and urine to pass through may be stressful because the animal is still eliminating in its living area and will be subjected to the odor.

Many laboratory animals can be cage toilet trained to use one particular area for their own health and well-being. Others, forced to live surrounded by their excrement, may develop the vice of eating their own feces (Hill 1966) or drinking their urine.

Direct or indirect (via odor) contamination and irritation by excrement may contribute to an increase or decrease in self-care or grooming. The former can lead to self-mutilation and the latter to skin infections; irritation of ocular and upper respiratory mucous membranes may lead to secondary infections. Regular cage cleaning and provision of bedding may reduce such problems. But with a slatted or wire-mesh floor, such actions will not eliminate the potential psychological stress to the animal from having to evacuate where it sits and sleeps.

Boredom may frequently underlie stool-eating (*coprophagia*) — which is to be differentiated from so-called *refection* in those rodents and lagomorphs that naturally eat their feces. Providing a little straw or hay to play with may reduce this problem in primates; for dogs, a ball or chew toy may suffice. More will be said subsequently on the need to enrich the sterile, stimulus-deprived cage.

Recently acquired animals that have lived free may react to cage confinement by refusing to urinate and defecate, and they soon become susceptible to further complications — i.e., cystitis, constipation, general malaise, lowered resistance to disease, and refusal to eat or anorexia. Confinement stress may be alleviated by increasing the cage size to provide sufficient space for various behavioral needs and natural functions. To deny this is to abdicate one's ethical responsibilities toward laboratory animals. They should be assured the best facilities possible, designed with scientific expertise and concern for their socio-environmental needs and right to humane treatment. If economic considerations make such a proposal unpalatable, no animals should be kept. The scientific rationale for this, that inadequately housed and stressed animals are of little value of research, will be elaborated upon subsequently (see Chapts. 3 and 8).

CONFINEMENT EFFECTS

Few studies have been done on the immediate and long-term effects of captivity per se on wild animals kept in laboratory cages for research purposes. The following summary of Steyn's (1975) study of the effects of captivity on wild baboons clearly illustrates that the stresses of cage confinement are significant and relatively long lasting:

> Baboons were trapped and transported to the colony within 3 days of being captured. Blood was collected on Tuesdays and Fridays for blood chemical determinations. The changes in albumin and globulin resulted in marked changes in the albumin: globulin ratio. Cholesterol values showed a sudden and marked drop and the values were still below normal at the end of 9 weeks. Blood sugar values increased to significantly elevated levels and marked changes occurred in the enzyme activity and plasma corticosteroid activity. Male and female animals differed in their response with regards to the values found in some parameters. A period of adaptation or conditioning of 8 weeks was found to be required for an animal to reach stability in its blood chemical values.

A wide range of behavioral abnormalities and changes in temperament and emotionality have been described in primates and other laboratory animals and attributed to cage confinement (Fox 1965; Krushinski 1962; Mitchell 1970; Sackett 1968; Thompson 1967). Cage confinement may not only increase abnormal stereotypic behaviors (see Fig. 2-2) but it may also cause increased timidity (Krushinski 1962). This, in turn, may lead to fearfulness and defensive-aggressive reactions when the animal is handled, making routine handling and restraint difficult — and sometimes dangerous — for both personnel and the animals. Increased aggression in a confined animal and in a crowded animal facility may be a pathological hypertrophy of the normal territorial defensive behavior (Hediger 1950), again making the animal extremely difficult to handle.

Cage confinement may also lead to other behavior *hypertrophies* such as *hyperphagia* and *polydipsia* (increased eating and drinking), which have been described in socially isolated rhesus monkeys (Miller et al. 1969). More extreme confinement, limiting physical activity for extended periods in constraining chairs, slings, and stocks, will rapidly produce gastric ulceration in a number of species (Ackerman et al. 1975; Ader and Plaunt 1968) or produce other stress reactions that may be detrimental to a given experiment if not controlled.

As a humane alternative to the primate restraining chair, several research institutions now use a jacket and swivel-tether system (see Fig. 2-3) to permit chronic monitoring, sampling, and infusion techniques (see McNamee et al. 1983). However, according to Kaplan et al. (1983), the heart rates of chair-restrained monkeys are elevated, indicative of physical discomfort and emotional distress. In over 80 percent of the

Figure 2-2

Confinement evoked stereotyped circling in a laboratory beagle.

animals studied following their attachment to a tether, heart rate measurements eight and 10 days following attachment was substantially elevated over pre- and postattachment periods. And of four monkeys tethered for a month or more, three failed to show heart rate declines to pre-tether levels. Beta-adrenergic blockade demonstrated that this was due to sympathetic arousal. Thus, even if several weeks' habituation are allowed, disturbances from tethering may persist.

Cage size has been demonstrated conclusively to be an important factor in environmental enrichment for rodents (Manosevitz and Pryor 1975). This study by psychologists using refined behavioral measures contrasts with a preliminary study of the effects of cage size on physical activity in beagles (Neamand et al. 1975). In the latter study, no significant effects were found. Investigators should be aware of the fact that unitary measures of behavior, such as activity, alone may be inadequate

Figure 2-3

An example of a more humane "replacement" alternative to the primate-restraining chair. This rhesus monkey has an "umbilicus" through which it may be injected at intervals without having to be forcibly restrained for long periods.

to evaluate the effect of a given environmental variable such as cage size. Multiple measures, including the frequency of occurrence of various behaviors, are often needed before significant differences can be demonstrated (Richter 1971). The limitations of using a single measure is exemplified by one study (Newton 1972) in which long-term confinement in beagles was found to have no significant effect on the musculoskeletal system (determined by calcium-47 kinetic analysis and assays of myofibrillar-specific enzymes). Such a study should not be used to support the notion that confinement in small cages has no effect on beagles. One would anticipate that musculoskeletal effects would only be identifiable following actual physical immobilization. However, young primates raised in small cages may show a retardation in motor development and manifest considerable deficit in locomotor coordination; and musculoskeletal and behavioral anomalies in farm livestock as a consequence of long-term confinement have been well documented (Fox 1983a).

Inferring cause-effect relationships from correlations between unitary measures amounts to bad research. One example of this is the unpublished doctoral dissertation of a student from a large state university. He found that dogs kept in very small cages run faster in maze-learning tests. Since these dogs performed better than dogs kept in larger cages, he concluded from this unitary measure and illogical correlation that confinement may not be detrimental — it may even be good for animals. That confinement might increase activity — rather than enhance performance — when the animals are finally free was never considered.

Fortunately, not all studies on cage effects are so poorly designed and narrowly conceived. Further studies and behavioral effects will be discussed in Chapter 5.

CAGE VARIABLES

Different cage designs can influence reproductive performance and body weight of laboratory mice. Eisen (1974) in summary reported as follows:

> A study was conducted on the effect of two cage regimes on the reproductive performance and growth rate of a random bred stock of mice derived from a four way cross. There was no effect of the cage regime on dam fertility, number born and percent preweaning mortality. Mean body weights of standard litters of six mice at 12 days of age were significantly greater in the polypropylene cages than in the wire cages. Mean body weights of males and females at weaning (21 days), 42 and 56 days of age were also significantly greater in the polypropylene cages. Phenotypic variances and coefficients of variation of 56-day body weight were larger in the wire cage regime for both males and females.

One useful study (Serrano 1971) compared the effects of cage covers, population, and activity on carbon dioxide and ammonia levels in mouse cages. In summary:

Figure 2-4

A considerable and potentially stressful build-up of ammonia can occur in closed propylene rodent cages (here shown with automatic water dispensers) when the cage lids are semipermeable pathogen filters. Frequent cage cleaning and low density stocking per cage are indicated.

To determine the effect of rod, wire-mesh, and fibrous-filter types of covers on diffusion or convection of gases produced in the cage, groups of 4, 8 or 16 mice were placed in cages, and samples of air from each cage were analyzed daily. Filter and mesh covers had a major influence on the composition of air in the cages, allowing the accumulation of CO_2, NH_3, and probably other gases to levels considerably higher than in cages with open covers. When the mice were active, or when the number of mice in the cage was doubled, the CO_2 level increased 50-100% above the original level determined for each cage cover. NH_3 was not detected until the 3rd to 6th day, depending on the number of mice per cage, and by the 7th day reached noxious levels under some covers. Limiting the number of mice per cage and frequently removing soiled bedding could prevent excessive levels of CO_2 and NH_3 from accumulating in protectively covered cages.

Routine cage cleaning therefore must be adjusted to the kind of cage system used.

Raynor et al. (1983) have shown that for rats in polycarbonate cages with filter covers contact bedding is useful in controlling ammonia production and that a raised perforated floorwalk insert significantly reduces the aerolization of bedding particles that the rats can inhale or ingest. This is important not only to improve the animals' microenvironment and reduce ocular and respiratory tract irritation that leads to increased susceptibility to respiratory disease (Broderson et al. 1976) but it is also advisable because contaminants in bedding can produce estrogenic activity (Weisbroth 1979).

In addition, pesticide residues in the shavings of treated wood, and endogenous volatile hydrocarbons in wood-derived bedding materials can act as inducers of liver miscrosomal enzymes (Vessel et al. 1976).

Different bedding materials can have profound effects on the reproductive performance of mice. Itturian and Fink (1968) reported:

> Pregnant mice exhibit a definite preference for a processed sawdust bedding material as opposed to a commercial deodorized cellulose. Thirty-nine percent of the mice forced to give birth on the cellulose bedding moved the nest when presented the opportunity. Nest moving did not occur in mice housed on sawdust. Furthermore, mice housed on the cellulose produced smaller litters, had diminished lactation, and the percentage of the progeny weaned was decreased.

More will be said on habitat preferences and more natural cage systems in Chapter 8.

Greenman et al. (1983) have shown that cage position is a significant variable affecting growth and food consumption. Body weight gains were lowest on the top shelf, highest on the next two shelves and became progressively lower as the shelf approached the lowest level on the rack. Differences in ambient temperature and illumination from shelf to shelf may account for these cage-position variables.

Cage design, specifically the type of flooring has a significant effect on muscle metabolism. Rats on wide grating (large spacing of floor grating as in a metabolic cage) show higher levels of creatine phosphokinase than rats kept on solid floors or on gratings with smaller openings (Frolich et al. 1981). Wide gratings may either cause muscle damage or enhance muscle tonus, the maintenance of balance acting as a form of endurance training or a potential stressor.

Obeck (1978) has implicated galvanized caging as a potential factor in the development of the *fading infant* or *white monkey* syndrome in rhesus macaques. Four offsprings in galvanized closures developed achromotrichia, alopecia, and weakness. Plasma copper values were depressed, while plasma zinc and liver zinc levels were significantly elevated compared to healthy controls housed in stainless steel cages.

Newton (1978) emphasizes that sanitation of animal rooms has implications beyond the control of overt disease. For example, liver enzyme systems are affected in rats that are in contact with different kinds of bedding and are kept in wire cages over dirty pans — for example, see Vessel et al. (1973).

Hidden diseases may be exacerbated due to stress synergism. One relationship of particular concern is the stress effects of cage ammonia and *Mycoplasma pulmonis* in rodents, which cause chronic respiratory disease, a potentially serious experimental variable.

Few studies have as yet been done on such questions as providing bedding or nesting material to satisfy certain behavioral/manipulative needs, particularly for rodents. In one government laboratory, a researcher showed me what he considered to be a fascinating behavioral phenomenon in his hamsters. Each hamster collected and piled its chow in one corner of its wire-mesh and wire-floored cage. When these piles were disturbed, they would quickly hoard every piece together again in a neat stack. In this example, the normal hoarding behavior may have undergone a pathological hypertrophy.* The hamsters could do nothing else since the cage system provided neither litter nor nesting material, which should have been provided for such highly manipulative and naturally nest-making rodents. For sanitation and ease of cleaning, the wire-mesh floored cages are preferred in many laboratory animal facilities. This is certainly a questionable choice since the absence of material to manipulate deprives the animal of stimulation and may lead to behavioral stress and the development of compensatory stereotyped actions.

Ethostasis

The concept of *ethostasis* is relevant here. By ethostasis I mean the adaptive execution of certain behaviors by the animal that help bring about and maintain physiological homeostasis and overall well-being. An animal, in order to maintain physiological homeostasis or regulation may execute certain behavior patterns. If the execution of adaptive behavior patterns is thwarted, then ethostasis would be impaired, and physiological homeostasis may not be maintained. Abnormal behavior, such as stereotypic actions, may bring about physiological homeostasis. But to conclude that the animal is normal when it is showing stereotypic behavior on the basis of an absence of demonstrable physiological abnormalities is illogical. This is like saying that a person who compulsively overeats because of some emotional anxiety is acting adaptively and is

---

*a phenomenon termed "hypertrophy of valency or values" by H. Hediger (1950).

perfectly normal if no physiological (metabolis/endocrine) anomalies can be demonstrated. Behavioral changes should be the first level of analysis and concern, but, too often, the significance of behavioral abnormalities are overlooked since there is a greater reliance and significance placed upon physiological indices and pathophysiological signs. As in the phenomenon of ethostasis, behavioral and physiological changes may not correlate: wherever possible, multiple measures (behavioral and physiological) should be made to evaluate the health and normality of the whole organism. Analysis of one system alone — e.g., blood profile or plasma cortisol level — does not tell us much about the whole organism.

It is indeed a major challenge to the laboratory animal scientist to sort out which physiological functions and behavioral indices may be used as diagnostic criteria of poor housing and social stress, and, as emphasized in this book, there is a wealth of unanswered questions in this field that warrants further research.

It is difficult to define normal behavior without knowing what the animal is like in the wild. Rather than rely upon testing laboratory animals to decide what is normal, one should incorporate studies of animals in their natural environment. One could then predict settings in which animals might be maintained more comfortably (e.g., if one knows that an animal in nature has a burrow and is nocturnal, one might question the practice of keeping such an animal in a cage constantly exposed to light without an area of relative darkness in which the animal can sleep).

Other factors in the laboratory animal surroundings including chemicals in the food and bedding and those used for sanitary purposes (Cass 1970), can have profound effects upon any research done on sick, contaminated, or otherwise chemically or phenotypically modified laboratory animals. The few studies that have been done on such problems demonstrate that laboratory living can greatly alter the animal's phenotype (Wagner 1971). Such laboratorification processes must be understood and controlled since they can, like physical diseases and other phenotypic anomalies (Festing 1977), confound the interpretation of research findings.

Lighting Effects

Light is an often neglected aspect of the animal's environment. One of the best illustrations of this is the discovery that albino rats become blind because of the intensity of light to which they have been exposed in the animal room (Weisse et al. 1974; see also Weihe 1976; Lay et al. 1978; Bellhorn 1980; Chignell et al. 1981; and Clough 1982 for literature reviews on the effects of light on animals' development, physiology, biochemistry and pathology).

In many animal laboratories, all albino animals may be blind since they lack a protective retinal pigment. A luminance of 30-foot candles or less is optimal; 150-foot candles can cause permanent damage within a week (Robinson and Kuwabara 1976; Ott 1974). Cage position effects in the typical "rat rack" setup may be aggravated in those rats in the top cages that are exposed to direct fluorescent or incandescent lighting (see Fig. 2-5). Indirect lighting below 30-foot candles is clearly indicated if researchers want to work with relatively normal-sighted rodents. How many researchers unknowingly use blind animals, and how this laboratory environmentally induced disorder affects the animals' behavior and physiology is impossible to tell without further research. We do know, however, that diurnal variations of illumination can produce potentially confounding effects; for example, continuous light may also over stimulate the reproduction system.

The effects of various light intensities can be dramatic. Porter et al. (1963) reported that when the cage lighting level was reduced from 500 lx to 5 lx, preweaning mortality rates in mice declined from 50 percent to 5 percent. However, many domestic strains of mice may be adapted to abnormally high light intensity. Bronson (1979) found that wild mice at 1000-2000 lx showed reproductive impairment while laboratory-bred mice were unaffected.

Photoperiodicity, the dark-light circadian cycle of illumination, affects breeding cycles in many mammalian species. A 12-hour light/12-hour dark cycle is linked with a four day estrus cycle in Sprague-Dawley rats, which increases to five days or more under a 16-hour light/eight-hour dark cycle (Hoffman 1973). Photoperiodically linked physiological activities can be disrupted by switching on the lights even for a short time during the dark cycle in several species (Clough 1982), a finding that necessitates the avoidance of any such disruptions by janitors and other laboratory staff working in the evening.

Stoskopf (1983) has emphasized that phototransition is one frequently neglected environmental stress on animals. He concludes that a sudden switch from light to dark and vice versa, without a natural transition of decreasing or increasing illumination, "may have considerably more impact upon the biological and physiological well-being of a captive animal than a simple startle response at the transistion. Improper

Figure 2-5

A cage system for mice, illustrating a marked difference in cage illumination from top to bottom of the racks.

transition can effectively eliminate important activities or modify them into ineffective parodies of the original behavior.''

Light wavelength has been shown to affect wheel running in mice (Spalding et al. 1969). Albino mice are more affected than black mice, but all mice are more active in darkness and red light, least active in blue, green, and day light and showed intermediate levels of activity in yellow light. Saltarelli and Coppola (1979) found that different types of fluorescent light, such as ultraviolet, cool white, full spectrum, pink, blue, and black, affect organ weights in mice in general and total body weight in male, but not female, mice.

From such findings, it is clear that it is important to know under what conditions foundation breeding stock are maintained by commercial breeding establishments that supply animals to research institutions. Genetic drift and phenotypic changes over generations, as well as the incongruities between the conditions under which commercial breeding stock are maintained and experimental animals housed, need further definition and attention.

The effects of electromagnetic energy waves as an environmental contaminant of the laboratory animal research facility warrant further evaluation (Mulder 1978).* Mulder summarized his review on this subject as follows:

> Reports in the literature vary with respect to the effects of electromagnetic energy waves on animal behavior. Factors considered in this review include visible and invisible light, plus variations in duration, intensity, and quality of light exposure. Reproductive ability, sex ratio of newborn, animal activity, and length of life were reported to be altered. Investigators describing seemingly similar conditions reported wide variations in results. Well documented and controlled research is needed to accurately measure the effects of light upon animal behavior.

Effects of Noise

Gamble (1982) emphasizes the fact that exposure of sound can stress animals and the consequences can be apparent for several weeks. Furthermore, the importance of holding purchased animals for a period of time in the experimental situation before use, or using homebred animals in situations as close as possible to those in which they were bred, needs to be recognized. Gamble highlights his extensive review on the effects of sound on laboratory animals with the following points:

1. Several methods of varying accuracy have been used to assess what sounds small laboratory animals such as rodents are capable of hearing. Most rodents can detect sounds from 1000 Hz (the frequency of the Greenwich Time Signal) up to 100000 Hz, depending on the strain, with usually one or more commonly two peaks of sensitivity within this range. Dogs can detect sound most easily from 500 Hz to 55000 Hz, depending on the breed.

---

*see also I.B. Arieff, "Microwaves: the silent invaders," Environmental Action (March 11-13, 1977).

2. Rodents also produce sound signals as a behavioral response and for communication in a variety of situations. Ultrasonic calls in the range 22000-70000 Hz are the main communicating pathway during aggressive encounters, mating, and mothering. Similar calls have also been recorded from isolated animals associated with inactivity, rest and possibly even sleep.

3. Very loud sounds cause seizures in rats and mice, or can make them more susceptible to other sounds later in life. This effect is possible even when animals are fully anaesthetized. Sound tends to startle and reduce activity in several species of animal. Even offspring of mice that have been sound-stressed exhibit abnormal behaviour patterns. Sound also elicits various responses in rats from increasing aggression to making them more tolerant to electric shocks.

4. Levels of sound above 100 dB are teratogenic in several species of animals and several hormonal, haematological and reproductive parameters are disturbed by sounds above 10 dB. When rats are chemically deafened the disturbance to their fertility disappears. Lipid metabolism is disrupted in rats when exposed to over 95 dB of sounds, leading to increase in plasma triglycerides. Atherosclerosis can be produced in rabbits by similar levels of sound.

5. It has also been shown in guinea pigs and cats that hearing damage is governed by the duration as well as the intensity of the sound and is irreversible. Work on chinchillas has demonstrated that sounds above 95 dB lead to this injury but that sounds of 80 dB have no permanent effect on hearing sensitivity.

Since the majority of laboratory animals have hearing thresholds quite different from humans, generally being insensitive to lower frequency sounds and being acutely sensitive to higher frequencies beyond our hearing ability, the importance of sound in the environment can be easily neglected. Reviews on this subject by Gamble (1982), Peterson (1980), Fletcher (1976), and Pfaff (1974) provide good documentation to support the need for greater attention to this environmental factor. Sudden noises, such as the clatter of metal cages being cleaned, can cause a 100-200 percent increase in plasma corticosterone in rats, while noise or music may be of value in protecting animals from extraneous sounds outside the animal room. Music has a recognized calming effect on farm animals, and studies have shown that rats reared with continuous music by Mozart subsequently preferred Mozart over Schoenberg. Rats raised with Schoenberg's less melodic and atonal music showed no preference for either, nor did rats raised with either continuous white noise or repeated 4KHz tone-bursts, when given a choice between the latter and the former (Oswalt et al. 1973). High frequency sounds from gas cylinders and recording devices can affect brain physiology and biochemistry, trigger seizures, or cause audiosensitization (Clough 1982).*

Thermal Influences

Thermal influences on laboratory animal husbandry and experimentation are both subtle and complex (Clough 1982). Ambient temperatures need to be recorded and controlled, especially in pharmacological, toxicological, and teratological studies. Variations in drug toxicity attributed to differences in cage population densities — i.e., crowding stress — may be due to differences in thermoregulation (Weihe 1973). It should also be emphasized that metabolic adaptation to a change in ambient temperature, as when animals are placed in new quarters, can take several weeks. Cage design, the presence or absence of bedding, and the number of animals per cage also influence the stability of the microenvironment within the cage.

Changes in body or core temperature in rats can be influenced by such factors as circadian rhythm, handling, stormy weather, and the presence of unfamiliar people entering the animal room; fewer variations in body temperature were recorded on nonworking days (Georgiev 1978).

Ambient temperature and humidity has a significant effect on the immune response mechanism. Rao and Glick (1977) found that chicks exposed to cold (45 °F) significantly increased antibody levels, while higher temperatures had a depressant effect. Mimicking natural circadian variations in ambient temperature, with a cooling off in the evening (where appropriate for the species) may be optimal and advisable for the proper husbandry of laboratory animals.

Ambient relative humidity plays a significant role in animals' thermoregulation, affecting food intake, general activity, and disease patterns. Low humidity is linked with ringtail disease in rodents, while high humidity potentiates ammonia production, both factors are linked to respiratory disease (Broderson et al. 1976). The viability of airborne microorganisms is generally lowest at a relative ambient humidity of 50 percent (Anderson and Cox 1967).

---

* Monitoring ultrasonic distress vocalizations of rodents could be a useful quantifiable indice of stress, such sounds being emitted by caged rats, for example, while others are being handled, injected, and experimented upon in the same room (David Secord, personal communication). Clearly such manipulations should not be done in the animal colony room, since they appear to cause distress to other animals.

Ventilation

Clough (1982) and Teelman and Weihe (1974) have provided a detailed review on air movement, which influences animals' thermoregulation as well as ambient humidity and temperature. More research is needed on this subject to develop environmentally engineered systems to provide for more even airflow regulation and monitoring thereof within animal rooms. Airflow is affected by the kinds of cages used (some types can cause deflection of airflow), cage position, and the convective air currents around the cages generated by animals' body heat. Air movement through metal ductwork diffusers and air conditioners influences the ionization of the air itself. Pollution-free air contains some 800-1100 positive ions and 600-900 negative ions per cm^3, while animal quarters have much lower levels (125 $\pm$ 20% positive and 110 $\pm$ 20% negative ions per cm^3) according to Krueger et al. (1971).

Forced ventilation systems, metal fixtures, plastics, dust particles, and lack of sunlight affect air ionization, causing a decrease in negative ions and a proportionate increase in positive ions. Such changes have been shown to adversely affect the growth, behavior, and disease resistance in animals (Krueger et al. 1974). Under controlled studies, the airborne transmission of Newcastle's disease virus from infected birds to healthy birds in adjacent cages was prevented by increasing the negative ion concentration in the air (Estola et al. 1979). The question of air ionization in laboratory animal housing, and the influence of fluorescent strip lighting on health and behavior (Ott 1974) warrant greater attention.

Studies have shown that spontaneous activity and learning ability in animals are influenced by air ionization, a high level of positive ions impairing short- and long-term memory in rats (Oliverean and Lambert 1981). Ion depleted air increases susceptibility to various respiratory infections such as PR8 influenza virus, *Coccidioles immitis* and *Klebsiella pneumoniae,* while higher concentrations of negative ions, or low concentrations of mixed charge with a predominance of negative ions, reduced mortalities (Krueger and Reed 1972).

Circadian Rhythms

Circadian (diurnal) rhythms can also have significant effects on behavior and physiology (Menacker 1969). The basic circadian rhythm of the animal is normally "in phase" with the laboratory light cycle (Richter 1971), and careful consideration should always be given to the fact that in many nocturnally active species, particularly rats, most studies are done during the daytime, which is their nighttime. Behavior, metabolism, and other processes may be quite different between daytime and nighttime. Reactions to infections and drugs may also vary as a result of the time of exposure or treatment.

In wild rodents and squirrel monkeys (compared with inbred laboratory rats) the activity rhythms of the people with whom they are in contact have a marked effect on their behavior. Seven-day cycles in spontaneous activity were reported (Richter 1976) as a consequence of the weekend reduction in human activity in and around the animal facility. The postweekend "Monday morning syndrome" in laboratory animals and personnel alike may be a significant variable in some experiments.

Fuller et al. (1978) have reported marked differences in cold response among squirrel monkeys kept at 28 °C under a light regimen of 12 hours light and 12 hours dark and others kept under constant light. When exposed to a reduced temperature of 20 °C for six hours, the latter did not adapt well and their body temperatures fell by about 1 °C. This is the first evidence of animals being unable to regulate a body function in the absence of circadian time cues, and it serves to emphasize how certain environmental variables may influence seemingly unrelated physiological processes.

In addition to other social variables detailed in Chapter 4, colony lighting conditions may influence the frequency of home-cage aggression in rodents (Kane and Knutson 1976), and the amount of day length can influence the rate of sexual development in mice (Drickamer 1974).

Ader (1965) showed that rats forcibly restrained during the peak of their circadian activity cycle were more likely to develop extensive gastric ulceration than if restrained during the low phase of their cycle. Ader concluded that the existing psychophysiological state of the animal is a major determinant of the response to some superimposed stimulation. Rats may thus perceive restraint as being especially intense during the peak of their activity cycle, a subjective factor that Ader's work revealed since the same degree of restraint during the low activity phase was less stressful.

Romero (1967) highlights the major effects of diurnal cycles on biochemical parameters of drug sensitivity studies in rodents, using research on the pineal gland as a model example. He states:

> Diurnal cycles in physical parameters in the environment modulate biochemical and physiological circadian rhythms in experimental animals, including cycles in the sensitivity to external influences. Environmental lighting synchronizes cycles of indole metabolism and melatonin synthesis in the rat pineal gland by modulating the activity of postganglionic sympathetic nerves. As a consequence, the sensitivity of

pineal N-acetyltransferase to stimulation by isoproterenol or by dibutyryl cyclic AMP varies diurnally. Also the capacity of actinomycin D to inhibit this induction varies with circadian periodicity. The cycles in sensitivity to isoproterenol reflect cycles in the system that regulates cyclic AMP production, and include variation in the availability of specific β-adrenergic binding sites, and in the sensitivity of receptor-coupled adenylate cyclase to catecholamines. Further, a variation in the response to dibutyryl cyclic AMP indicates in addition the participation of intracellular controls in the regulation of the sensitivity of N-acetyltransferase to catecholamines. The varying sensitivity to actinomycin D suggests a changing requirement for the synthesis of RNA as a function of prior environmental lighting conditions. The basic nature of these sensitivity changes suggests that diurnal cycles of environmental lighting may similarly affect other systems.

Feeding Rhythms

Two other studies point to additional sources of experimental variability. Constant — ad lib or free — feeding of rodents may not be natural. A wild animal has to forage for food and may be subject to intermittent periods of food shortage. Black-hooded rats have been shown to have a longer life-span after a regimen of intermittent fasting and feeding (Kendrick 1972).

Recent studies of animals in zoos, such as macaque monkeys, have shown that if their chow is scattered on the floor — ideally in hay or straw bedding — they have to spend more time working to find their food and, consequently, they spend less time in boredom-related activities such as stereotyped movements. There may also be a reduction in aggressive interactions. Hediger (1950) has been a strong advocate for providing captive animals with "work" in order to relieve the monotony of cage life.

Dietary Variables and Commercial Testing

Dietary requirements of laboratory animals have, to some extent, been well researched. Nutrition may affect social stability in group-housed animals; aggression levels in rats, for example, is influenced by the amount of Vitamin A in the diet.

Both diet and type of intestinal bacteria or flora are potential experimental variables that must be controlled in a variety of experiments. The nature of the diet influences the prevalence of certain microflora, for example, there are more *Clostridium welchii* with a high meat diet, more *lactobacilli* with a high grain diet. These variables can influence the toxicological and pharmacological effects of drugs.

Dietary contaminants such as aflatoxins from mouldy feed, nitrosamines in fish meal and enterobacterins in food may act as immunosuppressants or favor the growth of certain intestinal bacteria. The interrelationship between the external (laboratory) and internal (organismic) environments are extremely complex. Laboratory animal ecology clearly extends far beyond the microcosm of the animal in its cage.

Fouts (1976) expresses the following concerns over dietary variables:

> Few experimentalists seem to attach much importance to the standard feed that is used for either control or treated animal groups. Routine and regular monitoring of animal feed for food additives or contaminants is seldom done, and variation in composition of all components and contaminants from batch to batch of food and from one laboratory to another may well account for significant differences in animal responses to experimental manipulations — in terms of not only drug metabolism, but all other parameters, affecting animal responses, including cell receptor activities. The point then is not that diet is important and can have great effects, but rather what can and do we do about diet either to make diet a reproducible factor in our experiments or to minimize it as a source of effect?

The additional variables of social isolation, competition over food acquisition, and the biological value of a given diet warrant further study. These variables are particularly important when an animal, prior to testing, becomes anorexic because it is put on a different diet or is not adapted to its new cage environment or is not accustomed to being caged alone. It may be even more important in a chronic toxicity, carcinogen, or drug assay study since, if the animal becomes wholly or partially anorexic, nutritional imbalances and deficiencies may influence the treatment effects and lead to erroneous conclusions. Loading a rat with large doses of a test substance orally or via injection must be accompanied by rigorous monitoring of body weight and food consumption, and, where anorexia is a problem, highly palatable and concentrated dietary formulations may be needed. This aspect of good laboratory practice has long been neglected in the routine screening of drugs and other chemicals by commercial testing laboratories.

In a report on the control of diets in laboratory animal experimentation (Institute for Laboratory Animal Resources (ILAR) 1978) the following environmental factors were emphasized:

> Many other environmental factors can also affect a nutrition experiment. Most caged rodents practice coprophagy extensively. Even when kept in cages with raised wire floors allowing fecal material to drop into

the collecting pans, rats will consume fecal pellets as they are being voided. To prevent coprophagy completely, rats should be kept in cages that restrict them from turning or they should be fitted with tail cups to prevent access to fecal pellets. When coprophagy occurs, the intake of drugs under study can be altered by the recycling of fecal material. Certain vitamin deficiencies such as those of folic acid, biotin, and vitamin K are very difficult to produce in rats unless coprophagy is completely prevented or unless an antibacterial agent is used to prevent their synthesis by the gut flora.

The size and type of cage and the number of animals in each cage can affect experiments. Bedding materials may be consumed by animals that are kept in cages without raised wire floors. Although some species, such as mice, are usually kept with bedding, one must recognize that bedding can be a source of environmental contamination. It is inconsistent to feed animals highly purified diets and then keep them in environments where other sources of contamination are uncontrolled. Zinc-deficient animals, for example, can obtain significant amounts of zinc from galvanized metal cages and from rubber stoppers in water bottles.

Other environmental factors in rooms where animal experimentation is conducted can have important nutritional consequences. Ambient temperatures or ventilation drafts may affect energy needs and, thus, food intake of laboratory animals. Lighting cycles can affect food intake patterns, which in turn affect daily rhythms of certain enzyme systems. Similarly, the schedule of feeding or handling of laboratory animals may affect daily rhythms.

Drinking water can be an important source of both contaminants and chemical elements in an animal experiment. A careful investigator should be aware of the composition of the water supply, especially in experiments with minerals.

According to Tucker (1984), special low-calorie diets or a rationed food delivery system are needed for long-term studies in rodents since she found that overnutrition was a common problem, leading to gonadal atrophy, myocardial fibrosis, fatty degeneration of the liver and increased incidence of tumors.

Some examples of certain routine animal care practices and factors in the laboratory environment that need to be recognized and controlled as extraneous experimental variables will be given in the next chapter.

Chapter 3

Experimental Variables

A major problem in using animals in research is that, in the course of an investigation, certain variables may be unwittingly introduced because of the method of investigation. Such variables may have a direct influence upon the animal's response to a given treatment, and the difficulties in controlling such variables may seem insurmountable; however, they should not be ignored. The levels of plasma cortisol (a stress-related hormone) levels in rats, for example, will differ significantly between the first and the last animals taken out of a colony cage.

Transportation Effects

Stresses associated with transportation can have significant effects on laboratory animals prior to arrival at the laboratory animal research facility. M.E. Wallace summarized her findings as follows:

> The importance of various stress factors involved in boxing and transit of wild and laboratory mice on a 28 hour journey was studied. Transference from laboratory cage to transit box alone caused weight loss; under the best conditions the laboratory mice lost 5% of their initial weight and wild ones 8%. Deprivation of food resulted in absolute loss of weight; from this death ensued when 20% of initial weight was lost: the smaller wild mice died sooner than the larger laboratory ones. Water deprivation resulted in retarding recovery of weight lost; wild mice took longer to recover than laboratory ones. It also caused weight loss and, in conjunction with deprivation of food, poor condition and death. Transit itself affected percentage weight loss and wheat consumption; wild mice were affected differently from laboratory mice in both respects.
>
> Genotype is seen to be important not only in controlling initial weight and activity level, but also — and independently of weight — the total food requirement.

31

In light of her findings, she concludes that current literature giving guidance on shipment of small mammals is inadequate.

One of the most detailed studies of the effects of shipping stress on the immune function of mice (Landi et al. 1982) concluded that the immune system is impaired by shipping by truck and plane. Corticosterone levels were elevated and remained so 48 hours postarrival. The release of ACTH stimulated by the stress of transportation was believed responsible. The authors recommend, on the basis of these findings, that the mice be allowed to stabilize for 48 hours upon arrival to allow their immune functions to return to normal limits. Ideally, the newly arrived animals should be kept in an environmentally controlled facility separate from the main colony to prevent the spread of disease, the risk of which is enhanced by the immunosuppressive effects of elevated cortisol levels caused by transportation stress.

Restraint Handling and Treatment Variables

The actual restraint and handling of an animal to take a blood sample can influence the blood profile. Excitement while being caught and intense arousal during restraint can affect the blood packed-cell volume reading in dogs, as can feeding and associated excitement (Reece and Wahlstom 1970). One way around this problem is to identify the extent of the handling excitement variable as it affects dependent measures of a given study. An additional control group of animals that are used to being handled and restrained on a daily basis may prove advantageous. Riley (1981) found that reliable baseline measurements of plasma corticosterone can only be obtained within three to five minutes following initial disturbance of the animals by handling them. Furthermore, what he called "contagious anxiety" affects the levels of corticosterone in other mice that remained in the cage during the sequential capture of each mouse.

Bickhardt et al. (1983) have shown how a number of hematological parameters in rats are affected by the kind of sampling procedure adopted. For instance, significant differences in plasma protein and blood lactate concentrations were found between two rats kept in one cage when the first rat was decapitated twenty seconds before the second one. The authors concluded:

> Interindividual variances of haematological and metabolic blood constituents are influenced by the conditions of housing as well as the circumstances of handling for blood sampling. It is possible to reduce

the interindividual variation by standardization of sampling conditions. Quick decapitation of rats without previously disturbing the animals or touching the cages and a maximum bleeding time of 10 s may be useful for reduction of variation. Animals of different experimental treatment groups should also be bled in a strictly random order according to a formal experimental design in order to avoid 'significant' differences between groups which are purely an artefact [sic] arising from the conditions of bleeding.

In an earlier study, Gartner et al. (1980) evaluated several variables on 25 blood parameters in rats, demonstrating the dramatic effects of several routine procedures. They summarized their findings as follows:

> The effects were observed of moving male, adult Han:Sprague rats in their cages or of exposure to ether for 1 min on the plasma concentration profiles of 25 blood characteristics linked with stress and shock reactions. 5 min after the stress serum prolactin, corticosterone, thyroid-stimulating hormone, follicle-stimulating hormone, luteinizing hormone, triiodothyronine and thyroxin levels were elevated 150-500% compared with those in blood collected within 100 s of entering the animal room.
>
> Heart rate (telemetrically recorded), packed cell volume, haemoglobin and plasma protein content were 10-20% elevated 2-10 min after cage movement or 2-20 min after ether confrontation over those of controls sampled within 50 s, indicating circulatory and microcirculatory shock reactions.
>
> Serum glucose, pyruvate and lactate concentrations rose by 20-100% 1-5 min after cage movement and 1-15 min after ether exposure. Phosphate, calcium, urea, apartate and alanine transferases, alkaline phosphatase and leucine arylamidase were not altered significantly by either stressor, while potassium and bound glycerol fell for 1 min and 5-20 min respectively.
>
> The presence of a familiar animal attendant working in the room without touching the cages did not markedly affect the blood characteristics being studied.

The method of handling and restraint per se may influence a number of parameters and care should be given to this variable. Busch et al. (1977) showed that chemical immobilization may be the preferred method for a number of studies. They summarized their study as follows:

> The arterial acid-base balance and other selected physiologic measures of physically restrained and chemically immobilized nonhuman primates from the families Callithricidae, Cebridae, Cercopithecidae, and Pongidae were compared. The physically restrained primates had significantly lower pH, pCO_2, and base excess values, but they had significantly high pO_2, values, rectal temperatures, and pulse and respiration rates.

Of 56 physically restrained primates, 30 (54%) experienced severe metabolic acidosis, with pH values less than 7.2; 15 (27% of total) had pH values less than 7.1.

Two types of behavior were observed during the physical restraint of golden marmosets. Some of the marmosets were excited during restraint, with a great deal of struggling and vocalizing. The other marmosets were quiet and calm, with minimal struggling. The excited group had significantly lower pH, pCO_2, and base excess values, but significantly high pO_2 values, rectal temperatures, and pulse and respiration rates.

Primates immobilized with ketamine or tiletamine-zolazepam had a near normal acid-base balance and were handled more easily than the physically restrained animals.

Such innovations as the one shown in Figure 2-3 involving a harness and "umbilicus" for giving injections may help reduce the future need of restraining chairs, crushes, or chemical immobilization of primates.

The following summary of a unique study clearly illustrates how stressors from routine experimental procedures and from the animal quarters can influence the physiological state of research animals (Jacques and Hiebert 1972).

Laboratory animals can be maintained in a hypocoagulable state with suitable doses of anticoagulant without hemorrhage or with hemorrhage occuring only in a small percentage of animals. Stress, induced purposefully by the experimenter (e.g., hypoglycemia with insulin, 10 percent sodium chloride interperitoneally, electrical shock, frost-bite etc., in rabbits and rats) or unintentionally through conditions of animal care or experimental design, will precipitate internal spontaneous hemorrhage into body cavities and tissues. This can be quantified by recording incidence of hemorrhage, degree of hemorrhage and by mortality from hemorrhage for very severe stress. Daily subcutaneous injection of physiological saline, anesthesia, sedation have thus been shown to be stressful for rats, while determination of the bleeding time and workmen visiting the animal room constituted severe stresses for rabbits. Stress will similarly cause hemorrhage in animals treated with drugs affecting platelets. Hemostasis is dependent on (1) blood coagulation, (2) platelets and (3) vessel wall. Anticoagulants and deficiencies of coagulation factors interfere with (1). Thrombocytopenia and reserpine interfere with (2). Stress, changes in the adrenopituitary axis and local pathology interfere with (3). Spontaneous hemorrhage results when combined treatments or conditions interfere with (1) + (2), (1) + (3), (3) + (3), but not when the combined treatments cause only a single defect in hemostasis. Administration of anticoagulant drugs in suitable doses provides a simple test for stress in animal quarters or of experimental procedures, since internal hemorrhage is a definite indicator of stress.

These three relevant studies further emphasize the importance of recording all details of the rearing, care, and treatment of animals in biomedical research.

THE EFFECT OF HANDLING WEANLING RATS ON THEIR USEFULNESS IN SUBSEQUENT ASSAYS OF FOLLICLE-STIMULATING HORMONE (SHARPE ET AL. 1973)

Handling weanling female rats for three days prior to experiments using the Steelman-Pohley method of follicle-stimulating hormone (FSH) assay reduced the variability of their responses, significantly in two out of three instances. The results suggested that about twice as many non-handled rats would be required in an assay to obtain the same degree of precision as with handled rats. Variability was not significantly altered by handling in experiments using the Johnson-Naqvi method of FSH assay.

THE EFFECT OF SAMPLING TECHNIQUE ON ACID-BASE BALANCE AND OTHER BLOOD PARAMETERS IN SHEEP (MORGAN AND UPTON 1975)

The effect of four sampling routines — venipuncture, intravenous cannula, intravenous cannula following the administration of a tranquilizer (xylidino dihydrothiazine hydrochloride), intravenous cannula following exercise — were compared. Blood pH and base excess values were similar after venipuncture and cannula sampling, but higher ($P < 0.05$) after the administration of the tranquilizer and lower ($P < 0.05$) following exercise. Blood haemoglobin, haematocrit and lactate levels followed this pattern, while plasma protein levels were similar for all treatments except after exercise, where they were higher ($P < 0.05$). The recovery of various blood parameters to normal values after a period of exercise was also studied: acid-base balance had returned to near normal within 60 minutes, while haemoglobin and haematocrit levels had returned to normal within 10 minutes.

Little thought is usually given to the injection of a control substance (usually normal saline), but the control substance may have some effect upon the animal. Administering saline or blank injections to young rodents produces differences in maze-learning ability at maturity (Stein 1971). Other behavioral and physiological differences might also have been found, but, as in many studies, this particular investigation relied solely upon a single behavioral measurement; enhanced or impaired maze-learning ability could mean any of a number of things.

Behavioral disturbances have been shown to influence the eosinophil blood count in mice (Southwick 1959), a finding that is pertinent to studies involving eosinophil counts such as parasite and immunity research.

It should be emphasized that the animal's overt reaction to handling and restraint may be misleading. While one animal shows hyperexcitability and hyperactivity, another may be similarly intensely aroused but may overtly show *no* gross behavioral change. Its hypoactivity, which may border on tonic-immobility of fear-freezing catalepsy, may be mistaken for docile passivity.

If animals are to be handled frequently during the course of study, regular handling to accustom them to being caught and restrained should be instigated long before the investigation commences. Experimental variability and temporal changes due to habitation effects during experimentation would then be minimized through such *preconditioning*. For the same reasons, it is considered ill-advised to begin a study on recently acquired animals until they have adjusted to their cages and new surroundings.

The potential introduction of other experimental variables during the course of routine laboratory animal care are many and when identified and studied, often highly significant. The "queue" effect of treating animals sequentially is an often overlooked experimental variable. Treadwell[*] (personal communication), for example, found in a study of adrenal cortisol precursors that levels were lower in the last rats to be sacrificed. This effect was produced by taking rats one by one out of their colony cage in the laboratory and guillotining them in the same room. If rats were instead removed from their group one by one and decapitated in an adjoining room, this queue effect was eliminated. Dr. Treadwell terms this procedure "quiescent sacrifice," which exemplifies how close the correlation is between humane treatment and control of experimental variables.

Other Husbandry Variables

What of the frequency of cage cleaning per se since the frequency of human contact may have significant effects on behavior and physiology (see Chapt. 6)? Cisar and Jayson (1967) studied the effects of frequency of cage cleaning on rat litters prior to weaning. In summary:

> A study involving the comparison of twice per week cleaning of rat
> cages to once per week cleaning has been described. The total number of

---

[*]*C.R. Treadwell. George Washington University Medical School, Washington, D.C.*

cull animals and average weight gain were observed. The number of usable animals produced indicates that more frequent cleaning is of benefit in the production of weanling rats.

WEANING

The age of weaning young rats and mice may have a significant influence on subsequent behavior, development, and emotionality (LaBarba and White 1971; Milkovic et al. 1975). Susceptibility to gastric ulcers is influenced by the age at which rats are weaned (Ackerman 1975). This has been reconfirmed after controlling for nutritional influences that may be implicated as a factor leading to increased susceptibility following early weaning (Ader 1962). Weaning rat pups too early, for example, in 15 days rather than 22 days, has been shown to retard the normal maturation of behavioral and thermoregulatory responses to restraint stress (Ackerman et al. 1979).

POPULATION DENSITY

When animals are weaned, how many should be kept together in the same cage? Should different litters be mixed in order to maintain even numbers? Doolittle et al. (1976) summarized their study on this question as follows:

> The effects on body weight of mixing litters to attain constant density of mice per cage, as opposed to housing litters in separate cages, was studied. Mixing litters resulted in a decreased weight gain between 21 and 42 days of age and a decreased adult body weight at 63 days of age compared to housing litters in separate cages, whether the separately housed litters were allowed to vary in density or not. Mixed litter housing also increased the variance of the body weight measures among males. Housing litters separately, even if it entails variable density of housing, appears to be the preferred method for studies involving inheritance of body weight.

Les (1968) found that cage population density influences the efficiency of feed utilization and that optimal cage density may vary according to the animal's genetic strain. He reported that:

> The number of mice (1, 2, 3, 4, 5, 6, or 8) in a cage had an effect on weight gain in 2 of 5 inbred strains. There was a significant difference between population density groups in the ratio of feed consumed to weight gained. In each strain, 1 mouse per cage was least efficient in feed utilization, and 6 or 8 mice were most efficient. The differences between strains were more pronounced than the differences between

densities. In order of increasing efficiency the strains were: C57BL/6J, C3H/HeJ, A/J, DBA/2J, and AKR/J. These observations indicate that efficiency of feed utilization is dependent on population density, and that any attempt to define an optimum cage population density for mice must take into account the genetic differences between strains.

Housing animals in groups will influence their response to a number of drugs (Kasman 1965). Psychosocial stimuli — i.e., stimulation by cage mates — may produce prolonged systolic hypertension in mice (Henry et al. 1967) and may lead to renal and cardiovascular pathologies (Henry and Stephens 1969). Psychosocial stimulation has also been shown to influence the enzymes involved in the biosynthesis of adrenaline and noradrenaline. Catecholamine enzyme levels increased in colony-linked and regularly caged laboratory mice compared to socially isolated controls. Significantly, sudden stimuli such as evoking fear or aggression, were not found to cause any significant increase in catecholamines (Henry et al. 1967, 1969).

Several years ago, Chance (1946, 1947) reported his findings that social isolation and social aggregation influences the toxicity of sympathomimetic amines in mice. He later showed in rats that even routine gonadotrophin assays can be affected by social factors, very different data being derived from group-housed animals (Chance 1956).

The number of animals caged together has been shown to have other effects, depending upon the questions asked and the kind of experiment being conducted. Increased psychosocial stimulation will increase susceptibility to adjuvant-induced arthritis in rats (Amkraut et al. 1971). Conversely, social isolation may have significant effects upon the animal's response to a given treatment (Ellis 1967).

Studies comparing the responses of rats and mice raised in groups to those raised alone illustrate dramatically that the psychosocial variable can affect the test animal's response to a wide variety of treatments. These studies certainly call for a very thorough reevaluation of existing FDA, regulated drug-testing procedures for commercial products such as new pharmaceuticals and cosmetics. Simply using the old model of establishing an LD_{50} is no longer scientifically valid, especially if there is no control for psychosocial influences. An LD_{50} for a given drug may vary widely according to how many test subjects are caged together (Nutrition Reviews 1966). Maintaining the cage size rather than increasing cage size in proportion to the number of animals housed may or may not have a significant effect (see Tab. 3-1).

In some strains of rats, isolating test subjects can mean a decrease in the LD_{50}, an even control animals may develop pathophysiological

Table 3-1   Differential Housing and Susceptibility to Pathogenic Stimulation (from Ader 1967)

MEASURE	POTENTIATOR
Spontaneous mammary tumours	Isolation
Spontaneous leukemia	Isolation
Human adenocarcinoma	Isolation
Trichinosis	Crowding
Alloxan diabetes	Crowding
Rumenal ulcers	Isolation
Gastric erosions	Crowding
Anaphylactic shock	Crowding
Hypertension	Crowding
Spontaneous convulsions	Isolation
X-irradiation	Crowding
Encephalomyocarditis virus	Isolation
Amphetamine toxicity	Crowding
Isoproterenol toxicity	Crowding

Figure 3-1

Rats isolated in wire cages for a toxicological study: the stress of social deprivation is an experimental variable that such housing creates and that should be controlled for in the experimental design.

changes indicative of Selye's stress syndrome (Hatch et al. 1965). When using rats as test animals, it is easy to overlook the fact that they are highly sociable, gregarious creatures who may suffer emotionally and physiologically from social deprivation. (see Fig. 3-1).

The toxicity levels of a number of drugs have been shown to be influenced by prolonged individual caging (Wiberg and Grice 1965). Isolation stress in rats has been shown to influence myocardial electrolytes and epinephrine cardiotoxicity (Raab et al. 1968). Central nervous system depressants show decreased potency in mice after prolonged social isolation (Baumel et al. 1969). Baer (1971) has presented a detailed review of several studies that have shown how reduced psychosocial stimulation affects drug responses in rodents. One investigator applied the social isolation model as a neuropharmacological test (Barnes 1959).

Brian and Benton (1979) critically reviewed studies comparing rats housed individually versus group-housed rats, concluding that since rats housed individually do have some visual, olfactory, and auditory contact with each other, they are not truly isolated. Differences between groups should therefore be attributed not so much to crowding or isolation per se but to the influences of differential housing. It was emphasized that many factors such as the sex and strain of animals studied, prior housing conditions, prior history, cage design, group constitution, group size, and the duration of grouping or isolation are rarely investigated. The age at onset of differential housing and the interaction of concurrent tests should also be considered when evaluating the effects of differential housing on such physiological parameters as hormone secretion, adrenocortical activity, and estimations of localized neurotransmitters.

Stanislaw and Bruin (1983) have elaborated what is termed a "path analysis" design to evaluate the effects of differential housing in male mice. They summarized their findings as follows:

> Path analysis was used to examine the effects of grouping/individual housing, duration of differential housing (13 days or 10 weeks), and the age at which differential housing was initiated (at weaning or 4 months) on the physiology of male TT strain mice. Variables studied included body and relative ventral prostate, left testis and left adrenal gland weights, and plasma corticosterone level and $(Na+)/(K+)$ ratio. Compared with grouped counterparts, individual housing produced lower adrenal weights and plasma corticosterone levels, but higher prostate weights. This housing condition also suppressed the plasma $(Na+)/(K+)$ ratio, probably through an action on aldosterone secretion. The adrenal response to differential housing thus appears to be at a number of levels, involving at least two separate components. No evidence was found to support the notion that the gonadal response to grouping is mediated via the adrenal gland, although prolonged grouping does generate reduced testicular weights.

As Gough (1982) emphasizes, while the ideal laboratory animal should have standard, reproducible physiological responses, this ideal is difficult, if not impossible, to obtain. This difficulty can be significantly overcome, however, by adopting a controlled, reproducible environment and standard handling procedures to reduce physiological and other variations in the animals' phenotype.

SOCIAL CONTACT AND DEPRIVATION

At what psychophysiological level do these social deprivation or social grouping influences have their effect upon the organism? Brain biogenic amine metabolism has been shown to vary significantly between grouped and isolated rodents (Welch and Welch 1966). Such biochemical findings do not tell us what actual psychophysiological processes are involved in creating such marked differences in response to drugs; they are only symptoms. Differences in ambient temperature in grouped versus isolated rodents, rather than social deprivation per se, may lead to an increase or decrease in LD_{50}.

Physical contact and social grooming in all animals result in a marked bradycardia or decrease in heart rate. This bradycardia is indicative of a high level of parasympathetic arousal (Fox 1968), which may be a pleasurable, stress-relieving state of psychophysiological relaxation (see Fig. 3-2). It may be a significant motivating stimulus for social contact, and it may lead to social dependence in contact species. In other words, many species may rely upon being groomed by others to help maintain normal physiological homeostasis. Primates, for example, will groom more after there has been some conflict within the group, and this behavior may serve to relax or unstress them. Social grooming of con-

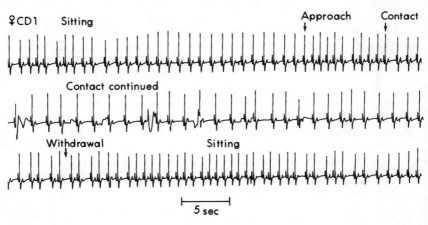

Figure 3-2

Physical contact (petting) produces marked parasympathetic arousal (reflected in cardiac bradycardia) in a dog.

Figure 3-3

Primates like these macaques in the Nilgiri forest in S.W. India and other mammals engage in much social grooming. They may be emotionally and physiologically dependent upon such social ethostasis.

specifics may therefore be regarded as a form of ethostasis, an adaptive behavioral response to facilitate physiological homeostasis (see Fig. 3-3). Also the presence of a conspecific and, in some species, eye contact and vocalizations (e.g., purring) can produce a similar physiological response. Such contact has been postulated in both infant and adult animals as being a potent motivating factor for gregariousness, reflecting a physiological dependence upon an optimal level of social stimulation to maintain, via ethostasis, normal physiological homeostasis (Fox 1968).

Withdrawal of such stimulation would be stressful in more socially dependent species, in infant animals, and in more gregarious rodent species.

These observations lend serious doubt to the validity of a number of experiments that use gregarious species, especially primates and rodents, kept in separate cages for convenience. The stress of sudden or continued social deprivation may have profound effects upon the animal's response to a given experimental procedure (e.g., radiation, induced cancer, or another disease). The ethical issue of humane treatment, especially in those experiments involving long-term social isolation in primates, should also be considered. See also Chapter 5.

Nerem et al. (1980) found that rabbits on a two percent cholesterol diet that were individually petted, held, talked to, and played with on a regular basis had a 60 percent reduction in the percentage of aortic surface area exhibiting atherosclerotic lesions compared to other rabbits that were given the same diet and normal laboratory animal care. This research shows how the routine treatment of laboratory animals may actually bias certain research conclusions, especially in toxicity studies and in research investigations of such multifactor diseases as atherosclerosis. More recently, social stress has been implicated in the development of atherosclerosis in monkeys.

Kaplan et al. (1983) reported that socially stressed adult male cynomolgus monkeys fed a *low* fat, *low* cholesterol diet developed more extensive coronary artery atherosclerosis than unstressed monkeys. The stress was induced by periodically altering group memberships by redistributing animals among three groups. The monkeys were redistributed once every 12 weeks in the first year of the study and once every four weeks in the following nine months. Reorganization of groups was selected as a means of inducing stress because previous reports had indicated that the introduction of strangers fosters a high degree of social instability in macaque monkeys. The results of this study suggest that psychosocial factors may influence the development of atherosclerosis. These two scientific reports illustrate a new dimension in biomedical research that has been called "behavioral medicine," and through which a greater understanding of the emotional and social factors involved in human disease and disease prevention may be more fully understood. Furthermore, such studies provide insights into the importance of social and emotional factors in the development of disease in animals. Researchers and others can no longer ignore the fact that animals are likely to suffer emotionally as well as physically, in ways more similar to us than we might otherwise wish to believe.

Diseases and Husbandry

The relationships between the husbandry of laboratory animals and the incidence of various diseases are well recognized, but specific examples have been poorly documented. The correlations are compounded by paradoxical effects. Social isolation may increase *or* decrease susceptibility, as may crowding. Social stress, often caused by the presence of a strange animal in the cage, increases resistance to *Trypanosoma brucii* in mice according to Ferguson et al. (1970). It can be more stressful to

house mice alone than in a stabilized group — as for certain test procedures. Mice alone in cages are more susceptible to encephalomyocar-
ditis virus, but more resistant to *Plasmodium berghei* (Friedman et al.
1969). They are also more susceptible to virus-induced tumors than are
those kept in groups of five. If mice are handled frequently, they will
develop higher salmonella H antibody titers than unhandled mice
(Soloman et al. 1969). Chickens maintained in a high social stress environment compared to those exposed to a low social stress environment
are more resistant to *E. coli* and *Staphylococcus aureus* and are more
susceptible to *Mycoplasma gallisepticum,* Marek's disease, and Newcastle disease virus and produce less antibody when injected with *E. coli*
"01" antigen (Gross 1972). Riley (1974) and Riley and Spackman (1976,
1977) reported a number of studies from their laboratory concerning the
relationships between husbandry, viral contaminants, and disease incidence, which are of critical concern in the development and utilization
of animal disease models. Riley's (1975) study of the relationship between husbandry and the incidence of mammary tumors in mice dramatically illustrates this point:

> Eighty to 100 percent of female mice of the C3h/He strain carrying the
> Bittner oncogenic virus usually develop mammary tumors within 8 to 18
> months after birth when studied under the usual housing and ex-
> perimental circumstances providing different degrees of chronic stress,
> mammary tumor incidence at 400 days was modified, with incidences
> ranging from 92 percent under stress to 7 percent in a protected environ-
> ment. The data suggest that moderate chronic or intermittent stress may
> predispose such mice to an increased risk of mammary carcinoma,
> possibly through a resultant compromise of their immunological com-
> petence or tumor surveillance system, and that adequate protection
> from physiological stress may reduce mammary tumor occurrence in
> mice.

Natural viral contaminants may act as additional stressors, interacting with handling or husbandry stress to compound and confound the effects of a given experimental procedure or disease model. Such biological
contaminants may lead to serious scientific misinterpretations (Riley
1974). Riley and Spackman's (1976) abstract of their study reveals such
complex interrelationships:

> The influence of biological stress in promoting the enhancement of
> tumor growth in a nonpigmented melanoma is demonstrated and
> analyzed. Similar effects were obtained with other stress-associated
> stimuli. Biological stress was imposed by infecting the tumor-bearing
> mice with a relatively benign murine agent, the LDH-virus, which is
> capable of causing a temporary increase in plasma corticosterone,

followed by thymus involution and T cell destruction. Tumor growth enhancement and thymus involution were also produced by the direct administration of a synthetic corticoid, dexamethasone, or by imposing a controlled anxiety-stress. The implications of these observations for the basic technical requirements in experiments that require a controlled or defined immunological status are discussed. The possible role of pregnancy in the exacerbation of certain neoplastic and other pathological processes is correlated with striking elevations in plasma corticosterone.

Antibiotics, often used therapeutically or for prophylaxis following surgery in laboratory animals, can alter cardiovascular reactivity. Tetracycline and neomycin cause hypotension and decreased cardiac output in dogs and rhesus monkeys respectively, and lincomycin results in arrhythmias in dogs (Adams 1976).

Immunological reactions may be influenced by a number of behavioral and/or emotional variables (Bogden 1974). It has recently been shown that immunosuppression may be behaviorally conditioned (Ader and Cohen 1975): rabbits were injected with saccharine and cyclophosphamidine, an immunosuppressant. The animals were then sensitized to foreign protein by injecting sheep erythrocytes. Subsequently, when injected *only* with saccharine and not with the immunosuppressant a marked decrease in hemagglutinating antibodies occurred. Conditioned physiological or psychosomatic reactions must therefore be considered as potential treatment variables.

This study serves to remind us that the interrelatedness of behavioral and physiological processes is extremely complex and cannot be properly investigated by an overly reductionistic and mechanistic view. Like making a single unitary measure of behavior, singularly reducing the organismic complexity to one or two physiological or biochemical parameters may be no less meaningless. The difference between the reactions of two animals in the same test group when handled is due to their prior exposure to handling and may account for the wide variance in test results. More important perhaps is the possibility that our understanding of drug effects and disease processes is too mechanistic and too narrowly focused at the molecular or biochemical level. This necessary reductionism must be balanced by a more integrated or holistic view of natural processes and variables such as psychosocial stimulation and circadian periodicity. The quality of animal care and animal research may then be improved, complementing a more enlightened view of human health and medical treatment. "Health" for man and animal is not, as some would define it, simply the absence of disease, nor are most diseases caused by one factor alone.

Chapter 4

Social Influences and Pheromones

One of the most profound determinants of mammalian behavior is the complex chemocommunication system of olfaction. But for Homo sapiens, a relatively anosmic species, this realm of animal awareness has been intangible and virtually ignored until the last decade.

With the help of electronic recording devices, the ultrasonic code of rodents, inaudible to us, is being broken (Meyer 1968). This is a relatively easy task compared to the complexities of deciphering the effects of pheromones, those exohormones that can influence the behavior and neuroendocrine systems of mammals.

Some knowledge of the effects of these pheromones is valuable in laboratory animal care. If unrecognized, or uncontrolled, they may have a significant effect on dependent variables in experimental procedures.

A particular significant finding concerning pheromones is that rats, when disturbed, release a "fear" pheromone (Valenta and Rigby 1968). The authors concluded that:

> Albino rats can reliably distinguish between the odors of stressed and unstressed rats. Five animals learned to interrupt an ongoing response when air from the cages of stressed rats was introduced into the test compartment, and to continue responding when air from unstressed rats was introduced. The discrimination does not seem to depend on recognition of odors of individual rats.
>
> The major finding of this paper that rats can respond differentially to odors of stressed and unstressed rats suggests the need for instituting experimental controls in those studies in which odor from a stressed animal might affect behavior of nearby animals. Previously such controls were not thought necessary. We are presently seeking to locate the odor source in the animal's body to assist us in determining whether the material has pheromonal activity and in its eventual chemical analysis.

When exposed to this chemical signal, other rats will show an alarm reaction. This phenomenon is particularly important when handling and treating rodents, especially when some pain or fear is caused by the experimenter. Other rats, awaiting treatment, may be already in a state of alarm triggered by the fear pheromone released by animals already tested or being tested. This could lead to a response variability between the animals tested first and those tested last. (Ultrasonic distress vocalizations may also affect the animals' physiology.)

In mice, a pheromone produced by the preputial gland can potentiate aggressive behavior (Mugford and Nowell 1971) and could lead to considerable social stress and disrupted social relationships in group-caged mice (MacKintosh and Grant 1966). Mice will respond differently to the odors of stressed versus nonstressed mice of either sex (Carr et al. 1971), a response that may aggravate social disorder when treated animals are placed back in the same group cage with nontreated control subjects.

Olfactory stimuli can have profound influences on mammalian reproduction (Parkes and Bruce 1961). The Bruce, Lee-Boot, and Whitten effects are well-recognized respectively as: pregnancy block in a recently inseminated female caused by the presence of or urine from a strange male; extended estrus and high incidence of pseudopregnancies produced by grouping four or more female mice together; inhibited cycling among females in larger groups, while a synchrony of cycling may occur if a male is introduced to them to stimulate estrus (Bronson 1967; Bronson and Chapman 1968; Eisenberg and Kleiman 1972; Marsden and Bronson 1965). Particularly intriguing is the fact that in extremely sensitive mice, especially those of a wild strain, merely tapping the cage or moving it around can block pregnancy as effectively as can the presence of a strange male. Lombardi and Vandengerg (1977) discovered that the social environment of the male mouse affects the sexual maturation of female mice, which is influenced by the male's urinary pheromone. They encapsulated these surprising findings in the following summary statement:

> Social subordination, which suppresses gonadal function in juvenile and adult male house mice, also suppresses the activity of an androgen-dependent urinary pheromone that accelerates the rate of sexual maturation in juvenile females. Pheromone production may also be suppressed by the presence of pregnant or lactating females. This suggests that the social environment may influence the fertility of population females by altering urinary pheromone activity in the male.

Drickamer and Hoover (1979) have shown that the urine of pregnant and lactating female mice potentiates sexual maturation in juvenile female mice. Juvenile mice produce a distinct odor which, in combination with their smaller size, effectively protects them from attacks by adult males (Taylor 1980). Lyons and Banks (1982) have shown that the ultrasonic calls given by rat pups can vary according to the odors to which they are exposed (such as their mother or a strange rat) some of which are pheromonal. A maternal pheromone acting as an innate stimulus for rat pups has been identified by Schumacher and Moltz (1982).

These findings serve to remind us that the neuroendocrine systems of animals are highly sensitive to social and environmental influences; in fact, the more these interrelationships between the organism and its environment are identified, the more we are impressed by the evolved coadaptations of the organism with its socioenvironmental milieu. As a result, we should be more concerned about ensuring that the regimen of laboratory animal care provides optimal environmental controls to avoid excessive or subnormal stimulation.

An important thought-provoking finding from Bronson's work (Marsden and Bronson 1964) is that highly inbred strains of laboratory mice may not show the Bruce effect. One possible explanation is that resistance to the Bruce effect evolved unbeknownst to the mouse geneticists, as an adaptation to being crowded in colony cages. Successive generations of mice, selectively bred for optimal fertility in a crowded environment, eventually lost the pregnancy-block mechanism that, in wild populations, probably serves as a population regulator. This classic example of "laboratorification," where a neuroendocrine and behavioral system is virtually obliterated, may be a warning that laboratory populations may not always be ideal or normal models of natural biological systems. More will be said on this point subsequently, with reference to genetics and phenotypic variability (see Chapt. 7).

The physical presence of an adult male mouse may significantly accelerate the onset of sexual maturation in females compared to females not raised with an adult male, which is the usual practice. Vandenbergh (1969) attributes this sociosexual phenomenon to the male's odor — i.e., a pheromone effect.

Vandenbergh (op. cit.) summarized his observations as follows:

> Previous work has shown that sexual maturation of female mice is accelerated by the presence of a male. This report identifies male odor as a critical stimulatory masculine agent. Groups of females in contact with 1) an adult male, 2) with a male behind a wire mesh barrier, or 3) the odor of a male display vaginal opening and first estrus about 15 days earlier than females exposed to a castrate male, forced activity, or no male influences. The data also suggest that odors derived from males exposed to estrous females are more effective than odors from solitary males in accelerating sexual maturation.

More recently it has been shown that the male's presence also influences growth and feed efficiency in young female mice, as well as sexual maturation (Eisen 1975; Fullerton and Cowley 1971).

Rodents are not the only common laboratory species whose behavior and development can be affected by pheromones. Various primate species, including man, produce potent pheromones that can influence sexual behavior and menstrual rhythms (Michael et al. 1971; Rowell 1967). These findings should be considered not only in relation to the effects of prolonged social isolation in confined cages and the absence or presence of mature males but also the significance of the pheromones produced by experimenters and by animal care personnel. Rats can distinguish familiar and unfamiliar human odors (McCall 1969), and primates sometimes become more difficult to handle when a female caretaker or researcher is menstruating. Subtle effects of body deodorants, perfumes, and aftershave lotions, not to mention animal room disinfectants and deodorants, remain to be investigated. More than one pet owner has reported marked sexual arousal in her dog or cat when she or other people are wearing particular perfume.* Considering the profound effects that natural pheromones can have on behavior and neuroendocrine function, we should be alert to the possibility that some synthetic compounds and other chemicals may have comparable effects.

The practical use of pheromones in animal husbandry is also beginning to be explored. The sow aphrodisiac called "Boar-mate," a testosterone metabolite from boar saliva, has now been isolated and can be used to encourage sows to stand for breeding.

To ensure that orphaned animals can be cross-fostered and will not be killed or rejected by the foster mother manipulate the pheromones: remove the mother and allow the orphans to mix with her offspring and acquire their odor (a pheromone); wipe the mammae of the mother with a moist cloth and then wipe it over the orphans to give them her odor; block the olfactory sense of the mother temporarily with vanilla or some other volatile oil.

Social Variables

One of the most frequently overlooked causes of phenotypic variability in a genotypically uniform strain of animals is the interindividual

---

*The musk in many perfumes, a potent pheromone from Ethiopian civet cats, has stimulated a number of pet cats to attack their owners.

variance created by dominance-subordination relationships — i.e., the "peck" order of a social group that is raised and caged together. As social relationships change, so will the behavior and physiology of individuals affected by such changes.

Several examples of these social hierarchy effects will be reviewed. Some might argue that caging animals separately would eliminate such interindividual variances if phenotypic uniformity is desired for experimental purposes. But in isolating animals, we create the problems of reduced psychosocial stimulation (discussed in the preceding chapter) and of social/environmental deprivation (see Chapt. 5). This dilemma cannot be overcome by raising members of the same sex together for the absence of one sex can influence certain behavioral and physiological activities. The solution may be to develop optimal social groupings just as we must develop the optimal environmental conditions described earlier.

Obviously one should never begin a study of animals kept in groups until their social organization has stabilized. Treatment of one animal may influence its social status and lead to a subsequent destabilization of the entire group. It is for these reasons perhaps that many animals are removed from their group for the duration of the study (or for their entire lives in some cases). Social isolation effects therefore are probably the most serious single class of uncontrolled variables in animal research; and in gregarious, socially dependent species, social isolation warrants humane concern as well. Social rank is also a significant variable; for example, socially low-ranking rats and other mammals tend towards adrenal hyperplasia. Reduced tolerance to parasites, increased susceptibility to disease, and possibly greater sensitivity to certain drugs and other experimental manipulations have been correlated with social stress and/or associated low social rank in several vertebrate species (Davis 1971; Gross 1972).

The stress associated with being low in the social hierarchy has recently been shown to lower fertilily in female talapoin monkeys. Higher levels of circulating prolactin and repression of luteinizing hormone production following estrogen treatment were found in monkeys of low social status (Keverne et al. 1978).

The effects of social interaction, hierarchical rank, and crowding stress on fertility, offspring survival, and disease susceptibility have been well-documented in rodents (Archer 1970; Christian and Davis 1964). The social position of an individual will influence its performance and other dependent experimental measures (Taylor and Moore 1975); for example, resting heart rate levels will vary according to the individual's social rank and will change with its change in social rank (Canland et al.

Framingham State College
Framingham, Massachusetts

1970). In primates, a correlation has also been made between dominance rank, aggressive behavior, and plasma testosterone (Rose et al. 1971; Rose et al. 1975).

SOCIAL FACILITATION

Behavior may be changed by group effects in other ways. One well-documented phenomenon known as "social facilitation" refers to the additive or reciprocally stimulating effects of individuals on each other. For example, courtship and sexual behavior may be contagious in many species of birds and mammals, leading to a synchrony of ovulation and of the production of offspring. Panic and flight reactions of one or two timid, or very alert individuals may, via this behavioral contagion, lead to a mass panic reaction in the colony.

In dogs (James 1953; Ross and Ross 1949) and chickens (Tolman 1968) social facilitation may lead to increased food consumption and increased growth rates in young animals, a significant variable in nutritional palatability studies. Efficiency of feed utilization in mice is affected by cage population density and genotype (Les 1968).

Great care should be taken to avoid disrupting social groups by introducing a strange individual or one that has been isolated from the group for experimental purposes for some time. "Closed" social groups are common in laboratory animals and the degree of closure and reluctance to accept strangers may vary according to the strain or breed of animals used (James 1951; King 1954).

The kind of social contact an animal has during early life will influence its social preferences and social compatibility in later life. The amount of contact with conspecifics and human beings during the early life of rhesus monkeys, for example, will influence social and sexual preferences at a later age (Pratt and Sackett 1967). Prolonged contact with the mother in an otherwise socially deprived environment may lead to reciprocal overattachment, both mother and infant maintaining a pathological dependence on the other for social stimulation (Jensen and Bobbitt 1968). Laboratory rearing should focus upon optimal peer and adult or paternal socialization (Mitchell 1968), especially in primates, in order to avoid subsequent social problems of hyperaggressivity, disruption of sexual and maternal behavior, and other potential problems following exposure to or isolation from conspecifics, human caretakers, or foster parents (see Figs. 4-1 and 4-2).

Significant variations can be found between groups of animals derived from litters of different sizes (Barbenhenn 1961). Raising large

Figure 4-1

Animals in the wild, like these Indian macaques, enjoy the fulfillment of life by simply being in the environment of which they are an inseparable part and for which they are evolved. Mother nurses the infant, while the troop leader threatens the author. The quality of social interactions will influence the physiology and behavior of each troop member and, thus, the social "ambience" and ecological adaptivity of the troop.

litters together or mixing litters may lead to crowding stress in certain strains; for example, tail lesions were correlated with crowding stress in one strain of mice (Les 1972):

> Lesions similar in appearance to bite wounds occurred in the tails of adult male and female C3H/HeJ mice. The incidence was only 4% among paired mice in breeding cages, but as high as 21% among weaned mice clustered in large cages in groups of 40. Age of onset among weaned mice ranged from 5 weeks of age upward. The age of most frequent onset among both females and males was 8 weeks. Tests for ectromelia antibody were negative as were all examinations for ectoparasites. Skin scrapings cultured for bacteria and fungi were also negative. The incidence was lowest among weaned mice kept in littermate groups with sexes separated. Healing of the lesions occurred when mice kept in groups of 40 in large cages were seperated into groups of 5 in smaller cages. The principal factor in the etiology of tail lesions appeared to be social stress resulting from interaction of cage size, cage population, and whether or not the mice were cage mates prior to weaning. The apparent dependence of the disease on social stress could make this a useful model for investigating the effects of stress on a genetically defined population of mice.

Figure 4-2

A rhesus macaque in a standard cage environment, illustrating the extreme degree of social deprivation that was not an intended aspect of the medical research being done on this animal.

Group size and sex will also influence organ weights, social behavior, and catecholamine levels in mice (Anton 1969; Anton et al. 1968). Prenatal influences have also been identified; social crowding during gestation will influence the behavior of offspring (Keeley 1962).

Social deprivation can have marked effects on the behavior, physiology, and response of the animal to various experimental treatments. This important aspect of laboratory animal care and experimental validity will be discussed in the next chapter.

Chapter 5

Social Deprivation and Isolation Effects

A great deal of research on the effects of social deprivation on the physiology and behavior of animals has been conducted over the past two decades. Much of this research, published in theoretical journals concerned with behavioral development, psychobiology, and comparative psychology has not been integrated at the applied level of animal care and experimental design. From a humane standpoint, such basic research demonstrates conclusively that social animals can experience psychophysical stress and emotional distress when socially deprived.

The effects of social deprivation should be considered at three levels (1) immediate effects caused by confining a previously free roaming or wild animal, (2) long-term effects associated with continued deprivation, and (3) *emergence* effects caused by the animal's removal from isolation for experimental purposes or return to its colony or social group when the study is over.

Immediate effects of being caged alone in relative social and environmental deprivation will vary according to age and species and, significantly, in relation to prior experience. Adaptation may be easier for those animals that have not been cage raised or have not lived a part of their lifetime under free or relatively free social and environmental conditions. In young mammals, especially primates and carnivores, early deprivation introduces the added stress of maternal deprivation and disrupted maternally regulated ethostasis discussed earlier.

Anaclitic depression and withdrawal occurs in infant monkeys following social isolation (Kaufman and Rosenblum 1966, 1967). Such predictable reactions have been instigated to develop an animal model of human depression (Harlow and Suomi 1971). This study, which is hardly original if not inhumane, at least emphasizes what profound behavioral and emotional changes can be triggered by such treatment. Physiological correlates associated with such anaclitic depression have been documented (Reite et al. 1974), and, interestingly, when a surrogate "swing" is provided many of the symptoms of self-directed comforting (presumably rhythmic stimulation to maintain parasympathetic arousal normally provided by the mother) are alleviated (Mason 1968).

Even a brief period of separation — a few days — from the mother can have long-lasting effects on subsequent development and behavior (Hinde and Spencer-Booth 1971; Hinde et al. 1966). Prolonged social isolation leads to more extensive impairment of social behavior, including abnormalities in maternal (Arling and Harlow 1967), social, sexual, and aggressive behaviors (Harlow 1959, 1962; Harlow and Harlow 1966, 1962).

Einon et al. (1981) found that social isolation in rats early in life has short- and long-term or permanent influences upon behavior. But this was not the case with other rodent species they studied — mice, gerbils, and guinea pigs. These differences were attributed to the play hypothesis, which holds that those who play together stay together. Only rats engage in long bouts of rough and tumble play between 20-50 days; mice, gerbils and guinea pigs do not engage in extensive and prolonged social play. Hence, if they are denied the opportunity to play, the deprivation has no marked effect on these species. In contrast, rats show increased timidity or aggression and, if denied the opportunity to play, are permanently affected.

Particularly significant for laboratory animal care and handling is the paradoxical effect of such social deprivation. The animal may become hyperaggressive and overdefensive of its territory and therefore difficult to handle, and, when finally caught and restrained, its physiological state may contraindicate any anesthesia, drug assay, baseline physiological, or biochemical tests. Conversely, the human caretaker may come to be regarded as a surrogate or social companion substitute, even for rats (Sloan and Latane 1974). Dogs and primates may become overexcited by the presence of a human being, which could create acute temporary physiological changes that may influence the direction of various experimental treatments. Aroused and anticipating social contact, like petting, they would differ behaviorally and physiologically from adult animals of the same species who have not, in spite of conspecific deprivation, developed a compensatory dependence upon humans. This variable (see other caretaker variables in Chapt. 6) can be compounded further by caretakers who favor some animals over others.

Figure 5-1

A laboratory primate recovering from a bout of self-mutilating hair-pulling: note lack of hair on shoulders and forearms.

During the acute phase of isolation in adult animals, and until the animals adapt to confined space and develop adaptive rhythms, normal rhythmic and maintenance behaviors will be disrupted to varying degrees. Ingestion, elimination, motor activity, sleep, and self-care may be affected. Transient anorexia and refusal to eliminate may lead to further complications. Sleep periods may increase, or motor activity hypertrophy into episodes of stereotyped hyperactivity. Grooming may hypertrophy in the absence of the physiological ethostasis of social grooming (Sade 1965; Terry 1970), and the animal may overcompensate for lowered input and may self-mutilate rapidly (see Fig. 5-1). Associated with this may be heightened pain threshold, causing the animal to appear insensitive to normally painful, noxious stimuli.

Steyne et al. (1975) found that two months' time was required for recently caged baboons to develop stable blood chemistry values. Other physiological and behavioral parameters may never reach normal levels, but may oscillate according to the animal's adaptation strategies to confinement in establishing and maintaining homeostasis and ethostasis. Unfortunately, the long-term effects of isolation on physiological processes have received scant evaluation.

The age at which a rat is isolated and the sex of the individual rat have been shown to influence the severity of the isolation (Korn and Moyer 1968). Rats raised in isolation prefer a familiar cage environment, while group-raised rats prefer a novel environment (Turpin 1977). This has also been demonstrated by the author in the dog, the practical significance of which will be discussed subsequently in relation to emergence effects.

Stress resistance may be lowered by isolation rearing. In one study, group-housed rats survived a period of swimming stress, while isolates, stressed for the same period, died (Rosellini et al. 1976).

In mice, isolation stress[*] may have a significant effect on endocrine function (Weltman et al. 1962; Weltman et al. 1968) and the blood levels of circulating leucocytes may be affected also (Suckler and Weltman 1967; Weltman et al. 1970). Weltman et al. (1968) summarized their studies of isolation stress on female albino mice as follows:

> The findings demonstrated that isolation produced significant behavioral abnormalities such as head-twitching, aggressiveness, increased locomotor activity and decreased white blood cell counts. The alterations in locomotor activity and white blood cells, consequently, reflect heightened metabolism rates and increased adrenocortical activity. Although isolation-induced aggressiveness appeared to hinder initial mating-behavior interactions with males, no apparent effects were noted on fertility and fecundity of the test females. The practice of caging laboratory animals singly should be carefully evaluated.

Baer (1971) in an extensive review on long-term isolation stress and its effects on drug response in rodents stated in summary that:

---

[*] *As emphasized earlier, social isolation effects may be compounded by changes in ambient temperature and difficulties in the isolated animal being able to maintain thermoregulation in the absence of cagemates and bedding material.*

General effects of isolation as compared to grouped rats and mice, resulted in behavioral changes (such as aggressiveness, head twitching, convulsions); lowered resistance to stress (stress varying with sex, length of isolation and strain); affected food consumption and weight gains; resulted in hematological abnormalities (especially leukopenia and eosinopenia); produced endocrinal changes (such as hyperadrenocorticism); differences in organ weights, and other related changes. In addition, the effects of drugs, especially those affecting the central and autonomic nervous system, were compared in isolated versus community caged rodents.

Some of the effects identified in rats following isolation stress are shown in Table 5-1, by Baer.

Another variable that may increase or decrease the effects of isolation is the breed or strain of the animal. A basically timid dog would be more severely affected than one that is more stable or outgoing as Fuller (1967) has shown. Thus the environment may exaggerate certain genetic (physiological and behavioral) traits, or the latter may buffer or compensate for some of the effects of the former.

Under conditions of isolation, the animal will eventually attain some degree of homeostasis and ethostasis. The degree of departure from the adaptive norm may only become apparent when the animal is placed in a more natural environment (e.g., a complex environment with novel objects and peers). This is the *emergence phase* from isolation and, like the initial phase of isolation, it is characterized by marked behavioral and physiological changes. Understanding this phase is particularly relevant to the control of experimental variables. An animal not used to being handled or exposed to the laboratory testing room or any place other than its familiar animal quarters may manifest, to varying degrees, clear signs of the isolation-emergence syndrome. To some extent this can be controlled by regular handling and exposure to different environments; the latter reduces the possible stress of *environmental dissonance,* as between rearing cage and testing cage, animal room and experimental room, etc.

Isolation-Emergence Syndrome (from Fox 1965)

Emergence from isolation in higher animals, such as the dog, is characterized by two types of reaction, depending partly on the age of the subject and on its breed — it must be added that timid breeds are more severely affected than outgoing ones.

One reaction is a mass fear response in which the animals freeze and adopt bizarre postures, defecate, urinate, and may even show defensive-

Table 5-1   Effects of isolation stress — rats
(from Baer 1971)

	Sex, wt., or age	Animals/cage	Stress duration	Isolation effects
R. Norwegicus	M 64g	4 litter mate trios: 1 isolated, 1 raised in cohabitation, 1 raised in all male group	Up to 16 days	a) Disorientation b) inability to achieve intromission in 2 or 3 copulatory tests with females
Wistar	M Weanling F (equal nos.)	½-isolated ½-10/cage	Up to wks.	a) Aggressive, Nervous, vicious b) ascending caudal dermatitis; c) enlarged adrenal cortex
Wistar	M Weanling F (equal nos.)	½-isolated ½-10/cage	13 wks.	a) Females-1) increased plasma corticoids, response to ACTH, hemoglobin values, packed-cell volumes, adrenal, thyroid, and pituitary wts., width of adrenal cortex; 2) decreased follicle in ovary, ovary, adrenal cholesterol. b) Males-1) Decrease in fasting level of live glycogen. c) Males & females-1) Decrease in circulating lymphocytes, spleen, thymus; 2) hyperadrenocorticism
Wistar	M 28 days F 28 days (equal nos.)	½-isolated ½-10/cage	Up to 16 wks.	a) Slower growth (especially Wistars); b) lymphopenia (especially Wistars); disappeared in Sprague-Dawley females after 15 wks.; c) alterations in organ growth and organ wts. to body ratios;

	Sex, wt., or age	Animals/cage	Stress duration	Isolation effects
Sprague-Dawley (Holtzman)	M 28 days F 28 days	½-isolated ½-10/cage	15 wks.	a) Sprague-Dawley females — increased packed cell volume and hemoglobin after 15 wks. isolation; b) stress varied with sex, length of isolation, strain
Sprague-Dawley	F Weanling		20 wks.	a) Increased activity (max. at 35 days); b) identical body wts. and activity at 20 wks.
Sprague-Dawley	F Weanling	Controls — 2-3/cage Test-1	Up to 14 mos.	a) Increased myocardial K and Mg; b) decreased myocardial Na and Ca c) increased corticoid production

aggressive *fear biting*; they may also be, in the layman's terminology, touch-shy, sound-shy, and sight-shy. The other type of reaction is one of hyperexploratory behavior, in which the dog runs around hyperactively, rather like a much younger naive pup, and approaches objects that normally would be avoided. Impaired pain perception has been reported in such isolation-raised dogs; for example, they would repeatedly stick their noses into a candle flame. It has been proposed that in this type of reaction, excessive arousal actually increases the pain threshold. The author's studies of EEG and the evoked potential of pups emerging from isolation into a more complex environment (Fox 1971b) reveal that the brain is in a state of overarousal, which may be a pathophysiological state, for spindle-like bursts of activity were recorded. These bursts disappeared rapidly as the subjects recovered from the effects of isolation. They had only been isolated for seven days, from four until five weeks of age, and recovery was evident in most subjects after a further four to seven days in the normal animal room environment.

Isolation for longer periods up to 16 weeks of age can produce almost permanent behavioral change; adaptation following emergence from isolation is protracted and symptoms of the isolation syndrome may persist permanently in innately timid, more susceptible individuals or breeds. Little protection from the syndrome was afforded by raising dogs in isolation in pairs (Fuller 1967).

The isolation syndrome has been emphasized because, when moved to a more complex environment such as the testing room or the laboratory animal facility, many dogs bred and raised for research purposes, under relatively impoverished conditions, will react to the novelty and complexity of the new surroundings in one of two ways described above. In addition to showing symptoms of the isolation-emergence syndrome, they may have received little handling and socialization early in life, which in no way enhances their usefulness as research subjects, especially in long-term experiments.

If pups are raised with plenty of human contact to ensure that they are socialized, but are not removed from their pens until 12 weeks of age, they show some of the symptoms of the isolation syndrome. Many actually prefer to remain in the pens even when the door is left open and, when first placed in an observation arena with various play objects, they withdraw and do not explore (Fox 1971b). Pups placed in the arena for a mere 15 minutes at five and eight weeks of age are *protected* by the prior exposure in that they actively explore the arena at 12 weeks of age and behave normally, while littermates who lack prior exposure show marked fear and avoidance behavior.

Sackett (1968, 1966) has found comparable effects in monkeys raised under varying degrees of deprivation. The practical implications of these experiments are brought home by the familiar statement that random-source or pound dogs are usually much easier to manage in the laboratory than dogs born and raised specifically for research. The latter are often dubbed "crazy or hyper," or "passive and timorous." It is not only socialization that influences these different reactions but also the fact that random-source dogs have been exposed to a more enriched and varied environment; they have prior associations that facilitate their habituation and adaptation to novel visual and auditory, and possibly olfactory, stimuli in the laboratory. Of course, random-source dogs with wide genetic variability and no known prior life history are of limited value for many research projects.* What we should consider is a type of programmed life history for specifically raised animals that have been selectively bred for research purposes. Some varied stimulation in order to prevent possible brain changes (see Chapt. 7) and behavioral impairment may be wise, not purely for humane reasons but for the validity and justification of using such animals for biological research.

Essentially, this issue of prior experience in a particular environment involves the animal's ability to adapt to a new environment. The narrower the range of prior experience, the more limited would be the animal's ability to adapt to more varied or totally different conditions. Each environmental change from the rearing facility to the laboratory animal facility to the animal research unit entails some degree of adaptation to psychophysiological stress evoked by change. Adaptation would be more protracted and psychophysiological stress more pronounced if there were a greater dissonance between consecutive environmental conditions or if the animal had had a restricted, experientially impoverished prior history and were suddenly plunged into a more complex environment. Consecutive environmental conditions should be comparable in their qualitative complexity to reduce dissonance and contingent adverse effects. And time should be allowed to enable the subject to adapt to the new conditions prior to experimentation.

Furthermore, they would most likely experience considerable difficulties adapting to the restricted and impoverished conditions of a laboratory cage or pen.

The Psychopathology of Isolation and Deprivation

Consider a wild animal suddenly being removed from all that it has learned — and all that it has evolved — to interact with, translocated from one socioenvironmental milieu to another that in no way simulates a natural environment or one that it is used to. One must seriously question the ethics and humaneness of such treatment, especially in the higher primates and random-source dogs. In many zoos and laboratories we see bizarre behavior patterns emerging from the animal's maladaptive attempts to adjust to confinement. Its fear is overcome through habituation, gentle or predictable handling, and food reward, but, in the frustration of captivity, thwarted attempts to escape may become stereotyped fixations in which the animal paces or weaves backwards and forwards. Other abnormalities may develop — automutilation, hyperphagia, coprophagia, hyperaggression, hypersexuality, and disruption of reproductive maternal behavior (Meyer-Holzupfel 1968).

It should also be emphasized that social isolation eliminates social grooming, which for species such as mice is essential for the control of skin infections and ectoparasitic mites and the maintenance of a healthy coat. Dystrophic mice, housed in isolation, may have even more extensive problems since normal self-grooming may be inadaquate (see Fraser and Waddell 1974).

Stereotyped movements may also develop as a means of providing self-comfort or varied stimulation; indeed, even children hospitalized for extended periods will develop such patterns in order to enrich their environment by varying their sensory input and motor output. Monkeys and dogs raised under restricted conditions frequently develop these stereotyped movements. We may postulate a mechanism of perceptual-motor homeostasis, where the organism either seeks stimulation or provides its own to maintain some optimal level of complexity. The optimal quality and quantity of stimulation may be lower in an animal raised earlier in relative isolation than in one raised under more natural conditions because the *set point* is higher in a feral animal. An animal placed in an environment in which perceptual input is lower both qualitatively and quantitatively and in which motor activity is restricted may therefore experience a perceptual-motor homeostatic imbalance (see Figs. 5-2 and 5-3). Psychophysiological depression, anorexia, increased susceptibility to infectious diseases, and psychosomatic disturbances may occur during the initial stages of adaptation. Adaptation to this situation essentially involves institutionalization; the set point is gradually lowered and the animal adapts to a lower level of stimulation. Indeed, this has been a

Figure 5-2

A standard-caged, socially deprived chimpanzee showing fear and withdrawal; prolonged deprivation may lead to stereotypic behavior, depression, or anorexia.

long-recognized problem in many mental hospitals; by the time the original problem is cured, the patient has adapted to the relatively monotonous and impoverished environment typical of so many over-crowded and understaffed institutions and the clinicians now have to deinstitutionalize and rehabilitate the patient.[*]

*see R. Sommer, *Personal Space*. (New Jersey: Prentice-Hall, 1969)

Figure 5-3

Deprived of companions and stimulation, a depressed, isolated monkey begins to mutilate itself. *Photo: Courtesy of Dr. H. Harlow.*

The adaptation period may be prolonged in animals derived from random sources or wild conditions. Recently captured monkeys may take up to 12 months to develop some degree of physiological stability. There is a clear advantage in using animals raised for the laboratory under stand-

DISSONANCE THEORY OF STEREOTYPY

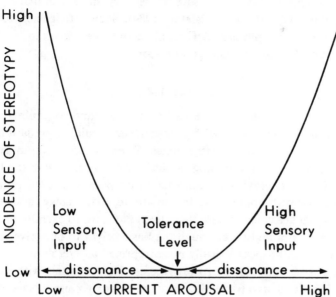

Figure 5-4

Relationships between arousal level and degree of stereotypy illustrate the homeostatic function (or ethostasis) of stereotyped behavior patterns. With low arousal (e.g., in isolation) or intense arousal, the frequency of stereotyped actions increases.

ardized, relatively impoverished cage conditions, for their adaptation period will be considerably shorter. However, they may be so phenotypically changed that they are of limited value in research (see Chapt. 7).

While stereotyped behaviors may develop as an adaptive strategy to compensate for reduced stimulation, they may also be seen when the animal is under more intense or novel stimulation (see Fig. 5-4). This intriguing paradox, also recognized in autistic children, points to a dual role of stereotyped behavior. Stereotyped behaviors seem to maintain some degree of homeostasis and ethostasis by (1) increasing stimulus input by self-stimulation in isolation and (2) by acting as a filtering or blocking device of incoming stimuli so as to prevent stimulus overload. Presumably, under normal rearing conditions and environmental complexity, the nervous system is adequately attuned to regulate its excitory state without the need to elaborate stereotyped motor actions. What this would seem to imply, therefore, is that the presence of stereotyped actions is a clear indicator of a suboptimal environment and that the animal is attempting to compensate for sensory and social inadequacies (see also Fox 1983a and Wemelsfelder 1984). Such deficiencies, like any nutritional or other physical deficiency, should be corrected in the interests of both the animal and good research.

Exercise

Many people claim that exercise is important for animals, but animals in nature that are well-fed, warm, not afraid of predation, and not sexually frustrated do not exercise. Exercise per se is an anthropomorphic concept, an unbiological activity at variance with the law of conservation of energy. Wild animals either play with each other, by themselves, or with appropriate inanimate objects, engage in grooming or other social activities, or else they sleep. No drive to exercise has been recognized by ethologists, although the basic drives to be active and explore may be anthropocentrically misinterpreted as exercise.

The answer may not be to provide confined animals with exercise devices alone, such as a treadmill, since the value to many species of such stereotyped, compulsive activity is questionable. The answer is varied stimulation such as social interaction, objects to explore and manipulate, and sufficient space to satisfy basic locomotor activity needs. Dogs might be walked around the animal facility, leash trained, exposed to trucks and dollies, exposed to strangers, and introduced to a variety of audiovisual stimuli of varying intensity and complexity. This would be especially advantageous and appropriate where long-term experiments were to be conducted in which the subject would have to adapt to a new set of complex and novel stimuli. Rodents may enjoy the opportunity to explore tunnels and ramps in "play pens" containing various novel objects and manipulanda. Primates could be provided with play objects, operant devices to "work" in order to break the *taedium vitae* of a barren cage, and they should have sufficient space to satisfy their locomotor activity needs, especially for brachiation.

Mather (1981) proposes that the wheel-running activity of caged rodents is not related to boredom or the need for exercise, nor is it simply a reflection of general activity. Rather, such activity may reflect an urge of the caged animal to explore areas beyond the boundaries of its cage. Overcrowding, thirst, hunger, and sexual arousal increase wheel-running activity that, under noncaged conditions, would lead to increased exploratory and appetitive behavior. Wheel-running activity in cage-confined rodents may therefore be a general response to the frustration of exploratory behavior directed toward a perceived goal that cannot be attained (e.g., food or a mate outside the cage).

In conclusion, we should be mindful of how we alter the socioenvironmental structure of laboratory animals before and during experimentation. Adaptation may be facilitated by selective breeding, socialization, handling (see Chapts. 6 and 7), and rearing under standardized socioenvironmental conditions that match conditions under which the animals will be kept prior to and during experimentation. If the experiment involves confinement or even more extreme variables, such as those experienced in a space capsule in which the subject must execute certain procedures while experiencing weightlessness, it is imperative that psychophysiological adaptation and stability to these environmental conditions be established prior to countdown. Simulate take-off before actual experimentation, otherwise there will be compounded interacting and uncontrolled variables that cannot be separated from the dependent variables of the experiment.

In the next chapter, other variables that may greatly change the animal's behavioral and physiological phenotype will be detailed.

Chapter 6

Handling, Socialization, and Caretaker Effects

L aboratory animals are, by virtue of their use, exposed to varying degrees of human contact. The contact necessitated by experimental purposes, such as taking blood samples or administering an injection or other treatment, usually entails handling and/or restraint of the animal. Other forms of contact may be less obvious, but they are no less influential upon the animal's behavior and physiology. Routine cage cleaning, feeding and watering procedures, and the mere presence of people in the animal room facility can cause measurable effects on the animals.

Of most immediate and practical concern is ease of handling and restraint; this is a result of the animal's degree of prior habituation and, for many species, the degree of socialization or attachment to man.

Handling animals also entails their subsequent release, and the act of releasing an animal may give it a sense of competence or control (see also p. 116, discussion on learned helplessness). As farfetched as this notion may seem, this conclusion was reached by Richter (1957) in his studies of rats' ability to endure the stress of being placed in a tank of water and having to swim or drown.* Rats forcibly restrained and then placed in the water gave up their efforts to survive and drowned after some 30 minutes. Others that were restrained, allowed to escape, then recaptured and released a few times before immersion swam an average of 60 hours before drowning. Though this kind of research is questionable on humane grounds, it does indicate that the effects of repeated handling may have beneficial consequences in subtle ways and help immunize or inoculate animals against the harmful effects of the *helplessness* syndrome (see p. 116).

It is to be hoped that any replication of this study would employ the new fluoride compound (artificial blood) that is so oxygen rich that mice inhale it without drowning.

Limited or suboptimal human contact early in life, especially during the critical period of socialization (Scott 1962) between five to 10 weeks of age, will result in a dog that, at maturity, will be difficult to handle (Freedman et al. 1961). If it is from a timid or shy breed, it may react fearfully and resist capture, but it will submit passively when restrained. It may give the mistaken impression, by virtue of its passivity, that it is docile and unafraid. Physiological measurements — plasma cortisol levels and heart rate, for example — would indicate otherwise. A dog from a more outgoing breed may behave fearfully but aggressively — the typical fear-biter that is a hazard for anyone to handle.

Socialization/Handler Habituation

In order to avoid hazards to both laboratory personnel and the animals, who otherwise may be rendered behaviorally and physiologically in no suitable state for any meaningful experimentation, early socialization with people is essential. Play, grooming, food reward, handling, and restraint — i.e., leash and table training — early in life will make a dog easier to handle and to train later in life (Pfaffenberger and Scott 1959). It will also be more adaptable to many experimental procedures involving frequent human contact such as restraint (in a conditioning harness), specific performance (running on an exercise treadmill), or working for some operant reward. Fear will not only affect performance and physiological base-line measures but it will also block the animal's ability to learn and greatly limit its capacity to adapt to many experimental procedures. Therefore, for many experiments involving dogs as subjects, early handling during the critical socialization period should be considered essential if not mandatory for good research (see Fig. 6-1).

It should also be remembered that, following early socialization, some regular human contact must be maintained; otherwise, the dog may regress and become people-shy or "kennel-shy." In other words, without reinforcement, the bond with humans may be broken, especially in dogs caged with other dogs. The same holds true for cats and most other domestic animals.

In domesticating the dog, selection in favor of docility and dependence, associated with trainability, has been strong. Consequently, it should be borne in mind that a dependent, human-attached dog may suffer emotionally when deprived of human contact. This suffering would be aggravated further by isolating the dog from its own species, as may be dictated for certain experimental purposes. The emotional and

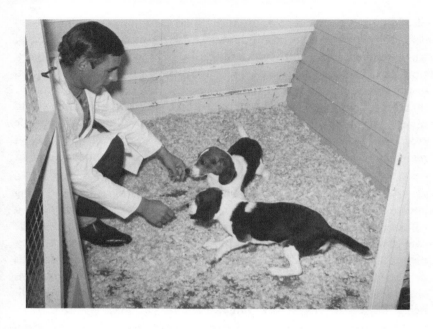

Figure 6-1

Inadequate human contact during early life results in a fearful beagle that may be difficult to handle, while its socialized litter mates are friendly and tractable.

physiological consequences of such ill-advised treatment have been detailed earlier. It is to be reemphasized here that such deprived dogs, when handled, can be difficult to restrain, not because of fear or aggression but because of overexcitement. Behavioral and physiological disturbances, including hyperactivity, excessive care-soliciting behavior (barking, jumping up, licking), hyperthermia, cardiac dysrhythmias, and other autonomic disturbances (excessive salivation, urination, penile erection) may be triggered by human presence and/or handling. A regimen of regular handling and exercise would help eliminate some of these variables.

As Dr. Tom Wolfle has shown with his NIH program for breeding and rearing Pointers for biomedical research, humane sensitivity and a full recognition of the social, emotional, and environmental needs in the care of laboratory animals can make them more adaptable, easier to handle, and also more reliable subjects for research.* Research conclusions derived from animals that are not treated humanely and whose environments are not conducive to their behavioral and emotional well-being may be of little, if any, value.

Although the above observations pertain to dogs, a species in which the most detailed studies of socialization have been conducted, the same basic principles hold for all laboratory mammals, including rats, mice, rabbits, cats and nonhuman primates. Like the dog, these species undergo a period of socialization early in life, the critical period varying according to the species. As in the dog, delayed socialization with humans until after this optimal attachment period will make the establishment of a social bond difficult if not, especially in wild species, impossible. While it may be debated whether or not such a social bond is desirable for experimental purposes, the lack of socialization towards humans will not only make the animals difficult to handle but may also introduce an added social/emotional stress that could be detrimental to experimentation.

Those vertebrates that are relatively mature at birth — i.e., chickens and guinea pigs — have a very short postnatal attachment period during

---

*D.C. Secord and J.C. Russell (Lab. Anim. Sci. 23: 567-571, 1973) present evidence that purebred dogs (labradors) may be better for research purposes than conditioned mongrel pound dogs, since the latter showed greater heterogeneity in several biochemical and blood measures, some of which were a reflection of their stressful prior history. However, Secord agrees that purpose-bred, purebred dogs that have not been properly socialized and have been raised in the impoverished conditions of a cage or pen, are not good experimental subjects (personal communication).

which time imprinting occurs (Salzen 1967). In amphibians, reptiles, and various invertebrates frequent human contact may lead to habituation, rather than emotional attachment. Flight and defensive reactions in these species can be gradually reduced through handling.

PSYCHOPHYSIOLOGICAL EFFECTS

Some of the subtle but profound physiological effects that the presence of a human can have on a dog have been documented (Gantt et al. 1966; Lynch and Gantt 1968; Lynch 1970). Holding, stroking, and even making eye contact with a dog can evoke a marked slowing of its heart rate. Differences in reactivity and cardiac activity have been identified in Pointers of stable and unstable temperament lineages (Murphree et al. 1967). A low resting heart rate, often with cardiac arrhythmias can be an early indicator of unstable temperament in the dog (Murphree et al. 1967). In contrast, dogs of a more stable and outgoing temperament have a higher resting heart rate.

Changes in heart rate as an indicator of sympathetic/parasympathetic arousal and homeostasis or tuning have been reviewed extensively in many vertebrate species, including man (Fox 1978). The relevance of these effects to the present discussion is that social or human contact and the emotions associated with such contact have profound effects on the organism's basic physiology. Rats interacting with each other have been shown, during affiliation, to undergo marked autonomic arousal (Joy and Latane 1971).

As a consequence of handling and other treatments early in life, the *tuning* of the autonomic nervous system can greatly modify an animal's phenotype (Fox 1971b). Gellhorn (1967) has emphasized the relative dominance of the sympathetic nervous system over the parasympathetic nervous system, or vice versa, and maintains that this dominance has a profound effect on behavior physiology (see also Fox 1978). Genotypic differences in autonomic tuning between species have recently been recognized (Mason 1984). Titi monkeys and squirrel monkeys respond differently to stress, the latter being active, tense, or excited and the former appearing depressed and becoming inactive and withdrawn. The squirrel monkeys, exhibiting greater sympathetic dominance, have been shown to be psychosomatically predisposed to hypertension and heart disease, while the titis, with greater parasympathetic dominance, are especially prone to diseases attributed to breakdown of the immune system.

The heart rate also varies in wolves and squirrel monkeys according to their social rank — generally the higher the rank the higher the rate —

and in pups of different temperament (reviewed in Fox 1981). Handling early in life also produces enduring effects in temperament and resting heart rate (Fox 1971), and it also enhances disease resistance in chickens (Gross 1984). Handling per se has a profoundly stimulating and potentially beneficial effect on the parasympathetic nervous system (Fox 1981, 1983 a & b), especially in sympathetically aroused, stressed, or overtuned animals. Conversely, some sympathetic arousal is needed in breeds or strains that are more parasympathetically tuned. Just as some parasympathetic arousal is beneficial to varying degrees, so sympathetic stimulation, such as social stress, can be highly beneficial (Gross 1984). With these thoughts in mind, let us reflect upon the disease susceptibility patterns in titi and squirrel monkeys and their linkage with their temperament, early experience, and species-typical, ecologically coadapted social structure. While they may provide models for sympathetic or parasympathetic psychogenic disease in man, they also reveal the complexities of physical health and psychological well-being. In summation, the heart rate is affected by genetic, developmental, neuroendocrine, sensory, cognitive, emotional, and socioecological influences.

By focusing more research on the autonomic nervous system and its connections with the emotions and psychogenic disease, along with the role that the social environment and heredity play in health and disease,[*] we may better husband and breed domesticated and laboratory animals and conserve wild animals in captivity. Most *domestogenic* diseases in animals (Fox 1983a) are caused or aggravated by human-introduced variables that reflect the inadequacies in our dominion over animals and overall planetary stewardship.

HANDLING AND GENTLING

Prior to the development of emotional, pain/pleasure associations via social experiences with conspecifics and human caretakers, the autonomic nervous system can be influenced by other environmental factors. Some of these are associated with handling, but during the immediate postnatal period in rats and mice these reactions are not linked with emotional/social reactions because the latter brain centers are not

---

[*]*The extreme temperaments of certain breeds of dog, and the way in which they are raised, may be linked with characteristic diseases, which in turn may correlate, as in Mason's titi and patas monkeys, with an autonomic nervous system imbalance that predisposes parasympathetic or sympathetic psychogenic dis-ease.*

sufficiently mature. But, since the autonomic nervous system and adrenal-pituitary axis are relatively mature, the neonatal mammal is sensitive to a range of environmental influences. The subsequent development of social behavior and emotional reactivity can be profoundly influenced, indeed directed, by such early environmental influences on the vegetative nervous system. Essentially the genetic and early experience determined tuning of the autonomic nervous system and adrenal-pituitary axis (Morton 1968). This becomes the template or basis for the subsequent development of temperament such as emotionality, reactivity towards handlers, physiological responsiveness to physical and emotional stress, and diseases — i.e., the emotional-behavioral phenotype. Further details of this dynamic interplay between the organism and environment, which may result in great physiological and behavioral phenodeviance, will be given in the next chapter. In the context of this discussion it is particularly relevant to the effects that a caretaker may have on young animals during their initial postnatal period. Routine handling and other procedures during the course of animal care warrant careful scrutiny and several research studies on these questions could be of value in this applied area of laboratory animal ethology and husbandry.

For example, handling or gentling a rat during its pregnancy may result in offspring that are less emotional and easier to handle. Husbandry methods can alter the behavioral and physiological phenotype; for example, one operator may talk to and handle the rat when he opens the cage to change bedding, food, and water, whereas the other operator avoids contact. Automated cage systems reduce the amount of human contact, (see Chapt. 7 for further details). This handler effect can be produced prenatally or postnatally during the first few days of life (Ader and Conklin 1963; Morton 1968). Even in adult rats, handling or exposure to an unfamiliar environment can affect behavior, plasma corticosterone, prolactin, and growth hormone levels (Brown and Martin 1974). Handling the mother or handling the offspring may cause the mother to groom her pups more; such maternal and environmental influences will affect the adrenocortical response to stress in weanling rats (Levine 1957). This stimulation early in life may also accelerate sexual development (Morton et al. 1963).

Some of these handling effects are not unique to rodents but also have been demonstrated in dogs (Fox 1971b) and cats (Meier and Stuart 1959).

Bradycardia or decreased heart rate is an indicator of a more generalized systemic shift in sympathetic/parasympathetic activity toward parasympathetic arousal. This physiological response may be associated with the anticipation of pleasant physical contact (e.g., petting). Paradoxically, bradycardia has been recorded in wild and unsocialized canids and is associated with passive submission and *tonic* immobility (i.e. "playing possum"). It has been hypothesized that it may be a behavioral and physiological precursor (a phylogenetically more ancient response) of the passive submission associated with pleasurable and friendly social contact (Fox 1978). The former response pattern has been identified in many species of reptiles, amphibians, and birds.

Phenotypic Changes

Differences in temperament (e.g., fearful, friendly, defensive, or outgoing) can have a genetic basis. Although experiences in early life may contribute to the genesis of such behavioral variance, the role of heredity in influencing the threshold of response and the subsequent developmental direction that such responsiveness may determine should be considered. For example, a basically timid dog may react fearfully towards strangers. Such reactions, when present early in life, may ensure that a pattern of avoidance/flight or defensive aggression becomes deeply ingrained; the older the animal, the more difficult such habitual responses will be to subdue or decondition. Optimal socialization early in life will help buffer such innate tendencies in the development of the animal's temperament. However, we should know which tendencies are being buffered and to what extent overt behavioral reactions are being subdued. In other words, the behavioral phenotype may be misleading since it may mask subtle genetically and experience-determined physiological reactions. Marked differences in behavior, emotionality, ease of handling, improved learning abilities, and faster maturation of EEG activity over nonhandled controls were identified in both laboratory cats (Meier and Stuart 1959) and dogs (Fox 1971b).

What these findings imply is that caretaker effects of handling must be controlled; otherwise, a great variance among individuals of the same strain (genotype) or species may be created. This human variable must be regulated as stringently as are other aspects of animal care such as breeding, nutrition, and cage size. Infantile stimulation — i.e., human handling — may be advisable if the animals are to be handled and/or exposed to human contact later in life; otherwise, excessive arousal may occur, rendering the animal physiologically unsound for many experimental purposes. A regimen of handling should be instigated in animal facilites as a part of sound animal care; this is an important, but often overlooked, aspect of animal husbandry (Denenberg and Whimbey 1963).

The ways in which laboratory animals are raised and handled can also lead to the introduction of significant experimental variables. For example, handling infant mice early in life will influence their resistance to leukemia (Levine and Cohen 1959). In rats, resistance to implanted malignant tumors is similarly affected by their early rearing (Ader and Friedman 1965). Such experimental variables may be inadvertently introduced by the caretaker's frequency of cage cleaning, whether or not the nest is disturbed, whether or not the pups are removed into a clean cage, and how the mother reacts to such disturbances. Smotherman et al. (1977 a & b) have shown that if rat pups are returned to the mother after a period of separation, but in a wire basket, the mother showed an elevation in plasma cortisone 20 minutes later. No such elevation was seen if the pups were accessible to the mothers. Significantly, the magnitude of corticoid elevations and the intensity of maternal behavior in these conditions correlated with the severity of treatment (shock or handling) the pups received when removed from their mothers.

Manuck et al. (1983) showed that those cynomolgus monkeys that had a marked increase in heart rate following the repeated stress of the experimenter's displaying prominently and threateningly before the target animals a large "monkey glove" (used to catch them with) also had a higher incidence of atherosclerosis. Other monkeys on the same moderately atherogenic diet that showed less cardiac reactivity to the experimenter stress had far less extensive atherosclerosis. The high heart rate reactors were also "significantly more aggressive, more ponderous, and had greater heart weights than did the low HR reactors."

Personnel

Another handler/caretaker variable not to be overlooked is the element of changes in personnel. While technicians may be equally trained how to care for and handle research animals, each person *is* different. Some individuals may have a particularly good way with cats or primates, and some animals may become especially attached to certain people. This again may introduce significant variance and would presumably be best controlled by rotating personnel in a large facility so as to dilute the effects of exposure to one person alone on the animals' social adaptability. Having the same caretaker over many months may result in some dogs becoming shy of strangers — for example, of the experimenter or of another laboratory technician. Varying personnel ex-

Figure 6-2

Rhesus monkeys in small laboratory cages express fear and apprehension towards humans, and their emotional and physiological state after handling introduces a serious variable to many critical studies.

posure would presumably provide a broader and more varied socialization base, making the animals more adaptable and accepting of other people. While this has obvious relevance when dealing with dogs, cats, and some primates, it may not seem worth considering with rodents. Research has shown, however, that rats can discriminate not only con-

Figure 6-3

The presence of a caretaker, feeding time, or other arousing stimuli causes this rhesus macaque to strike at and chew on its left hind foot.

specific odors (Morrison and Ludrigson 1970) but also that the presence of a familiar or unfamiliar caretaker can have a significant effect on their behavior (McCall et al. 1969). The discrimination between different personnel is based upon olfactory cues and, this being so, one may generalize with some certainty that all laboratory mammals should ideally receive as varied human exposure as possible if, in later life, they are going to be handled and perhaps even cared for by other people.

Other Aspects of Socialization

Many studies have shown how inadequate socialization or imprinting — caused by rearing animals in isolation or socializing them with an alien peer or foster parent — may cause respective deficits in social behavior and modify social and sexual preferences. It is a common problem in zoo animals — ungulates, carnivores, primates, and various species of birds — that have been hand raised with little or no socialization with their own species. When later put with their own species, they may withdraw, appear antisocial, and not join or be accepted by the group. They may show offensive or defensive aggression, frigidity, or inadequacies in care of offspring. There may also be interference in the sequencing of action patterns in their appropriate motivational context: a conflicting motivation may suddenly be seen in a dog that mounts a sexually receptive female and then suddenly bites the scruff of her neck. There may be a hypertrophy of basic drives or a lowering of the threshold of particular action patterns to the extent that inappropriate or trivial stimuli may release behavior such as flight or fight reactions.

It has been shown experimentally in both dogs and primates that lack of opportunity to socialize with peers interferes with later sexual and maternal behavior. When isolation-raised animals are first introduced to each other, extreme reactions of fear and defensive aggression or of inquisitiveness and social investigation interfere with other activities such as copulation. With careful handling and gradual socialization, such experimental animals may eventually recover from the effects of isolation rearing. Harlow observed that orphaned rhesus monkey mothers raised by surrogates recover much of their normal maternal responses to their second offspring, while the firstborn are severely mistreated. Experience, therefore, plays a major role in recovery or rehabilitation of species-characteristic behaviors.

The type of early social experience can have surprising consequences. Both dogs (Fox 1971b) and rhesus monkeys (Sackett et al. 1965) will prefer, as social play partners, conspecies who have had the same prior rearing history. Thus animals raised only with people, with people and their own kind, or exclusively with their own kind will, when given free choice, select an animal that has the same rearing history. Such interindividual compatibility based upon the type of early socialization has also been shown to influence sexual preferences (Sackett et al. 1965). Practically speaking, these findings have considerable relevance in setting up groups or communal colonies of animals since greater compatibility and reduced social conflicts are potentiated by ensuring that the animals have had a similar prior life history of socialization.

Methods of rearing and handling early in life clearly influence the emotional reactivity of animals when they are handled in later life. Prior handling greatly facilitates later handling: in rats, this is due to a reduction in emotional reactivity via the adrenal-pituitary axis. If instigated early in neonatal life, the neurohypophysis may be permanently affected so that ACTH is released in a graded fashion to increasing intensities of stress rather than in an all-or-none fashion as occurs in nonhandled controls (Levine and Mullins 1966).

Handling or, more correctly, gentling of older animals results in increased docility, partly as a result of habituation of the emotional fright, flight, or fight responses. Again, early handling of some strains has a greater effect than in others, indicating that the direction of effect is influenced by the genotype-environment interaction.

We should also not forget that the onset of gonadal activity may increase intraspecific aggression and act as a dispersal mechanism in some species. This endocrine change, as seen in pet ocelots and raccoons that suddenly become aggressive toward their handlers, is worthy of further investigation in relation to the proposed enduring nature of socialization and the interplay of ecologically adaptive dispersal mechanisms among various species.* Such behavior contrasts with the enduring attachment towards handlers in other species, particularly birds, which, at a later age, may regard the caretaker as a mate.

While these details, upon final analysis, may appear excessively fine grained and not particularly relevant to some experiments, they are, nonetheless, measurable variables that have been shown to influence a number of experimental factors. Plasma cortisol levels, susceptibility to radiation, and stress tolerance to cold or to induced diseases or neoplastic growths can vary widely not only as a function of age, sex, and genotype but also in relation to the animal's prior handling, exposure to people, and earlier socialization or habituation. The relevance of this, in relation to programming the life history of the research animal in order to control for phenodeviance, will be considered in the next chapter.

As hamsters mature, they prefer to live alone, while isolating a guinea pig from its herd may be stressful.

Chapter 7

Genotypic and Phenotypic Variables

S everal aspects of genotype-environment interactions in laboratory animals will now be described to emphasize that the practical implications of such interactions cannot be ignored if the quality and validity of biomedical research on animals are to be improved.

Fouts (1976), in presenting an overview of environmental and genetic factors affecting drug and chemical effects, concluded that:

> We do indeed recognize that the environment affects our experimental results and that effects of environment in our animals can be both dramatic and subtle. What we acknowledge is not, however, translated often into practice; and many of our data are confounded by environmental effects that we do not control, are unaware of, or for which we make no provision. Much of the information we do have is anecdotal rather than substantive, and much of what we need to know remains unstudied. Thus, this field of environmental and genetic factors affecting the response of laboratory animals represents an exciting area of biological research for future generations. Its appeal lies in the following: 1) small changes in environmental condition and genetic constitution can produce large alterations in the responses of the animal; 2) only a portion of the environmental and genetic conditions that cause such changes in laboratory animals have been identified, or once identified, adequately quantified; and 3) systematic investigations of such variables can result not only in closer correlation between animal models and physiological or disease states existing in man but also in discovery of new biological principles.

One intriguing report showed that in rhesus monkeys the sex of the fetus determines how frequently its mother gets bitten in a colony group. This study by Erwin and Anderson (1975) demonstrates the complexity of feedback systems between organisms and their socioenvironmental milieu:

Fifteen pregnant female monkeys were observed and the frequencies of 14 categories of agonistic behavior were recorded. Predictions of sex of foetus were based on relative frequencies of aggressive and submissive behaviors. Correct predictions were made in 11 of 15 cases (P < .06). The relative aggressiveness of females carrying male foetuses (by contrast with those carrying female foetuses) suggests that the secretion of androgens by male foetuses may masculinize the behavior of the female host.

(It remains unclear, however, whether "masculinized" mothers are more aggressive or more intimidating because of possible pheromonal changes.)

Other researchers have demonstrated a number of variables that may influence the developing organism such that a phenotypically different animal may be created. Such deliberately created phenodeviance illustrates the point that if we do not know what environmental influences are present during development, the animal remains an unknown factor. Knowing its genetic lineage is irrelevant if such environmental influences are not identified and either controlled or deliberately introduced so as to create a known phenotype (see Figs. 7-1 and 7-2).

In an elegant series of studies, Henderson (1970, 1976) has shown how laboratory rearing procedures can obscure genetic influences on behavior, while short exposures to enriched environments can increase genetic variability in mice. What these carefully designed studies imply is that the laboratory animal environment has a profound effect on the genetic influences that determine the phenotype that is expressed.

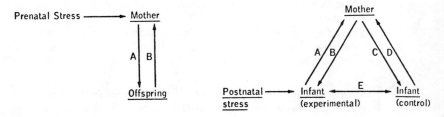

PRENATAL AND POSTNATAL INFLUENCES ON BEHAVIOR:
"FAMILY CIRCLE EFFECTS"

Figure 7-1

Schema of various feedback relationships that may affect mother and treated and nontreated offspring. (From Fox 1971a.)

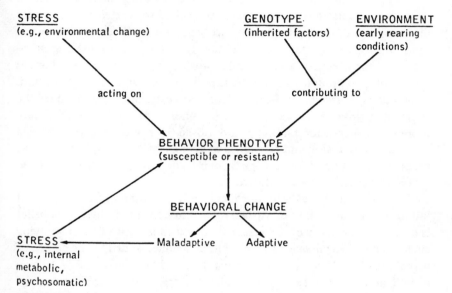

Figure 7-2

Schema of interrelated variables that may contribute to phenotypic variance and behavioral (and/or physiological) changes. (From Fox 1971a.)

This becomes even more complicated, as Henderson has shown, when we deal with different inbred strains; all of those studied had low scores for investigatory behavior and their hybrids all had high scores. Thus inbreeding per se may repress certain behaviors, as can certain methods of laboratory rearing. Henderson's studies make one wonder what a highly inbred and standard-caged rodent represents since it is both genetically and environmentally repressed.

How much actual change has occurred genetically in laboratory animals over generations in the absence of selection for specific heritable traits, rather than primarily phenotypic changes that buffer the genotype, is an open question. Yet it is surely important to know to what extent laboratory animals have been modified genetically, since domestication or "laboratorification" certainly has resulted in marked differences between wild and laboratory Norway rats. Price (1984) defines domestication as "that process by which a population of animals

becomes adapted to man and to captive environment by some combination of genetic changes occurring over generations and environmentally induced developmental events reoccurring during each
generation.''

Significantly, Connor (1975) attempted to model the domestication
process in populations of wild house mice raised for 10 generations under
different conditions. He found no behavioral differences between
random-bred tenth generation wild mice raised in a naturalistic environment and those raised in standard laboratory cages. Phenotypic changes
attributable to domestication in this species were insignificant since both
populations differed significantly from domestic mice raised under the
same conditions. However, a third population of wild mice that were
inbred (brother-sister matings) and raised in standard cages showed
male-male aggression and resistance to capture by humans; body weight,
investigation of intruders, escape from intruders and vocalization elicited
by being handled were unaffected.

A common belief still prevalent today is that inbred strains of
laboratory animals are less variable than random-bred ones. This belief
is as illusory as many of the research conclusions derived from studying
such animals. The reasons for this will be detailed shortly. The choice of
using certain inbred strains is often justified on the basis of known
genetic anomalies or specific biological models, but the common use of
inbred strains selected in order to reduce variability (so that results will
be consistent and so that fewer animals will be tested and less work required) is scientifically untenable if environmental influences are not
controlled. Also, the relevance of data from a small segment of the total
potential variance of a population is questionable since a characteristic
of normal animal populations is wide genetic variance with considerable
phenotypic uniformity (see Fig. 7-3).

The effects of the same rearing regimen can be quite different on
animals of different genetic backgrounds. Freedman (1958) illustrated
this important point and the complexity of the genotype-environment interaction in his study of four different breeds of dog. Each breed differed
according to the way in which it was raised (either permissively or
disciplined). Permissive rearing (or disciplinary rearing) did not have the
same effect across all breeds, but the final outcome was a consequence of
genotype and rearing history unique to each breed.

Other environmental influences have been shown to have profound effects on the physiology, anatomy, and behavior of a variety of laboratory
animals. These studies emphasize that we cannot adhere to the blind faith
that the genome will ensure normal development and the expression of a

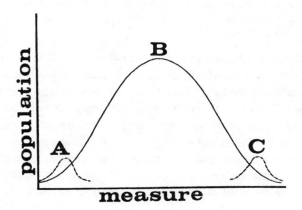

Figure 7-3

One of the pitfalls of using inbred strains is that measures derived from them (e.g., A & C) are not representative of a normal, more heterogenous population (B). For further discussion see the text. (From Fox 1971a.)

normal or standard phenotype. Through interactions with the genetic template during development, epigenetic changes may be created by environmental influences during critical or sensitive periods of development, resulting in a very different final phenotype.

One dramatic example is the sensitizing effect of noise in the animal house that, if mice are exposed during a receptive stage of development, will result in susceptibility to audiogenic seizures in adulthood. Iturrian and Fink (1969, 1968) summarized their findings as follows:

> Sound-induced convulsions continue to be a subject of great interest. It is possible to produce a high incidence of sound-induced convulsions in mice without the use of genetically susceptible strains, dietary, chemical, or surgical manipulations. Seizure susceptibility in weanling CF #1 mice depend on the interval between the first and second exposure to sound. Proper selection of age of audio-conditioning and the condition-test interval produces seizures of predictable incidence and severity.
>
> However, housing conditions during the experiment are most important. A routine fire drill, a busy telephone, noise from garbage cans or metal cages, electric drills, and barking dogs are examples of extraneous sounds that markedly change the incidence and severity of the convulsions observed. The audiosensitive period and the growth rate are influenced by various sounds generated in the animal room. Thus, environmental conditions must be rigidly controlled in such investigations if the results are to be reproducible.

Two different problems are raised by the data. One is the question of the mechanism(s) involved in the response to stress that develops the facilitated audiosensitivity. The other is whether the noise of metal equipment being banged about is a more serious disadvantage than has generally been recognized.

Even the basic physiological and behavioral response to pain can be modified by the way in which an animal is raised. Deprivation rearing can lead to a heightened pain threshold and an apparent insensitivity to pain in dogs (Melzak and Scott 1957) that may be misinterpreted as docility. Also, in rats, rearing in restricted or enriched environments will influence pain-avoidance behavior (Lore 1969). One may wonder, since such threshold shifts are related to the animal's general state of arousal, how such variance in excitatory state influences the results of basic neurophysiological studies and product testing, particularly of analgesics.

Riley (1981) has demonstrated that subnormal psychosocial stress caused by caging female mice singly, dramatically impaired lymphosarcoma tumor regression. He attributed this to the immunosuppressive effects of *hypostress,* in contrast to the *eustress* of caging mice in groups. Group living had a clear protective effect on the development of lymphosarcoma and influenced the phenotypic expression of disease. Gross (1984) has made similar observations on chickens since social isolation generally increases susceptibility to bacterial and parasitic diseases, while social grouping has a protective effect: social stress, however, increases susceptibility to viral diseases.

Riley's (1975) work on the development of mammary tumors in C_3H/He mice that carry the oncogenic Bittner virus as an indicator of the environmental effects of differential rearing is particularly instructive. A range of 92 percent incidence in the most highly stressed mice compared to a seven percent incidence in the least stressed and a respective median latent period for 50 percent of the mice to develop tumors in 276 days and 566 days are dramatic findings. The most stressed were parous females housed in groups of four to six in stainless steel cages in open racks in an animal room where other routine activities such as handling other mice and cage cleaning went on daily. The least stressed group consisted of nonparous females housed at the same density in plastic cages in ventilated, protected racks. Riley concluded that multiple-stress factors, including noise, odor, dust, pheromones, potentially infectious aerosols, and chronic anxiety in the former group were responsible for differences in tumor growth and incidence, illustrating how genetically influenced disease can be affected by the phenotype-modifying influence of the environment. This holistic approach is the basis of behavioral medicine (Weiss 1971) and will be discussed in more detail in Chapter 11.

Brain Development

Charles Darwin (1915) observed that the brain size of the domesticated rabbit is much smaller than its wild counterpart, a difference he attributed to a lower degree of stimulation in the domestic phenotype. Such an observation may appear ridiculous since one would assume that the development of the brain is dependent only upon genetic programming and good nutrition. As in all organ systems, however, the environment plays a significant role; brain development is environmentally dependent as well as genetically predetermined. Rosenzweig et al. (1972) have confirmed and extended Darwin's observations, using the laboratory rat to show that standard laboratory rearing conditions will produce rats with reduced brain size and other anomalies indicative of an environmental repression of genetic potential. Rats raised in groups in enriched cages with various manipulanda develop larger brains and exhibit other neurologic and behavioral differences in comparison to those raised either alone or together in otherwise barren standard cages.[*]

Similarly, in mice, postweaning environmental enrichment or deprivation will influence both emotionality and brain weight (Denenberg et al. 1969). Even more selective deprivation will influence brain activity, emphasizing that the rearing environment helps attune the organism's innate potentials. The unity of organism and environment is inseparable.

The rearing environment can affect brain functioning. For example, Pettigrew and Freedman (1973) reported that:

Kittens were reared in a planetarium-like visual environment that lacked straight line contours. Cortical neurons were subsequently highly sensitive to spots of light but not to straight lines, in marked contrast to those from a normal cat. If linear contour processing is an innate function, it appears to be subject to substantial modification by early visual experience.

---

[*]*Marian Diamond and co-workers have also found that rat pups from parents raised in enriched conditions have increased body weight at birth and increased cortical thickness as they matured. Three generations later, rats raised in standard cages from "enriched parents" continue to have greater body weights and larger brains.* Psychology Today. *(Nov. 1984): 68.*

It is obvious that if it is not known what influences are present or absent in the laboratory animal environment, it cannot be known what environmentally or experientially influenced structures and processes are present or modified in the animal.

Captive-born and -raised ground squirrels housed in an enriched laboratory environment were, according to Rosenzweig et al. (1982), closer to ground squirrels that matured in the wild in some, but not all, brain measures compared to others kept in an impoverished — i.e., standard, sterile cage — environment. Brain weight measures and total RNA in brain sections of the enriched animals equaled wild animals, both being significantly above the impoverished ground squirrels. However, in brain RNA per unit of brain weight, the wild squirrels had significantly higher values than either the enriched or impoverished ones.

Floeter and Greenough (1979) have demonstrated that rearing conditions affect brain development, in the rhesus macaque, as assessed by the dendritic branching in cerebellar Purkinje cells. They reported that:

> Sixteen monkeys, *Macaca fascicularis,* were semirandomly assigned to and reared for the first 6 months of life under one of three conditions. Six monkeys, three males and three females, reared in isolation had a very limited sensory and motor environment, having been enclosed in a 1-m^3 Plexiglas cube contained within a sound-attenuating vault. The I monkeys neither saw nor had physical contact with another monkey during rearing, and there was little in the cage to encourage manipulation or play. Six monkeys, five males and one female, reared under social conditions were housed in wire cages also about 1-m^3 in size. Cages for pairs of monkeys were adjacent, and 4 hours of play were allowed each day between pairs of monkeys. Social monkeys also had the opportunity to see and hear other monkeys and people. . . . Four colony reared monkeys, two males and two females, were housed in a seminaturalistic setting, — two interconnected large rooms with monkeys of all ages and both sexes. Several large fixed structures and smaller manipulable toys were present for play.

These three rearing conditions varied both the social and physical complexity of the animals' environment. (It should be pointed out that in many primate laboratories, the conditions are comparable to a state somewhere between the first two conditions described above.)

The authors also found that:

> In the colony-reared monkeys, spiny branchlets of Purkinje cells were more extensive in the paraflocculus and the nodulus than they were in the other two groups. Granule cell dendritic branching in the paraflocculus and nodulus did not differ across groups. In addition, Purkinje cell somas were larger in the uvula and the nodulus of the colony

animals than in the other groups. These data indicate that the social and physical environment during development influences the morphology of cerebellar Purkinje cells.

Generations of inbreeding under one set of variables in one laboratory may create a pattern of random genetic drift in the colony quite different from that of another laboratory animal facility that ostensibly has the same strain or breed of animals. The genotype-environment interaction may therefore create significant variance between different research colonies.

Genetic factors play an important role in the metabolism of various drugs, toxins, and other substances. This subject has been reviewed by Nebert and Felton (1976) who summarized their findings as follows:

> Gene differences may alter an individual's response to foreign compounds by affecting their absorption, binding, distribution, excretion, biotransformation, or drug-drug interactions. Genetic differences in the metabolism of xenobiotics among inbred strains of various laboratory animals and model systems are reviewed. The inbred mouse has been studied most extensively. Genetic differences in toxicity are shown to be caused by various environmental pollutants in several inbred strains of mice and in siblings of the $(C57BL/6N)(DBA/2N)F_1 \times DBA/2N$ backcross, in which the phenotypes "aromatic hydrocarbon responsiveness" or "nonresponsiveness" had been predetermined. This trait of "responsiveness" — which refers to the capacity for induction of cytochrome P_1450 and numerous monooxygenase activities by certain aromatic compounds — segregates almost exclusively as a single gene among offspring of this backcross. All nonresponsive mice ingesting benzo/a/pyrene (about 125 mg/kg per day) die within 4 weeks, whereas the survival of responsive mice receiving the chemical orally is not significantly different from that of control mice; the apparent cause of early death in these experiments is toxic depression of the bone marrow. The life span of animals exposed to certain environmental pollutants can therefore be markedly influenced by a single gene or a very small number of genes. The same genetic trait can be either beneficial or detrimental to the animal, depending on whether detoxification or metabolic potentiation occurs. There also may exist genetic differences in man's susceptibility to toxicity or cancer caused by the numerous foreign compounds in his environment.

Vessell et al. (1976) provide a useful summary of their studies of environmental and genetic factors affecting the response of laboratory animals to various drugs:

> Only some of the diverse factors that can affect drug disposition and response in laboratory animals have been identified at the present time. These numerous factors contribute to large day-to-day variations

that have become a major problem impeding investigation of drug disposition and response in laboratory animals. Although these variations render many experiments difficult to interpret and produce large discrepancies in the literature, few published investigations using laboratory animals provide sufficient details to permit replication of the studies under similar conditions with respect to these variables. Thus, the importance of these variables in affecting results is apparently insufficiently recognized at present. Two commonly overlooked variables affecting the activity of hepatic microsomal enzymes (HME) in rodents and hence the rate at which rodents eliminate from their bodies many foreign compounds are the bedding under the wire mesh cage and the relative cleanliness of the environment. Numerous chemicals present in relatively low concentrations in the environment of the animal room can significantly alter HME activity. Representative of these chemicals are aromatic hydrocarbons in cedarwood bedding, eucalyptol from aerosol sprays, and chlorinated hydrocarbon insecticides, each of which induces HME activity, whereas ammonia generated from feces and urine accumulated in unchanged pans under cages may inhibit HME activity. Chloroform, identified as an environmental contaminant of the water and air of certain cities, exhibits sex and strain differences with respect to toxicity (LD_{50}) in mice. After intraperitoneal injection, twice as much chloroform accumulated in the kidneys of males from the sensitive strain (DBA/2J) as from the resistant (C57BL/6J) strain. First generation offspring were midway between parental strains both with respect to LD_{50} and renal accumulation of chloroform.

Other studies have identified other environmental variables that may influence psychophysiological development (Bronson and Chapman 1968). Stress during pregnancy in rats may result in a persistent alteration in the turnover of brain noradrenaline (Huttunen 1971). Similarly, early experiences will influence the later behavioral/emotional/physiological characteristics or *phenotype complex* (Ader and Plaut 1968; Ader 1968; Shaefer 1971). The direction or magnitude of effect will be influenced not only by the genotype but also by handling the mother and affecting her behavior towards the offspring and vice versa (Barfield and Geyer 1972).

One of the more startling, if not disturbing, conclusions from these studies is that an environmental influence affecting one generation can be transmitted from that generation to several succeeding generations (Denenberg and Rosenberg 1967; Denenberg and Whimbey 1963a) because environmental influences affect the mother's endocrine system, which in turn affects the developing neuroendocrine system of the offspring.

Developing and Integrating Nervous System

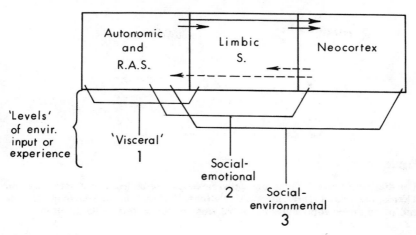

Figure 7-4

Schema of relationships between stages of development of the central nervous system and the times when various type of environmental influence have their greatest effect. 1) Handling early in life affects the adrenal-pituitary, autonomic, and reticular-activating systems. 2) Development of social attachments correlates with the development of limbic (emotional) centers. 3) Social and environmental influences affect brain (cortical) maturation. (From Fox 1971b.)

In the light of this, it would be highly advisable to create structured and carefully programmed environmental input to ensure that a known phenotype will be produced (see Fig. 7-4). Without experimentally programmed life histories (Denenberg and Whimbey 1963b), the variance and unknown qualities of laboratory animals will continue to cast dubious shadows on many of the research conclusions that are drawn from them.

The Dramatype (Russell and Burch 1959)

The studies discussed above converge on a single critical conceptualization, namely, the *dramatype*. This term was coined by Russell and Burch in their book *The Principles of Humane Experimental Technique*. Figure 7-5, borrowed from this classic text, shows the relations between certain variables discussed in this chapter. Russell and Burch (op. cit.) state:

> By the dramatype we mean the pattern of performance in a single physiological response of short duration relative to the animal's life-

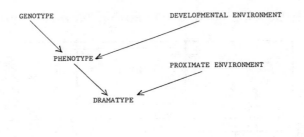

THE DETERMINATION OF THE DRAMATYPE (from Russell
                                        and Burch 1959)

Figure 7-5

The diagram shows the relations between certain variables. It is a *path diagram*. That is, the arrows represent causal relations. Variation in the system at the back end of an arrow contributes to the variance of the system at the front end.

time; for instance, the reaction to a hormone of its target organ, or the reaction of the whole organism to a poison. Variation in such responses is, in its turn, the joint product of two factors. One is the phenotype itself. The other is the *proximate* or immediate environment in which the response is elicited. Dramatypic variation thus depends on the animal's more stable properties, phenotypically determined, and on the environmental conditions in which these are expressed in action.

If we wish fully to control the variance of physiological responses, we must therefore proceed as follows. First, we must control the phenotype, and this in turn may be done by *breeding methods* together with influence on the environmental conditions *in which the animals are reared*. Second, we must control the environmental conditions *in which the animals are tested*.

Those interested in further details on the design and analysis of experiments, efficient statistical analysis, and economic reduction in the number of animals used for experimentation and routine test procedures such as bioassay are to be referred to this book.

Apropos of selecting a representative sample of animals for a study (such as a toxicity study) it might be concluded on the basis of the arguments presented on page 97, that a heterogeneous stock should be used in order to obtain a broad inductive basis. These authors argue to the contrary, suggesting that fewer animals would be needed if several different homogeneous samples of pure strains were used or preferably F_1 hybrids, and if the variance between samples were allowed for. Without application of these well-established principles of behavioral genetics, the investigator would not be able to make a relatively precise statistical evaluation of error.

Russell and Burch make the following important point:

It must not be concluded that one particular breeding policy is now established at the expense of all others. On the contrary, each bioassay problem must be tackled on its own merits. There are several reasons for this. In general, hybridity is advantageous quite apart from its effect on uniformity, because it confers increased "vigour" — better viability and general health and toughness under all conditions. Even this advantage may be cancelled in practice if it is accompanied by *behavioural* vigour to an extent that makes handling difficult. In general, any breeding policy is bound to have effects on characters other than those primarily envisaged, and these side-effects may be sources of trouble in practice.

More important, the relative contributions of genotypic and environmental variation differ in different characters. Hence the finding that hybrids are more uniform than relatively homozygous material is by no means universal for all characters.

. . . our policy must depend upon the relative importance of the two components of variance in the characters with which we are concerned. The genetic contribution is in effect twofold. *BOTH* genetic heterogeneity between individuals *and* the relative homozygosity of each individual contribute to phenotypic variance. The former factor acquires weight with characters whose variation is mainly genetically, the latter with those whose variation is mainly environmentally determined. For the former kind of character, inbreds and F_1 cross-breds will tend to be more uniform, for the latter random-breds and F_1 cross-breds. The F_1 cross is more generally advantageous because it combines the best of both worlds, its individuals being relatively heterozygous and relatively genetically homogeneous. But the exact relations will differ for each character.

Russell and Burch go on to cite key studies which show that the use of inbred strains of animals for response uniformity is a traditional illusion. Greater uniformity of many response indices are to be obtained from F_1 (first generation) hybrids — a conclusion reflected in the later work of Henderson cited earlier in this chapter. Inbred mouse strains have been shown to have greater variability in estrogen and nembutal assay than random-bred colonies, and the latter had more variability than the F_1 progeny of crosses between inbred strains.

In their thought-provoking discussion, these authors also emphasize that adverse environmental conditions can increase phenotypic variability, while optimal conditions will diminish it. + They state, "In the further-

---

+ *See Appendix II for further details of proven dramatypic influences that support the contention that the humane ethic and good biomedical research with animals are interdependent and not mutuallly exclusive, nor is their complementarity unattainable, overly idealistic, or impractical.*

ance of phenotypic uniformity, breeding methods, however excellent, will not avail unless supported by control of the developmental environment." When the ramifications of dramatypic variance are ignored, research on animals will be of dubious value and validity (see Ashoub et al. 1958 and Biggers et al. 1958). It follows that physiological uniformity is likely to be one of the rewards of good laboratory animal husbandry, this being a positive benefit to science and a practical justification for upholding the humane ethic.

Chapter 8

Alternatives and New Directions

From the foregoing review of the many variables that are often un-controlled in the research animal and the laboratory environment, the concerns of scientist and humanitarian find a common ground. There is a clear need to improve the conditions in which research animals are kept and to critically explore and evaluate alternatives and new directions for the future.

One good start would be to determine to what degree the various laboratory animal species have been modified genetically by inbreeding and genetic drift and phenotypically by environment. How representative are they, genetically and phenotypically, of normal, nonlaboratory raised and bred conspecifics? And how valid are the animal models created and many of the tests conducted on such animals, which are used increasingly in research, product development, and safety testing? What natural biochemical, hormonal, and behavioral processes have been altered via the process of "laboratorification" and what abnormal stresses are imposed upon such animals, which, unbeknown to the investigator, might modify the effects of experimental treatments (see Fig. 8-1)?

Several studies have been done to determine what effects, if any, domestication or "laboratorification" has had on the laboratory rat. (For a general review see Boice 1973; and Price 1984.) Differences in temperament, learning ability, and reactivity, as well as neophobia, neophilia, and avoidance of noxious/poisoned bait have been attributed to both intentional and incidental effects selecting laboratory rats for docility.

We may begin by asking the laboratory animal certain questions in the form of carefully designed ethological experiments. This way we may discover what normal physiological processes, needs, and behaviors have been intensified, suppressed, or otherwise altered in the process of rear-

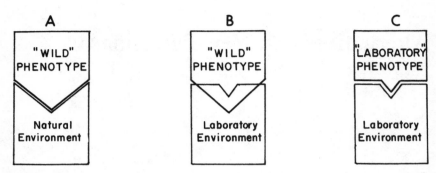

Figure 8-1

Schema of adaptation or laboratorification to the laboratory. Critical stress and transitional adaptation phases. Not all animals may reach phase C, especially if they are fully mature when captured. Over successive generations, artificial selection to standardize the phenotypes characteristic of the captive colony is atypical because it has been modified and adapted to an unnatural environment. Foundation animals that reach phase C are more likely than others to breed in captivity, and the reproductive rate would be an important selector for a genotype that more closely approximates the adapted phenotype. Where adaptation involves the innate or genetic capacity rather than early experience or socialization, such a selective "laboratorification" is highly probable.

ing, cage-confinement, and general care in the laboratory animal environment (see Dawkins 1976; Kavanau 1977; and Duncan 1978).

For example, an animal may be given a choice between two cage environments, one being dark, the other light, or one containing bedding or some material to manipulate while the other is empty. Hamsters at the FDA animal facility in Washington, DC are reportedly larger and healthier if they have a pile of pellets placed in their cages than if they have to chew them through the bars of a food container (Dr. R.A. Zaldivar, personal communication). Hamsters enjoy pouching and stacking pellets in one corner of their cages. This is a natural behavior that is frustrated when food is available only through the bars of a dispenser. Even more significant improvements might be evident if such animals were provided with some bedding material.

With a suitable battery of tests, we may be able to quickly determine what environment the animal favors. Given some choice, the animal will be able to maintain normal ethostasis and thus avoid the negative stresses of a suboptimal environment. This would provide a more normal animal for research since the dramatypic variance described in the previous chapter would be reduced. In a subjective sense, the animal would be happier in an environment to which it is preadapted and within which it can develop and express more of its natural range of behaviors as well as satisfy many of its basic needs. One would anticipate that with the provision of an optimal environment, the animal would be physically and psychologically healthier and such provision would satisfy our ethical obligation of humane care as it applies to the housing of animals for research purposes.

Skeptics might argue that a highly inbred laboratory rat, for example, is preadapted to the laboratory environment. As such, it is quite content in an otherwise empty wire cage. A casual observer might agree, seeing no signs of stress or of physical or behavioral pathology in the caged animal. But we have not asked the animal, which one can do quite easily. Some examples will be given shortly. It should be emphasized that domesticated and laboratory animals are not degenerate forms of their wild counterparts. Although this is an all too common view or unconscious attitude, there is no scientific evidence to support it. Domestication and "laboratorification" may alter the threshold and intensity of certain behaviors and either intensify or reduce various motivational or drive states and needs associated with such complex behavioral systems as territoriality, sexuality, and aggression. Some reduction in the size of adult structures (e.g., teeth, hair, and horns) may be interpreted as degeneration, but such changes may instead be due to infantilism (neoteny or paedomorphosis) a not uncommon consequence of domestication (and of evolution in man also). The unconscious or mistaken belief that laboratory animals are inferior or degenerate, artificial, manmade creations may, in fact, be responsible for their being treated more indifferently and less humanely than other animals.

Lockard (1968) went so far as to state, in reference to studying the domesticated laboratory rat, that "It is at least a waste of time, if not outright folly, to experiment upon the degenerate remains of what is available intact in other animals." Regardless of such prejudice, wild animals raised under impoverished conditions may be no less degenerate and even less reliable than domestic animals that are better adapted to captivity (i.e., have greater inclusive fitness) and are raised under more enriched conditions.

Huck and Price (1975) showed that the development of behavior in domestic laboratory rats is more highly buffered against locomotor and perceptual deficits in behavior than first generation wild rats born in captivity. Furthermore, early experience in an enriched environment had less effect on the growth and open field behavior of domestic rats than the wild ones, which seemed more dependent upon such environmental contingencies. Price (1984) concludes, "In nearly all cases, behavioral differences between wild and domestic stocks are quantitative in character and, in most instances, are best explained by shifting thresholds based on genotypic changes, the effects of the captive environment on behavioral development, or both."

The view that laboratory rats and other domesticated animals are inferior degenerate life forms with no instincts left, other than those associated with eating, drinking, sex, and maternal care, accords with and confirms the seventeenth century view that animals are mere unfeeling, reflexively mechanical automatons. Such a regard for laboratory animals is scientifically untenable and may be the basis for much of the inhumane and unethical treatment of these animals by some investigators, and, significantly, is often associated with poor and frequently meaningless research.

Over 40 years ago it was shown that the "degenerate" white rat, if given a choice, prefers to explore a maze rather than remain in its own cage. The animal's need for varied stimulation, its drive to explore, and its obvious enjoyment of having access to something more stimulating than a small, barren cage were dramatically demonstrated (Nissen 1930): Dramatically because the investigator placed a highly electrical grid on the floor to block the rat's access to the maze. The rat, however, crossed the grid and preferred to be subjected to painful electrical shock rather than be denied the opportunity to spend time outside of its cage in an exciting maze.

Since this study, other investigators have shown how other laboratory animals such as rhesus monkeys and dogs will work willingly in order to obtain visual access to companions or to a more interesting environment outside their barren cages (Fox 1971). (This may be done with the Butler box device in which the animal presses a bar or plate that lifts an opaque screen so that the animal can see out of its cage for a short time period. In this way, social motivation can be quantitatively measured.)

Cage size for rodents is a significant factor in environmental enrichment (Manosevitz and Pryor 1975) and can affect body weight and weight gain in mice (Doolittle et al. 1976). The effects on exploratory behavior of rearing rodents in a free environment have been demonstrated (Zimbardo and Montgomery 1957). Littermates raised in standard cages were more exploratory than those raised in the free environment when they were placed in a novel situation. The greater response

Figure 8-2A

Figure 8-2B

Rhesus monkeys (A) and a baboon (B) in standard laboratory cages in a U.S. government research facility, illustrating the extreme degree of social and environmental deprivation that is scientifically and ethically unacceptable.

to novelty in the relatively deprived animals reflects the effects of rearing under standard but suboptimal conditions. Other investigators have shown that free environmental experience in laboratory rats leads to improved learning ability (Forgays and Forgays 1952) — i.e., a more normal environment produces more normal rats.

In dogs, access to a novel or enriched environment is essential for normal development of exploratory behavior (Fox and Spencer 1969). Pups deprived in standard pens, even when in social groups, show fear and avoidance in novel situations later in life. What is exciting and enjoyable for some becomes fear-evoking and noxious to others, depending on their rearing history — a very clear phenotypic or dramatypic difference.

Even greater differences have been demonstrated in rats and mice raised in an enriched — i.e., relatively natural — environment compared to those raised under standard, but suboptimal, cage conditions. Brain weight, cell density, cortical thickness, acetylcholinesterase, and cholinesterase activity are affected, and enriched animals are generally healthier, more curious, and have superior learning abilities (Ferchmin et al. 1975; La Torre 1968; Rosenzweig 1971). These detailed studies would seem to imply that the standard laboratory cage environment may not produce an animal that is normal in any shape or form. What is needed to improve the quality of animals for research is greater attention to creating optimal environmental conditions. Conditions are generally suboptimal, tending to repress and otherwise modify the development and attainment of normal brain and behavioral functioning.

Chamove et al. (1982) assessed the effects of deep wood-chip litter in improving the husbandry of eight primate species. The results showed that the use of such litter material is an inexpensive way to increase environmental complexity and overall welfare in the indoor housing of primates. The presence of wood chips decreased fighting and increased general activity, exploratory behavior, and time spent on the ground. With time, the litter became increasingly inhibitory to bacterial growth. In addition, the use of frozen foods improved food distribution and reduced fighting in most situations, particularly when the food was buried in the litter.

Environmental enrichment can also be provided for a variety of species by using electrical and mechanical manipulanda (Markowitz 1982). Such devices need not be restricted to captive zoo animals since they do have a place in the design of laboratory animal housing facilities.

Kavanau (1967) found that captive white-footed mice spent inordinate amounts of energy and time resisting experimental manipulation — i.e., imposed regimens. If experimenters turned the lights down, the mice would turn the lights up and vice versa. It is therefore probable that providing laboratory animals with manipulanda, so that they can experience some measure of control, may enhance their well-being and physical health and, as shown by Markowitz (1982), it facilitates the early recognition of illness. Such animals should, theoretically, be easier to handle, and they should suffer less stress while being physically restrained. For example, frequent handling results in more than simple habituation — the animal learns that it will be released after a given duration of handling. In the process, it acquires a sense of competence and control.

Wallace (1982) describes the Cambridge mouse cage, which is designed to more fully satisfy the species behavioral and experimental requirements. She contends that a major obstacle in the design of optimal restricted environments for laboratory animals has been the notion that animal and human needs are invariably conflicting. By listing known and suspected animal needs separately from a list of human needs — i.e., for husbandry and experimentation — better designs can be developed when the two listings are compared and adjustments are made to enhance compatibility (see Tab. 8-1). The author contends, "This kind of thinking process ought to underlie the design of all restricting environments for animals in the 80s, when one hopes that it has at last become respectable to consider animal needs as well as those of human beings."

When given a choice, laboratory raised animals will seek out the environment or an artificial facsimile for which they are best adapted and within which they can satisfy their various physical and social needs. Habitat preferences have been demonstrated in laboratory mice. When they are given the habitat of their choice — i.e., a more optimal environment — their reproductive performance was enhanced (Itturian and Fink 1968). When given a choice of artificial woodland or prairie habitats, prairie and woodland species of deer mice raised in the laboratory and never exposed to their natural environment selected that environment for which it was preadapted. Laboratory raised prairie and woodland subspecies of deer mice chose a simulated prairie and artificial woodland habitat respectively (Wicker 1963).

Few such elegantly simple preference studies have been conducted on the various species that are kept for research purposes.* This is surprising since such animals might be healthier, happier, and more repre-

---

*For cage-preference studies in single-caged rats, (see Weiss and Taylor 1984).

Table 8-1a.　List of Animal (Mouse) Needs (from Wallace 1982)

BEHAVIOR	REQUIREMENTS
Activity	A living space permitting exploration, exercise, grooming and social interaction where territory can be marked; containing material providing sensory stimulation and adaptable for sleeping and nesting
	Dry, ventilated, and cooler than animal's body temperature
Eating	A balanced diet: hard enough to wear down growing teeth; and accessible enough to satisfy appetite and exercise paws, jaw, and the sense of smell
Drinking	Water (or moist enough food): with easy access, but ensuring a dry living space
Sleeping	A discrete area: for retention of body heat, and for social huddling (which may be a tactile need)
	Low light intensity
	"Mousey" smells (possibly desirable to the mouse?) and external noise should be controllable
Defecating	This seems to accompany activity and therefore can occur anywhere but the nest, so the nest area should be identifiable to the mouse
	Space restriction limits supply of food and water, so these must be inaccessible to excretory organs
	Activity areas should allow ventilation to dry out fecal pellets.
Urinating	An area away from the nest — restriction hinders territorial marking and escape of attacked males, so hiding places are desirable
	Use of urine for communication in mouse social groups, including females, seems desirable
Nesting	An area where nest temperature can be controlled
	Bedding must be suitable for chewing and manipulating — the mouse uses bedding to form a "sweater" inside a "windcheater," *i.e.*, the bedding insulates, but the confines of the bedding must be conducible to the exclusion of drafts around the time of parturition, and permit a gradual increase of air exchange during rearing of young
	(Note that "draft" and "air exchange" refer to air exchanges between activity area and nest area, not between the cage and the animal room)

Table 8-1b.   List of Human Requirements

CRITERION	REQUIREMENTS
	In Relation to the Animal
Confinement	Cage parts must fit such that there is no crack or hole big enough for the smallest active mouse to get through
Productivity	Maximum number of weaned young per female; this consists of maximum ova shed, minimum implantation and antenatal loss, minimum female mortality at parturition, and minimum mortality of young to weaning
Health	Cage conditions must complement the "macro-environment" to ensure certain disease-free levels
	In Relation to the Cage
Hygiene	Materials and parts must be easily washed and/or autoclaved
	The cage and its contents must be dry enough to discourage the growth of pathogens and fungus
	The cage and its contents must not be smelly
Cost	Materials and their manufacture must be cheap
	The design must be easy to mass-produce with a minimum of hand labor
	The part must be durable in use — washing, storing, assembly and handling
Comfort for the Handler	No sharp or rough surfaces
	The parts and the whole must be light to carry
	The cage must be easily put on and removed from shelves
	The lid must be easily put on and taken off
	The contents must be easy to inspect, with or without the removal of the lid
	Ease of servicing, handling and storing
Design Should Be Adaptable	The parts must be easy to clean, stack and store, and easy to assemble and dismantle
	The design should be adaptable to accessories concerned with research (*e.g.,* behavioral); with cleaning (*e.g.,* vaccum cleaning); with handling (*e.g.,* the chute); and with recording the status of the animals inside in terms of breeding and treatment

sentative of normality if they were to be provided with a more natural environment (Fox 1966). Further evidence to support this contention will be presented shortly.

Lawlor (1984) gives some useful examples of how a behavioral approach to rodent management can do much to enhance their comfort and well-being in laboratory facilities. One is a simple test of fearfulness. After pulling the rats' cage a few inches, the scientist uses the time taken before the rats stand up to investigate as a useful index of how used they are to being handled. The longer the latency (from 10 to 25 or 30 secs), the greater the fear. (Females are generally less fearful than males.) In studies conducted to determine what kind of cage design best satisfies rats' behavioral needs, Lawlor showed that many designs have insufficient height from the floor of the cage to the top. This interferes with standing and rearing up, which are aspects of investigatory behavior. She found that rats need a cage height of 20 cm. Thus, the Council of Europe's Convention on Laboratory Animal Standards of 14 cm height for rats is inadequate since some of their behaviors are distorted, inhibited, and possibly frustrated.

Infant monkeys raised in isolation show a marked difference in their choice of visually stimulating objects compared to those raised under more standard conditions (Sackett 1966). While the latter will work hard — for instance, in the Butler box apparatus described earlier — for the opportunity to look at complex visual patterns, the former prefer to look at less complex patterns. The deprived monkeys may be developmentally retarded.

Studies have also been conducted using the same quantifiable behavioral indices to compare wild, free, and caged groups of animals. Baboons show a higher frequency of such behaviors in captive groups (Rowell 1967), although no significant qualitative differences in behavior were noted. Under more restrictive conditions where space, manipulanda, and conspecifics are reduced, the quantitative and qualitative changes become increasingly apparent compared to the norm. The genesis of the stereotyped behaviors described earlier is one class of actions that are qualitatively different from the norm and that may show a quantitative shift depending upon what environment factors have been subtracted or added (Berkson 1968). The baboon study by Rowell (op. cit.) demonstrates the feasibility of applying direct observation and ethological analysis of behavioral data to determine the extent to which a given method of laboratory housing affects behavior and social relations.

Behavior studies of social groups of primates and other laboratory animals are not simply academic games without practical application. Some recent studies have demonstrated how valuable behavior research can be in the husbandry and production of primate colonies. Bernstein and Gordon (1977) synopsized their work showing the importance of behavioral studies and improved primate husbandry. In summary:

> The existence of an active behavioral research program using animals in primate breeding colonies was considered to be not only a compatible multiple use of animals, but a way of materially improving the management and efficiency of the breeding colonies. In colonies of monkeys specifically established for behavioral research programs directed at the examination of social relationships, incidental breeding resulted in levels of reproductive success equivalent to or greater than that normally experienced in colonies devoted entirely to breeding. Behavioral research revealed patterns of seasonality, fostering, kidnapping, and infant care that would otherwise have escaped notice and that would significantly influence culling and management choices in a breeding colony. Many young males and certain low-ranking adult males actively contributed to reproduction. Females born and reared in the colonies were the most productive, exceeding wild born or other introduced females in reproductive efficiency. Specific recommendations for establishing, expanding, and culling of nonhuman primate breeding colonies were derived from the behavioral research.

Knowing the social dynamics of the group and its space requirements can do much to rectify problems of fighting and injury without having to resort to the old safe way of placing animals in separate cages or in abnormally small social groups. This was shown by Erwin (1977), who summarized his findings as follows:

> Several experiments and surveys were conducted in a large colony of pigtail macaques (*Macaca nemestrina*) to determine some of the influences of spatial and social factors on aggressive behavior and risk of trauma. Female subjects exhibited more aggression when they had access to two-room suites than when they had access to single rooms. The frequency of aggressive interactions among females was positively related to the number of females per group. The presence of one or more males in groups inhibited aggressive interaction among females. Less aggression occurred among females in groups containing infants than in groups containing no infants. Provision of cover by introduction of concrete cylinders into rooms reduced aggression among members of stable groups. Subjects in newly formed groups composed of unfamiliar animals sustained fewer injuries than did those in groups formed by merger of groups or subgroups of familiar animals.

The practical problem of disrupted sexual behavior in a breeding colony can arise from early social deprivation. Again, behavioral research can contribute significantly to rectifying this problem, as Goldfoot (1977) showed in his study entitled "Rearing Conditions Which Support or Inhibit Later Sexual Potential of Laboratory-Born Rhesus Monkeys: Hypotheses and Diagnostic Behavior." This important study was summarized as follows:

> Sexual behaviors of adult rhesus monkeys reared in infancy under severe, moderate, or minimal social deprivation conditions have been studied at several laboratories. With severe deprivation conditions (weaning at birth; no peer contact) reproductive success for both sexes was very low, and rehabilitation efforts did not appear to be promising. Moderate deprivation conditions (weaning at 3-6 months; limited daily contact with peers) eliminated many of the neurotic behaviors associated with severe social deprivation, but reproductive success was still quite poor (25-40% male copulators; females poor mothers). Rehabilitation was possible in some instances. Minimal laboratory deprivation conditions (mother-infant rearing in penned groups; weaning at 8-12 months with further peer group socialization) resulted in high copulatory probabilities of the offspring. It was hypothesized that for eventual reproductive potential to develop, rhesus infants needed complex social environments in which aggression and fear among peers occurred only at low levels, and that the closer one came to duplicating the naturalistic social environment of the monkey, the better chance one had of producing reproductively capable animals. Diagnostic behavioral categories were given to help researchers assess the psychosocial development of rhesus infants. It was suggested, in particular, that weaning not be carried out until the development of the foot clasp mount in the infant male was a regular part of the behavioral repertoire.

Automatic recording devices are also available for measuring some behaviors such as general activity (Neamand et al. 1975), but it should be emphasized again that simply measuring one parameter or univariate difference between two different treatment groups may be of limited value. Suffice it to say that the science of ethology should be applied to evaluate what social and environmental criteria might be incorporated into a practical design of laboratory animal husbandry to create optimal conditions in the name of good science and humane ethics.

Economically, savings will be significant. Maintaining colonies of various species under varying degrees of seminatural conditions can cut the costs of caging, personnel, and other maintenance expenditures to a fraction of the usual amounts. This is especially true for primate colonies (Banerjee and Woodward 1970; Hoffman and Stowell 1973). See Figure 8-3. In addition, the animals are generally healthier and happier in well-

Figure 8-3

Seminatural primate facility at the Regional Primate Center, University of California at Davis.

integrated social groups than in sterile laboratory cages (Fox 1970; Fox 1966; Stara and Berman 1967). The incidence of diseases is usually lower, mortalities are fewer and since ethostasis is not limited, stress-related behavioral and emotional disorders will be minimized. Also, reproductive potential may be maximized.

For example, maintaining an outdoor cat-breeding colony will reduce suffering from disease and transportation stress, and it is a better option than purchasing animals as needed from random sources for research. Nuclear breeding colonies of various laboratory animal species conducted to supply research institutions within a close radius, and modeled after the regional primate centers, would be ideal. Contrast these summaries of two systems, one, a random source supply, and the other, a centralized breeding colony. Soave (1974) reported that:

> Mortality rates were followed for five years in cats purchased from random sources and used for medical research. The mean annual mortality was 31%, with a range from 22-42%. Sex of the animals or season of the year did not influence the death rate. The majority of deaths, 89% occurred in the first three weeks after receipt of the cats. During

the period of the study the total number of cats at risk was 2294; 695 died and 200 of these were necropsied, and laboratory examinations were performed. Enteritis accounted for 44.5% of the deaths, and respiratory disease was the cause of 28%. The remaining 27.5% of the deaths were due to a variety of causes.

It is principally for these reasons that humane organizations, notably the Humane Society of the United States, are basically opposed to the use of discarded and surplus pet animals for research. Animals bred and raised for research are also more adaptable, are generally of a known lineage, and will usually be exposed to minimal stresses in transit from the laboratory animal colony to the research laboratory. The demand for lost and abandoned pets for teaching and research has also resulted in illicit procurement from animal shelters and actual theft of pets, a fact well-recognized and partially rectified by the Animal and Plant Health Inspection Service division of the USDA.

Stara and Berman (1967) have shown how effective an outdoor — i.e., seminatural — environment is for maintaining a large and healthy cat colony. They summarized their study as follows:

> A feline colony of 200 to 300 animals has been established for both acute and long-term radiobiological studies. The advantages of using the feline species for radioisotope metabolism studies in the embryo and the growing offspring are its fertility, number of offspring per litter, personal hygiene, lack of noise, relative resistance to bacterial infections, length of pregnancy, and life span. The reported disadvantages, specifically respiratory virus diseases, have been reduced by housing the animals year-round under outside environmental conditions. Handling and reproductive problems have been largely eliminated. Construction and management practices are discussed. Both conception and survival rates in this colony can be compared favorably with domestic feline colonies elsewhere. The growth rate of the animals falls within statistical limits with five other growth data in the United States and England. Over a period of two years the cat has proven to be a satisfactory experimental animal for this type of research.

Such seminatural colony systems might also be developed for other laboratory animal species, including guinea pigs, rabbits and rodents. Such systems, as in many of the regional primate centers, are well-established. Banerjee and Woodard (1970) presented conclusive evidence to support the contention that outdoor housing is the method of choice for primates, reporting that:

> A comparison was conducted of survival, physical condition, reproduction, and cost of housing of rhesus monkeys in outdoor and indoor facilities. Survival in the outdoor pens averaged 80-90%, which was the

same as for the indoor monkeys. Body weight gain in the outdoor monkeys averaged 62% increase, in comparison to 43% gain in the indoor monkeys over the same time period. The outdoor monkeys showed significantly better reproductive performance than did those indoors. The cost of maintaining the outdoor monkeys was considerably less than for maintaining monkeys indoors.

Providing domesticated and laboratory animals with a more natural environment could result in what Price (1984) terms "feralization." Nikoletseas and Lore (1981), for example, found that domesticated Norway rats raised in cages that contained burrows were more aggressive toward strange rats than rats reared in standard laboratory cages without shelter. The social organization of wild house mice changes from territoriality to a highly polarized social dominance hierarchy if their living space is reduced (Butler 1980). Clearly socio environmental influences do affect the phenotypic expression of behavior. The tameness and docility of gerbils is affected by the physical design of their cages. Clark and Galef (1977) showed that if gerbils are provided shelter — i.e., burrows — early in life, they show more avoidance towards humans than those raised in open cages. The enriched environment reinforced the development of the flight or escape response. However, this might have been overcome by frequent handling. In subsequent studies, Clark and Galef (1980, 1981) demonstrated that gerbils raised in cages with shelter had later eye-opening, slower growth rates, later sexual maturation, and larger adrenal size compared to those raised in open cages, indicative of feralization. The open-cage environment produced changes hitherto considered to be genetically linked consequences of domestication. Clearly, the rearing environment can have a profound effect upon animals' phenotype.

Riley (1981) describes the low-stress animal housing that was developed in his laboratory in order to control environmental variables that influence the immunocompetence and development of neoplasia in mice (see also Riley and Spackman 1977). He found a 10 to 20 fold increase in base-line plasma corticosterone in mice housed in conventional, communal animal facilities compared to those kept in individually ventilated shelf units in a relatively sound proof environment. Thus, the need for quiescent, protective animal facilities must be recognized especially for studies involving the immune system of animals.

One of the founding fathers of the study of primate husbandry and behavior in captivity was Robert Yerkes, after whom the federal government's Georgia primate center is named. His pioneering studies ultimately facilitated the exploitation of primates for medical and other

Figure 8-4

Standard laboratory cage for a chimpanzee in a government research facility. Note extreme obesity of the spatially restricted and socially deprived animal.

commercial and intellectual purposes. How far the husbandry and care of captive, laboratory primates has deviated from what Yerkes urged almost 60 years ago is self-evident. In 1925, he wrote:

> Undoubtedly, kindness to captive primates demands ample provision for amusements and entertainment as well as for exercise. If the captive cannot be given the opportunity to work for its living, it should at least have abundant chance to exercise its reactive ingenuity and love of playing with things.
>
> The greatest possibility of improvement in our provision for captive primates lies in the invention and installation of apparatus which can be used for play or work.

Yerkes, in appealing for the provision of apparatus that can be used for play or for work, intuitively recognized the importance of pro-

Figure 8-5

Adult chimpanzees in the wild play indulgently with an infant and an old male, obviously deriving pleasure from each other. Sociable animals cannot be regarded as normal when confined for years in a laboratory cage (see Figure 8-3). *Photos: S. Halperin*

viding captive primates not only with a more enriched environment but also one over which they can exert some control. As will be shown, lack of environmental-instrumental control, like environmental and social deprivation can have a profound effect upon animals.

Learned Helplessness and the Importance of Predictability and Control[+]

In the laboratory, lack of both control and predictability has been shown to cause elevated plasma cortisol levels, immunosuppression,[*] and gastric ulceration in a series of experiments on *learned helplessness* in dogs that entailed the repeated administration of 5 mA of inescapable shock (Overmeier 1981). Furthermore, such dogs showed poor motivation and a decrease in the ability to learn a simple avoidance task, such as jumping over a barrier to avoid shock after a warning signal is given, compared with dogs that have not been previously subjected to inescapable shock. In series of studies with rats, Weiss (1971) demonstrated the connection among environmental control, predictability, and the incidence of gastric ulceration in rats. A high incidence of ulceration was found in rats that could neither control nor predict shock.

The findings of Laudenslager et al. (1983) that, when rats are unable to avoid electrical shock, their immune response is suppressed, while those able to escape from shock and, thus, control their stress did not show immunosuppression, supports the thesis that learned helplessness does increase disease susceptibility by its effect upon the immune system. MacLennan and Maier (1983) demonstrated that amphetamine- and cocaine-induced stereotypy in rats was enhanced when the animals were given inescapable shock, but, when they were able to control the duration of foot shock, they showed no more stereotypy than did nonstressed rats. In summation, if animals have some control over stressors, they *are* better able to cope.

Inability of animals to exert control over pain or other stressors appears to be a prominent feature of a variety of research studies in which emotional reactions were observed to have been heightened. Stroebel

---

[+] *From M.W. Fox (1983a).*

[*]*Immunosuppression, with associated reduced resistance to disease, has recently been demonstrated in rats subjected to conditions associated with learned helplessness (Visintainer et al. 1982). It was shown that those animals subjected to inescapable shock had a lower rate of rejection to implanted tumors than rats who received escapable shock or no shock.*

(1969) produced marked behavioral changes in rhesus monkeys, including lassitude and weakness, lack of interest in the external environment, movement stereotypy, and almost continuous masturbation and self-mutilation in some animals as a result of preventing them access to any means of controlling their immediate environment. Previously, the animals had been trained to press a lever to control aversive stimuli such as high temperature, bright light, loud noise, and mild shocks. When the control lever was retracted so that it could be seen but not manipulated, even in the absence of further physical stressors, the behavioral anomalies cited above emerged after an initial period of frantic reactions and then they subsided.

Additional features of learned helplessness in the laboratory include passivity, impaired motivation ability and difficulty in learning that responses can produce relief, lack of aggression, weight loss, appetite loss, and social and sexual deficits, generality of helplessness across a variety of situations, norepinephrine depletion, and increased cholinergic activity (Overmeier 1981). These signs have been observed in dogs, rats, and primates, and they may also be found in farm and captive zoo animals. Use of anticholinergic drugs and norepinephrine stimulants, as well as of the immunization to stress that can be fostered by permitting the development of mastery over the environment, have been proven by Seligman (1975) to be effective in alleviating this syndrome in laboratory animals. The causes and ramifications of these findings would constitute a fruitful area for further applied research related to laboratory animal husbandry as well as to primates and other wild species kept in captivity.

WORK AND THE SENSE OF EXTERNAL CONTROL

Joffe et al. (1973) demonstrated that animals raised in an environment in which they learned to exercise control over feeding, access to water, and amount of light by pressing appropriate levers grew up to be more exploratory, self-confident, and less anxious than animals that received the same food, water, and lighting changes, but had no control over their environment. Thus, early experiences in control and competence can lead to a reduction in anxiety under subsequent stressful circumstances and can also serve to immunize against adult helplessness. It is noteworthy that animals will choose situations in which they must respond instrumentally — i.e., through work — for food over those in which they receive food without any effort on their part. This is solid evidence that animals derive pleasure from the reward of effective instrumental responding and that, in the process, they become immunized against learned helplessness because, through their mastery of the task, they gain a sense of control and competence. Therefore, it seems like a good idea to reevaluate the methods used to feed farm, zoo, and laboratory animals in light of well-documented findings in rats, pigeons, and humans.

According to Dantzer and Mormede (1981), recognition of one of the most important interrelationships between hormones and behavior arose from the realization that animals develop coping processes — i.e., systems of psychological defenses and coping devices that enable them to minimize their emotional reactions to threatening and frustrating stimuli such as tonic immobility, displacement behaviors, and stereotypies. In this study of the neuroendocrine correlates of displacement activities in pigs, Dantzer and Mormede found that when hungry pigs were compelled to undergo the frustration of intermittent food delivery, but were provided with a chain hanging within reach, they would exhibit stereotyped chain pulling in the interval between food deliveries. At the same time, they showed no increase in cortisol production, even though the chain-pulling behavior had no influence on food delivery. In contrast, when the chain was not provided, the animals had high rates of cortisol production — i.e., they were under stress associated with frustration induced by a sense of lack of control or predictability of their environment.

In summation, it would appear that the happy and more adaptable animals are those that have been raised, from early life, under conditions that tend to reduce the development of learned helplessness. Under these conditions the opportunities are increased for the animal to exert some degree of control over its environment, thereby reducing what Seligman terms "negative cognitive set" in which "helpless animals and men have difficulty learning that responses produce outcomes." That animals choose, when given the choice, to work for food rather than receive free food clearly indicates their preference for, and the rewards of, having some control over their environment and the resulting knowledge that their responses to it are not futile.

Stress, defined as an ineluctable reaction to any condition, stimulus, or experience that disturbs homeostasis, may be reduced through proper environmental design of husbandry systems that allow animals the opportunity to mobilize their adaptive, stress-reducing behaviors. Similarly, learned helplessness, as demonstrated experimentally in dogs by Seligman (1975) and Overmeier (1981), *could be prevented in captive and confined animals* by providing them with opportunities to exert some measure of control over their environment, usually by means of operant devices (Markowitz 1982).

It may seem highly anthropomorphic to imply that when an animal is subjected to unpredictable and inescapable trauma, it is susceptible to developing chronic anxiety and even gastric ulcers and that fear of the unknown and lack of behavioral control can result in a state of learned helplessness that is analogous to human depression (Seligman 1975). This state in animals involves marked changes in physiology and behavior that can be clearly distinguished from simple habituation and conditioned fear reactions. These changes influence the animals' motivation, ability to mobilize adaptive responses to a variety of stressors, and level of associated resistance to disease. Research studies support the theory that learned helplessness is widespread in captive wild animals and in farm animals raised in confinement, and is therefore of economic as well as scientific and humane significance.

As Markowitz (1982) has shown with captive species, operant devices that provide animals a degree of autonomous control are valuable in reducing aggression, facilitating routine husbandry procedures, and assisting caretakers in recognizing early signs of sickness or physical injury. It has been shown that the state of anxiety can be alleviated by providing animals with *safety-signals* that enable them to predict or anticipate some disturbing event, and helplessness can be avoided by some opportunity for instrumental/operant control over their environment (see also Markowitz and Stevens 1978).

Predictability of daily events and caretaker activities, safety signals such as a caretaker turning on music or lights a few seconds before he enters the animal room, some degree of autonomous control over obtaining food and avoiding pen mates, and immunization through routine handling would, on the basis of these research findings, all be of potential benefit in reducing anxiety and helplessness in laboratory animals, in preventing immunosuppression, and increasing disease resistance (Laudenslager et al. 1983). The extent of the usefulness of these practices can only be determined by further applied research. Recognition of the phenomenon of learned helplessness broadens the scope of concern for animal welfare, and scientific evidence clearly indicates that improvements in pen or cage design and appropriate environmental enrichment may significantly improve laboratory animal health and psychological well-being. With judicious handling, including the association of unpleasant treatments (e.g., injections) in the context of activities that the animals enjoy (e.g., being fed and groomed) can make the appearance of the handler/caretaker itself a positive signal and help reduce anxiety.

To return to the issue of the acquisition of animals for research — while primate breeding colonies may reduce the impact of wild populations harvested for research,* it is to date still cheaper for the investigator to import captured animals than it is to buy captive-bred ones. Only three regional primate centers have accreditation with AALAC; the others have inferior facilities that must surely be a national disgrace to the biomedical research establishment. Universities associated with such centers are reluctant to provide funds to improve or expand existing facilities, and unfortunately, NIH grants provide no funds for any construction costs. This serious flaw in funding research, where animal care and facilities take second place to research productivity, should be rectified on humane grounds as well as on practical grounds, since the former may affect the latter.

Better monitoring by the USDA is urgently needed in the procurement and transportation of animals to research laboratories and universities. I have seen the facilities and operations of federally licensed dealers supplying animals for research that, on the basis of inhumane and insanitary conditions, should have had their state and federal licenses revoked. Some state and federal veterinary inspectors are either ineffectual, incompetent, or indifferent.

The source of supply should also be better regulated. Stealing pet cats and dogs and selling them, even under USDA license, for research may be difficult to prove, but it is a highly suspected and probably widespread practice in some areas, particularly in Pennsylvania.

Many cats and dogs are acquired from city pounds and animal shelters. For humane reasons, since they are not preadapted to living in a laboratory cage (as would be beagles raised for research), and for practical experimental reasons as well, if these unwanted pets are to be used for research, they should be used only in acute, terminal studies and essential teaching exercises. Long-term confinement and little human contact for the animals may be both inhumane and contrary to the interests of science since such animals, under deprivation stress, could potentially affect the validity of any given study, especially if the effects of such stress are not adequately controlled. Of course, adequate control would be costly in terms of personnel time and redesign of cages to

---

*As many as 80 percent or more of primates caught in the field have died in the past, prior to arrival at U.S. laboratories.

simulate a home environment. Frequent human contact with cats housed together in small colony groups and with dogs that were formerly kept as pets is preferable to solitary cage confinement. This is not suggested as an endorsement of using ex-pets for research purposes; but is offered as a humane alternative until such time as the use of animals in research can be effectively improved via reduction, refinement, and replacement. Ideally, only those cats and dogs preadapted to laboratory life should be used in long-term studies, and then sparingly!

At the 1977 regional National Capital Area AALAS meeting Dr. H.M. Marsden stated that many research proposals and published reports do not incorporate environmental considerations in the research design. The animal-environment interaction is not adequately addressed in much behavioral research. Research in *designed habitats* for laboratory animals is much needed. An investigator may argue that his research does not necessitate the animals' being behaviorally and physiologically normal and, therefore, having been raised in an environment most appropriate for the species. If this is the case, then his research may be invalid, or he may just as well have worked on some other species of lower sentience or used an *in vitro* system. Dr. Marsden

Figure 8-6

Millions of animals are used for routine testings: improved experimental designs and test alternatives are needed — replacement, reduction, and refinement — on humane and economic grounds. In these stocks, rabbits not infrequently break their backs as a result of struggling to escape while being used in the archaic Draize eye-irritancy test. *Photo: USDA.*

Figure 8-7

These and other baboons may be kept in these neck-restraining stocks for up to 90 days in the course of experimentation. Alternatives to such inhumane treatment should be implemented.

stated that for good behavioral research, the animals' environment must be considered, and he agreed that for good biomedical research, the environmental variables must likewise receive full consideration in the research design and the formulation of conclusions.

There have been a number of review articles published over the last 15 years that addressed various aspects of environmental effects on animals used in research (Clough 1982; LASA 1965; ICLA 1971; NRC 1978; Fox 1971a; Fox et al. 1979; Brown 1970; Conalty 1967; McSheehy 1976; Newton 1978). These publications reflect a growing awareness of the complexities of using animals reliably and optimally in biomedical, psychological, toxicological, and related research. The need to translate this awareness into responsible action is mandated by three concerns. First, the conditions under which laboratory animals are housed have not been improved equally in various research testing and teaching institutions over the past 15 years. This means that the experimental variance among institutions and difficulties in replicating others' findings necessitates otherwise needless repetition. The second concern is related.

Namely, the relevance of findings continues to be limited, not by scientific expertise, but by uncontrolled environmental variables that increase inter-experimental variance. The final concern is over the welfare of animals kept under suboptimal conditions and the needless suffering and killing associated with the repetition needed to confirm others' findings and to resolve conflicting findings.

Many of the new insights about how socioenvironmental factors affect laboratory animals not only increase the importance of laboratory animal and animal welfare science but also broaden the horizons of biomedical research, holistic medicine, and veterinary medicine. We have learned that a sterile, isolated, and behaviorally impoverished environment, just like one that is filthy and overcrowded, is not conducive to human or animal health and well-being. Nor is it conducive to good research. The physical and psychological requirements of all species must be understood and either provided for or deliberately manipulated as part of the experimental design. The greater the understanding of, the greater will be the control of extraneous, independent variables and identification refinement of the dependent variables of the experiment.

Figure 8-8

An all-too-common small laboratory animal facility, reflecting the need for better standards and more effective enforcement of animal care codes. *Photo: USDA.*

Furthermore, in discovering how similar and how different animals and humans are, scientists will learn how these differences can be better controlled and these similarities more accurately identified and effectively manipulated to model human diseases. Hence, we realize the importance of applied sciences such as comparative physiology, biochemistry, and ethology. But, until recently, the ethology of laboratory animals and their behavioral or socioenvironmental requirements have received scant attention. Hence, their welfare continues to be in jeopardy while animal welfarists push for *alternatives* and more effective standards through legislation and antivivisectionists debate animal rights and raid laboratories to liberate the animals. At the same, the animal research industries mount a costly defense, consisting of PR campaigns and more intensive lobbying to maintain public and government support. While some suspect a growing anti-science sentiment in society, the voice of reason must prevail. The dialectic between laboratory animal experimentation and antivivisectionism can be resolved. Some points of reconciliation that I recently noted in a letter to the *New England Journal of Medicine* (1984, 325-326) follow herewith:

RECONCILING HUMANE CONCERNS
AND LABORATORY ANIMAL RESEARCH

To the Editor: Attempts by various humane societies *to secure better federal legislation* to improve the welfare of laboratory animals and to reduce the numbers being used *have caused intense polarization between them and the biomedical-research establishment.* However, there are some common concerns that cannot be ignored. *Standards of care for primates, kept in social isolation in cages 0.6 by 0.9 by 1.2 m reflect a Cartesian attitude that ignores the social and emotional variables and correlated physiologic changes that result when group-living, socially dependent monkeys are kept under such impoverished conditions.* (These animals often acquire abnormal behaviors, such as self-mutilation, repeated masturbation, rumination, polydipsia, bulimia, and stereotypic movements, which ethologists regard as pathognomonic of frustration and emotional distress.) *The validity of research findings derived from animals kept under such conditions is surely to be questioned on scientific as well as humane grounds.*

Another potential area of common ground is between those in the biomedical-research field who have expressed concern that there is *too much emphasis on treating disease and not enough on preventive medicine* and persons (including me) who contend that the primary focus of animal research should be not treatment but prevention of human disease.

Italics are those of the author.

Organ transplants, fetal surgery, and vaccines against cancer may soon be commonplace, thanks to animal research, but as our environment becomes increasingly pathogenic, can we regard this as medical progress and can we continue to legitimize the exploitation and suffering of laboratory animals? Certainly, people who are sick should not be denied the best possible treatment, but if greater emphasis were placed on disease prevention, such potentially dangerous interventions would not be necessary. In addition, a reduction in the number of animals needed in biomedical research would be likely.

For these reasons, which are quite distinct from the antivivisectionists' abolistionist view, we should all question how real the need is for continued animal research and animal "models" of human disease. This is a potential area of common ground where the complementary concerns of healers and humanitarians may help to reconcile the present polarization that exists over the use of animals in biomedical research.

Another essential improvement that is urgently needed, as emphasized in the introduction to this monograph, is in the description of how animals used in a research project are husbanded. Davis (1973) provides a sample of the kind of description that should be included in all scientific publications* involving live animal research:

Three weeks before being used in these experiments, males weighing between 28 and 30 g were selected, assigned alternately to groups, and placed individually in plastic, topless cages measuring 28 × 18 × 11 cm. For 2 weeks before the experiment, the mice were handled daily.

The bedding in the cages (pine shavings) was changed weekly. Food (Sivad Blox) and water were provided ad libitum. The environmental temperature was maintained at 21 ± 0.5 C and the relative humidity at 50 ± 20%: there was 100% fresh-air exchange (20 air exchanges per hour). The photoperiod was controlled to provide dark (0.1 lux) from 2000 to 0800 hours and light (10 lux) from 0800 to 2000 hours; there was no twilight.

For these experiments mice *(Mus musculus)* of the High-Bree strain were purchased from Controlled Mice Company. The mice were produced by females kept five in a cage with one male. After being weaned, the progeny were caged in groups of six, three males and three females. At the age of 120 days, they were shipped by truck to our laboratory, a distance of x miles.

References to an earlier publication detailing how the animals were husbanded would suffice in subsequent research publications. Without such published details, needless repetition and difficulties in replicating

---

To excise such descriptions in order to reduce pages and publication costs surely cannot be justified.

others' research will continue to jeopardize the advancement of science and the reduction in the numbers of animals used in research. (see also *Laboratory Animals* 1985, *19:* 106-108. Guidelines for specification of animals and husbandry methods when reporting the results of animal experiments by the Working Committee for the Biological Characterization of Laboratory Animals.)

In conclusion, the ways in which laboratory animals are kept, with often total disregard for their social, emotional, and environmental needs and the research variables introduced by such lack of consideration mirror our limited knowledge and approach to questions of disease and health. When we are wiser about the latter, there will be a dramatic reduction in the numbers of animals needed in research. Already, we are recognizing that many of the questions concerning cancer are environmental (and political/economic). While great progress has been made at the molecular level in biomedical research, excessive mechanistic reductionism has led to a neglect of the more moral aspects of health and disease — those behavioral, emotional, social, and environmental variables that are as much overlooked in basic biomedical animal research as they are recognized as the "unknowns" that require investigation in the real world of health and disease — i.e., medical practice outside of the laboratory. Progress in biomedical research will be limited and remain at a relative impasse until these moral aspects are addressed. We need to ask new questions in research that embrace these aspects of the totality of living systems. Mechanistic reductionism has reached an impasse because animals are not Cartesian machines. They are living, sentient systems with behavioral, emotional, social, and environmental needs. To ignore these aspects of any whole animal used in research — as distinct from certain of its tissues or organs — is contrary to the best interests of biomedical research. Thus, the ethical and related issues raised by those who have humane concern over the care and use of laboratory animals are consonant with the best interests of biomedical research progress and, consequently, can no longer be ignored.

As we become more aware of the many variables entailed in the care and management of animals for research, the need for a reformation in traditional procedures and present standards will be more widely accepted. Indeed, even the choice of certain species for particular studies may be based more upon tradition or convenience than upon sound scientific rationale (Lockard 1968). In fact, in a number of studies, animals may not be needed at all, or at least in reduced numbers (Gould 1977). Improved statistical design, as well as improved rearing conditions to enhance phenotypic stability and uniformity and reduce interindividual variability or dramatypic changes (Russell and Burch 1959), will help meet the basic ethical injunction of animal research. Namely, one must aim constantly towards reduction of the numbers of animals needed, refinement of techniques and laboratory animal husbandry, and experimental replacement (Gould 1977; Russell and Burch 1959).

Postscript

It may be erroneously concluded that the author's premise that environmental sources of stress should be minimized to prevent experimental variables fails to recognize that this in fact may be unnatural, for surely these animals in their wild habitats are exposed to a wide variety of environmental stresses with which they continuously have to cope. An anonymous reviewer of an earlier draft of this manuscript, a veterinarian with 18 years involvement with laboratory animals in biomedical research, stated that, "Obviously the latter types of stress are different from those encountered in the laboratory, but my point is that exposure to various types of stress may be more natural than exposure to no stress at all. Also, such premise fails to take into consideration that the severely maimed or otherwise ill patient for whom much of the experimental data from studies using laboratory animals hopefully will benefit are also under various forms of environmental and emotional stress, particularly if they are hospitalized and removed from their normal environment (e.g., home, place of employment, family, friends, and colleagues). Who is to say that the adequately caged and cared-for animal is not more analogous to the incapacitated or ill human patient than the animal that is artificially isolated from most forms of environmental stress?"*

"The author seems to feel that various laboratory animals ought to be provided considerable freedom of choice to decide their own caging environment. This, to me, also seems to be extremely idealistic for who among us human mortals would not choose a larger tract of land with a larger home with servants and a life free of any forms of stress if offered such opportunities. I feel he is totally unrealistic in this regard."

It should be clearly understood that it is my belief that all stress factors to which laboratory animals are exposed should not necessarily be eliminated but rather (1) identified and controlled for in the experimental design, (2) eliminated if they cause physical or psychological suffering unless such factors are a vital and, therefore, necessary and

---

This is a classic example of reversed anthropomorphic reasoning.

unavoidable part of the experiment, and (3) a stress-free environment can, as Gross (see references) has shown, jeopardize an animal's welfare and health.

The analogy between an environmentally stressed human patient is dubious, to put it mildly. A close and accurate approximation of animal models of human disorders is only possible when environmental and experimental stress factors are identified, controlled, and selectively introduced in the experimental design creating such models.

The reviewer's final point that the author's views on designing more natural environmental conditions are "totally unrealistic" employs the arguments of economics and reverse anthropomorphism. The latter mode of thinking is best exemplified by those who see little wrong with raising farm and laboratory animals in small pens or cages because people also have to and can adapt to similar conditions — e.g., living in high-rise apartments and crowded cites. Thus, it is argued, if we must bear certain privations, there's no reason why animals shouldn't either, and if we can adapt, so can they. Such reverse anthropomorphism misses the entire point of designing optimal environments for laboratory, zoo, and farm animals, not simply because such improvements are conducive to bettering the animal's welfare, but because, from the point of sheer utility, such environmental enrichment can result in healthier animals that would be better models for a variety of research investigations than those raised and housed under conditions of social, physical, and environmental deprivation. As for economic concerns, naturally a golden mean must be struck between what is ideal and what is realistic. Economic savings may also be significant since research findings derived from animals raised under conditions of deprivation and where environmental and stress variables are neither identified, controlled, or selectively introduced may be neither valid, relevant, or reliable, thus necessitating futher experimentation and validation, and so entailing further waste of time, money, and resources.

Chapter 9

Behavioral and Ethical Aspects of Pain and Suffering in Research Animals

S uffering is a major and fundamental concern of Christianity. The powerful symbol of the crucifixion, of Christ suffering for humanity, is a constant reminder of mankind's potential for insensitivity and ignorance. Suffering is also a central concern of Judaism and Eastern religions and philosophies. Buddhism, for example, forbids the taking of *any* life without absolute necessity, and it teaches that ignorance and selfishness underlie unnatural, human-created suffering and can be overcome through understanding, compassion, and empathy. There is much unavoidable, natural suffering for which no one can be held responsible, such as an animal's being hunted by a predator or starving in the winter, or a mother's pain during labor or a child's mourning the loss of a parent or companion animal. But there is much unnatural, unnecessary, unjustifiable, and often avoidable suffering that man brings upon himself and animals alike. The politics of war and famine have been well-documented, and they have even been justified by some historians and politicians as necessary evils — the price of freedom and the natural regulation of human populations. Even stronger justifications are given for man-induced, unnatural suffering in animals. Economic necessity, scientific knowledge, human health, and other rationalizations deflect even the most carefully worded, unemotional criticisms by humanitarians, who are often put down as ill-informed idealists and sentimentalists. Concern over animal suffering per se is only too often demeaned as anthropomorphic sentimentality. Yet, on the basis of very extensive studies on the physiology and psychology of pain and suffering in man, subjective components turn out to be far more important determinants of the degree of pain or suffering experienced than the actual degree of physical trauma. In particular, the experience of physical pain is significantly influenced by mental attitude and such socioemotional factors as apprehension, fear, anxiety, and the presence or absence of supportive and comforting empathizers.

129

Suffering and Empathy

The literature on veterinary and farm animal husbandry is scattered with references on the importance of empathy in the general care of animals both in sickness and in health and also during postoperative recovery (Fox 1983a). Species that do respond positively to empathic handling include horses, sheep, cattle, pigs, poultry, dogs, and cats. Research by psychobiologists has also demonstrated that in the most common laboratory rodents — rats and mice — handling or gentling has a profound effect on the animals' behavior, emotionality, and resistance to disease and other stressors. What physiological/emotional systems are affected by gentle and empathic human care have not been thoroughly identified. As emphasized earlier, the pituitary-adrenal-sympathetic axis, parasympathetic, and immune systems have been shown to play an important role in these man-animal interaction effects.

In summation, objective scientific evidence irrefutably supports the fact that even if animals may not experience pain and suffer exactly as human beings do, many species respond to tender loving care in much the same way as human infants do. Physical and psychological pain and discomfort can be greatly mitigated via empathic care and appropriate handling in both man and other warm-blooded vertebrates. The similarity between the suffering associated with physical pain or separation from parents or companions in a preverbal child and an animal, such as a dog or rhesus monkey, may be greater than the suffering experienced by an adult human under similar circumstances. The adult has the advantage of experience and usually has the ability to reason and cope with his fear and anxiety.

What of an animal that is not emotionally attached to a person and has not had pleasurable or comforting experiences with a human caretaker? Without any affectional ties, there can be no bridge for empathy to be effective. Consequently, a captive wild animal or one not adequately socialized will experience more fear and anxiety in the presence of a person than one that is socialized to people (Scott and Fuller 1965; Lynch 1970). If that animal is suffering physically or psychologically, it is doubtful that human intervention, other than the administration of tranquilizers and analgesics is going to help the animal; in fact, human presence could aggravate the animal's suffering even more. This would be a significant variable in any meaningful study of such animals.

SUFFERING IN WILD ANIMALS

Research on wild animals involving some form of direct manipulation of the animal raises a number of ethical and methodological questions. It would be more humane to use captive born and raised, socialized animals than to use captive wild and unsocialized animals such as rhesus macaques and baboons. Similarly, as proposed by Dr. Tom Wolfle (personal communication) it is more humane and scientifically more prudent to use well-socialized domestic dogs than dogs that have not been properly socialized and are fearful or difficult to handle. Irrespective of whether an animal is wild or domesticated, if it is not used to being handled and subjected to various routine research procedures, the resultant physiological and psychological stress constitute actual and potential experimental variables. If these are not controlled, the quality of research, validity of data, and conclusions derived from such animals would be highly questionable (Fox 1971a).

Thus, it is in the best interest of good research, as it is of animal care in general, for researcher, veterinarian, and caretaker alike to be aware of the fact that all warm-blooded vertebrates have the capacity to experience pain and to suffer physically* and psychologically. Behaviorists have shown that it is possible to shape an animal to associate pain with reward so that it will self-administer painful shocks. While the ethics of such studies are highly questionable (Diner 1979), they do show that an animal will subject itself to considerable discomfort if there is a contingent reward. Knowing this is of great value in reducing conditioned aversion such as fear and anxiety that are associated with pain. Conditioned aversion can be eliminated if a reward is given after a painful manipulation.

Research dogs submit to having blood samples taken because it is rewarding for them to be petted and handled; rhesus monkeys can be trained to hold out one arm to receive an injection if they are immediate

---

*Recent research on endorphins and enkephalins in animals suggest that all sentient creatures have a "natural opiate" neuroendocrine mechanism to block painful sensations above a certain threshold. Even earthworms possess such a system (Alumets et al. 1979).

G.M. Cronin (1985) in his doctoral dissertation entitled The development and significance of abnormal stereotyped behaviours in tethered sows (Agricultural University of Waneningen, Holland) has found an important connection between abnormal stereotyped behaviors and endorphin production. Sows treated with naloxone (which blocks the brain's opiate receptor cites) stopped engaging in repetitive stereotyped actions and assumed more normal behaviors. These findings support the hypothesis that stereotypic actions are indicative of stress and help animals cope with physical and, or mental suffering by potentiating the release of endorphins as part of the coping strategy.

ly afterward rewarded with candy. This is a superior alternative to using a *crush* cage or other fear-reinforcing method of restraint.

Such shaping should be part of standard laboratory animal practice since it can do much to reduce an animal's fear and apprehension.

Ethology of Suffering

The surface phenomena of overt behavioral reactions and, in social species, the responses of conspecies to the distress of a companion can give a very accurate index of suffering. But some gregarious species, such as cattle, may show no overt response to a companion in distress.* Thus, while the capacity for empathy — i.e., care-giving or *epimeletic* behavior — and altruism does vary greatly between species, but its absence should not be interpreted as a lesser capacity to experience pain, fear, and anxiety. As Wilson (1975) and other sociobiologists have shown, altruism is closely related to kinship affiliations and survival of the group. Other strategies, such as mass stampede or mobbing of a predator, can evolve as no less adaptive patterns of group survival in response to danger. In those species in which there are close social bonds that persist into adulthood, there is a greater probability that altruistic reaction patterns will be incorporated into the animal's sociobehavioral repertoire and with them, the capacity for empathy. A state of fellow-feeling created by internal physiological and psychological sensations evoked by the distress of a companion may actually mimic the internal state of the one indistress. This capacity, according to the species, may be more or less dependent upon hormones (e.g., parental care) and socialization. In someanimals, social bonds persist from infancy into adulthood (e.g., baboons and wolves) while in others (e.g., raccoons and foxes) socio-fugaltendencies develop with maturity, and close social bonds tend to be seasonal, rather than continuous, during the reproductive phase (Fox 1974). The latter may therefore display less altruistic and empathic behaviors than the former except perhaps during courtship and caring for their young.

In considering the question of pain and suffering in animals, we must not, in our search for and analysis of physiological and biochemical

---

Such a lack of overt empathy in cattle and other animals does not mean that they are also physically insensitive to pain or cannot experience fear and anxiety. Likewise, rats eating the dead body of a packmate are not necessarily insensitive and uncaring toward each other. They engage in social play and grooming; the male has a subtle ultrasonic courtship song, the female does an elaborate courtship dance.

indices, forget the importance of the phenomenological surface: the animal's overt behavioral reactions such as distress vocalizations (e.g., chickens), including ultrasonic signals (e.g., rodents); alarm pheromones (e.g., rodents); and body posture displays of fear, defensive aggression, and passive submission (e.g., primates). These signals, to members of the same species, may, according to context, elicit flight or escape reactions such as collective defense in order to protect the one in distress or to mob the attacker or predator, discipline of the aggressor and protection of the one that is suffering (e.g., in wolves and baboons), caregiving behavior toward the one in distress, be it an infant who needs to be groomed or nursed or an adult who may be groomed, given food, or simply stayed with protectively.

Since the above reactions are evoked by the reflexive and innate reactions of an injured animal or one anticipating injury — i.e., conditioned or in a state of anxiety — we might mechanistically call them unconscious, automatic releasers of mechanical or unfeeling social responses. To speak of distress, empathy, and altruism as *shared* experiences between animals would be anathema to many scientists who adhere to Morgan's canon of avoiding anthropomorphism by interpreting an animal's behavior at the lowest or primary — reflexive or mechanistic — level. This *law of parsimony* has been severely criticized by Griffin (1977).

At best, it helps maintain scientific objectivity, yet its very basis is grounded upon highly subjective speculation, such as animals as Cartesian machines rather than upon fact. It is simply not good science to bias objectivity, observation, and interpretation with any preconception such as this mechanistic view of animal nature as being nonsentient and incapable of suffering emotionally and sympathetically with each other.

If one animal responds to the distress signals of another that is suffering, either on the basis of instinct, learning, or both, then the potential for empathy and altruism must be present because of the internal emotional and motivational states evoked by the one in distress.

Clearly, there is great natural variation between species, age classes, and seasons in the accessibility of one animal to another in terms of empathy and altruism. In terms of human accessibility, it is well known that a trusting, well socialized dog has a better prognosis under intensive care than one that is fearful and not socialized or one that is wild or feral.

Wild and feral animals are usually best left alone or, at least, interfered with as little as possible when sick or recovering from surgery. Less gregarious species, such as the domestic cat often do best when left to heal themselves with only minimal handling when absolutely necessary;

however, domestication and rearing patterns have created considerable variations in the species. In contrast, a more dependent dog benefits from almost continuous human contact.

It might be argued then that laboratory animals should not become bonded to people since they would become too dependent and not heal themselves independently. It would also be costly in terms of personnel time to have to minister to them. Such an argument does not hold, however, when one considers the fact that for many research studies the animals must be tractable and not overreact to human presence or handling. The animals may also be emotionally dependent by nature (e.g., dogs) or may have become socialized to people earlier in life. To deprive them, when in need, of appropriate humane care would be unethical and contrary to the interests of good research.

Researchers often become emotionally attached to their animal subjects, and this can be a painful problem when they have to sacrifice or otherwise divorce themselves from the animals. One way of avoiding this pain is for researchers to suppress their empathy and maintain emotional detachment, which can lead to a depersonalizing of their animal subjects.

THE QUESTION OF PAIN*

Individual differences in pain sensitivity within species are also well recognized. Beecher (1957), in a comprehensive survey of scientific literature on pain, concluded that "Pain cannot be satisfactory defined except as every man defines it introspectively for himself." The objective assessment of pain in humans would seem to be beyond the limits of scientific determination. Or perhaps it is the limitations of scientific methodology and objective attitude that prevents objective analysis of that which is principally a subjective phenomenon.

Perception of pain, as Breazile and Kitchell (1969) emphasize, is a "subjective analysis due to the activity of the central nervous system and as such involves a relationship between this activity and the mind," a point discussed earlier by Bowsher and Albe-Fessard (1962).

---

*For an excellent review of the ethical parameters and techniques of pain research in animals, see Dubner (1983). Analgesia is not as often provided as it is indicated for laboratory animals, especially following surgery. Flecknell (1983) recommends a recently developed analgesic buprenorphine for dogs, rats, rabbits, and primates since it has a longer duration (six to 12 hours) than morphine or pethidine. See also Flecknell (1985) Rollin (1985) and Morton and Griffiths for further discussion on pain in experimental animals.

Melzack (1972) reiterates this point by observing that:

The obvious biological value of pain as a signal of tissue damage leads most of us to expect that it must always occur after injury and that the intensity of pain we feel is proportional to the extent of the damage. Actually, in higher species at least, there is much evidence that pain is not simply a function of the amount of bodily damage alone. Rather, the amount and quality of pain we feel are also determined by our ability to understand the cause of the pain and to grasp its consequences. Even the culture in which we have been brought up plays an essential role in how we feel and respond to pain.

The mental state of the subject does, to a significant yet objectively unquantifiable degree, determine the degree of pain that is experienced. Pain becomes more tolerable when there is some indirect reward, such as a soldier being sent from the front line, or when fear, anxiety, or a sense of annihilation is resolved.

Research on endogenous opioid-mediated analgesic mechanisms is providing further insights into animal sentience. Miczek et al. (1982) find that, following an aggressive interaction between mice, the one that is defeated produces pain-killing opiates. This response is consistent and less physical stress — i.e., pain — is needed than with other stressors such as electrical shock. These authors conclude that the special biological significance of the defeat experience, and not simply the experience of being stressed, is critical to the occurrence of opioid-like analgesia. The subjective experience of defeat, associated with fear or anxiety, and the psychological, contextbound significance of the stress to the animal rather than its physical intensity influenced the degree of opioid-like analgesia that was produced. One of the most clear-cut correlations between behavioral and neurochemical responses and subjective emotional states has been reported by Herman and Panksepp (1980). Distress vocalizations were elicited in guinea pigs by brain stimulation. These forebrain-derived vocalizations were increased by systemic administration of naloxone and inhibited by analgesic periventricular gray stimulation. This procedure provides evidence of ascending endorphin-mediated inhibition of excitatory forebrain sites for distress vocalizations. The above study clearly demonstrates the validity of ethologists using subjective terminology to describe certain behaviors, "distress vocalization" being more appropriate than objective terminology such as "aversive vocalization" or "high-pitched call."

It is a curious fact that we have reached the point of denying the possible presence of humanlike states of emotion (e.g., pleasure and distress) and of intelligence (e.g., reasoning, insight) in nonhuman animals in spite of the absence of evidence to the contrary.

Nielsen et al. (1978) have found evidence for a late evolutionary appearance of brain receptors specific for benzodiazepines. These specific receptor sites are present in mammals, reptiles, birds, amphibians, and bony fish, but not in lower cartilaginous fish. Benzodiazepines are linked with librium and other anxiolytic drug effects on specific receptor sites, thus providing indirect biochemical evidence that all vertebrates, with the exception of the lower evolutionary order of fish, have the neurochemical capacity to experience anxiety.

Recent research on endorphins and enkephalins in animals suggest that *all* sentient creatures have a natural opiate neuroendocrine mechanism to block painful sensations above a certain threshold. Even earthworms possess such a system (Alumets et al. 1979). Ninan et al. (1982) have demonstrated the role of the benzodiazepine brain receptor complex in the affective behavioral and physiological expression of anxiety in primates.

Terman et al. (1984), in an extensive review of the mechanisms of stress-induced pain inhibition, emphasize that opioid analgesia can be induced in rats following front-paw shock while hind-paw shock causes nonopioid analgesia. Lower shock intensities cause opioid analgesia while higher intensities cause nonopioid analgesia regardless of whether front paws or hind paws are shocked. Brief but continuous shock and longer duration, intermittent shock yielded nonopioid and opioid stress analgesia respectively. Different parameters of even a single stressor can, therefore, have different neurochemical, endocrinological, and psychological effects, which, in their minds, makes Selye's conception of stress no longer tenable. These authors found that intermittent shock causing opioid analgesia had immunosuppressive and tumor-enhancing consequences, while nonopioid analgesia following continuous patterns of foot shock had no such effects. The authors concluded that these studies:

> . . . Reveal that seemingly minor differences in stress parameters (the same total amount of foot-shock applied intermittently compared with continuously) determine whether or not stress will be immunosuppressive and tumor enhancing, just as such parametric variations were seen to determine the neurochemical basis of stress analgesia. It also seems that these temporally different footshocks *mean different things to the animals* (italics mine). As mentioned above, stressing rats with the intermittent, but not the continuous, footshock causes certain learning deficits, or "learned helplessness," normally associated with inescapable shock. . . . It seems reasonable to conclude that the experience of

"helplessness" is important for the immunosuppressive and tumor-enhancing effects of stress we have seen, and that opioid peptides causing analgesia associated with "helplessness" are also involved in mediating these immunologic and oncologic effects.

It should be noted also that stress can have enduring effects that entail animal learning — i.e., consciousness. Rats, for example, learn to associate neutral environmental cues regularly preceding or accompanying stress with its aversive properties. When the rat was placed in a chamber where footshock had been administered often before, even though no shock was given, an opioid pain suppression response was evident, which is indicative of conditioned analgesia, a highly adaptive response.

Goodman and Gilman, in the standard reference work, *The Pharmacological Basis of Therapeutics* (1975) assert that:

> The effects of the benzodiazepines in the relief of anxiety can readily be demonstrated in experimental animals. In conflict punishment procedures, benzodiazepines greatly reduce the suppressive effects of punishment. *However, anxiety in the rat and man can hardly be equated* (emphasis added).

In light of the research demonstrating the close analogy of the physiological roles played by bradykinin, substance P, and the endorphins in a broad spectrum of invertebrates, this last sentence seems a rather premature and *speciesist* conclusion.

Gray (1982), in an extensive treatise on the neuropsychology of anxiety demonstrates less parsimony, stating that:

> A third important assumption is that human anxiety, or something very like it, exists also in animals and responds in much the same way to antianxiety drugs. This assumption is critical, not only for the arguments pursued in this book, but also for the whole research endeavour to which it belongs. For it is impossible to perform the great majority of the relevant experiments without using animal subjects. Yet many people will undoubtedly find this assumption hard to accept. It is commonly believed that anxiety is an almost uniquely human state, dependent on such complex cognitive capacities as the ability to foresee the future, to form a self-image, or to imagine one's own mortality. To the extent that this belief is correct, the present approach to the study of anxiety is totally misconceived, for the major inferences on which it rests have been drawn from experiments with rats, mice, cats, or, at best, monkeys. . . . Thus we must be particularly carefuly to demonstrate that this third assumption is correct.
> This demonstration will be made in two stages. . . I hope to show that the observed effects of antianxiety drugs in animals are consistent

with the view that these agents act upon a state that is closely similar to the human state of anxiety. Later. . . we shall apply a theory of anxiety based on animal experiments to the phenomena of anxiety in man. In the last analysis, this is the touchstone of the theory's success: the understanding it brings, or fails to bring, of human anxiety.

To postulate that animals do have an inner world of their own, within which they experience various emotional states is no less anthropomorphic than the fact that their circulatory or neuromuscular systems are fundamentally analogous to our own. It is ironic that while an experimental psychologist may claim to have an animal model analogous to separation anxiety or depression in man, the same analogy becomes anthropomorphic and thus invalid when concern is expressed over the animal's treatment and suffering.

There can be no grounds, therefore, for denying the probability that animals also have fundamentally analogous emotional states to our own and for rejecting analogy conclusions (Dow 1980). As Dow points out, a strictly scientific approach cannot prove that animals have feelings, but nevertheless there are arguments that lead to the so-called analogy conclusion. This is why a number of prominent biologists are concerned about animal welfare; it seems highly improbable that there should be no similarity between animals and humans when the physiological and behavioral organization of so many animals is so like that of man.

The eminent British neurologist, Lord Brain (1965) concludes that:

> I personally can see no reason for conceding mind to my fellow men and denying it to animals. . . . Mental functions, rightly viewed, are but servants of the impulses and emotions by which we live, and these, the springs of life, are surely diencephalic in their neurological location. Since the diencephalon is well developed in animals and birds, I at least cannot doubt that the interests and activities of animals are correlated with awareness and feelings in the same way as my own, and which may be, for ought I know, just as vivid.

It can be argued that animals do not have a conscious sense of self and that such a *self-less* mind is purely reflexive, instinctual, like an efficient biocomputer. Griffin (1976) and Dawkins (1980) attribute much of this attitude to the parsimony of behaviorism and the Cartesian perception of animals as unfeeling automata (Morris and Fox 1978). The concept of 'instinct', for example, has overtones of mechanistic reductionism, indirectly endorsing the Cartesian view. This Cartesian point of view is untenable because animals can discriminate themselves from others — chemically, tactilely, visually, kinesthetically, and auditorily —

and can recognize familiar objects from unfamiliar objects (Fox 1980c, 1982). Thus, they must have some sense of self, simply as a central reference point separating self from other.

Sambraus (1981) emphasizes the severe conceptual and methodological limitations of relying upon material — clinically and pathologically identifiable — indices of suffering. Sambraus uses the term *immaterial suffering* to describe suffering that may not be physiologically or morphologically demonstrable.

The mechanistic stimulus-response model of pain is simply not relevant. Bakan (1967) points out that pain is not a stimulus, but a sensation that is experienced: one responds to the sensation and to one's experience of the sensation, not directly to the stimulus as such. In other words, the organism, not the stimulus, is painful — i.e., full of pain. Pain is a subjective experience that cannot be measured objectively. This is not intellectual splitting of hairs, but rather a very fundamental distinction that scientists, particularly Skinnerian behavioral psychologists, fail to make. While, admittedly, stimuli of varying intensity may elicit responses of correlated magnitude, beyond a given threshold stimulus intensity becomesirrelevant. Threshold of pain may vary according to the state, expectations, etc. of the subject. Pain may even be closer to an emotional state than to a pure sensation. Bakan (op. cit.) concludes that "pain is so thoroughly associated with the individuality of the organism that Skinner must either abandon pain from his scientific purview or distort it." He observes that pain demands interpretation because it is "blind" to the external world. A person may describe pain as "nagging," "stabbing," or "drawing" but these are merely verbal attempts to interpret the emotional impact of the sensation. Skinner and other scientists make the classic error of attributing to the sensation the characteristics of the stimulus.

ARE ANIMALS MORE SENTIENT THAN HUMANS?

When a baby is suffering, it can be extremely difficult to console. But as it matures and becomes socialized and develops an empathic bridge, a kiss from its mother will help alleviate its suffering. At a later age, the child can be told why it is suffering, for instance, it is having an injection for its own good. The child is, thus, taught to reason. Such objectification of pain, as Bakan (1967) proposes, significantly helps the individual to cope with personal suffering.

First, love and, then, understanding are involved in coping with personal suffering. Suffering will be greater when love is absent or when the effectiveness of tender loving care is attenuated by an immaturity of the symbiotic bond with the mother. Suffering will also be greater in a child who has not yet attained the age of reason. Therefore, it may be argued that with increasing maturity we develop more effective means of coping with suffering. Since animals may lack the ability to reason and to understand what is going on and since they cannot be told that all will be well, they may actually suffer more than adult humans who have the ability to reason that certain painful ministrations are for their own good. A good example is a terrified steer who fights for his life in a re-straining chute even though he is being vaccinated for his own good. If animals are not socialized to people, they cannot be consoled and are, therefore, more likely to suffer like a presocialized baby. This is the sec-ond argument to support the notion that animals may often suffer more than human beings.

One who is regarded as having a highly emotional or unstable tem-perament — hypersensitive and often overreacting to sensory and social stimuli — would presumably suffer more than a person with a more mature, inhibited, or stoical temperament (termed "internal inhibition" by Kurtsin, 1968).

Since many animals, such as cats, dogs, and primates, belong to the former category and most of us adult human beings belong to the latter, temperament is a third reason why animals may suffer in certain contexts more than most humans. It may be argued that people can suffer more than animals when it comes to anxiety or worrying about some future, possibly catastrophic, or painful event. However, animals also, as Pavlov and other animal psychologists have shown, can anticipate pain and show anxiety or conditional emotional reactions. While we can rational-ize and otherwise cope with certain anxieties, animals generally cannot. Like a neurotic, paranoid, or psychotic person who cannot cope with anx-iety, animals are more likely to suffer in this dimension (Russell and Burch 1959). It may be concluded that in many contexts, animals are like-ly to suffer more, rather than less, than we in four dimensions: (1) lack of emphatic bridge; (2) inability to reason or to objectify suffering; (3) lack of internal inhibition, becoming wholly submerged by overwhelming emotional sensations when under stimulus control; (4) inability to cope with anxiety.

Skolnick et al. (1984) have gone so far as to develop an animal model of human anxiety, demonstrating that behavioral changes analogous to the human state of anxiety can be produced by biochemical manipula-tions. They summarized their study as follows:

The ethyl ester of Beta-carboline-3-carboxylic acid (β-CCE) has a high affinity for benzodiazepine receptors and can antagonize some of the pharmacologic actions of benzodiazepine in rodents. Administration of β-CCE (2.5 mg/kg) to chair-adapted, male rhesus monkeys (7-9 kg) elicited a behavioral syndrome characterized by extreme agitation, head and body turning, distress vocalization and other behaviors which might be termed 'anxious'. Concomitant increases in plasma cortisol, epinephrine, norepinephrine, heart rate, and mean arterial blood pressure were observed. Pretreatment of animals with the benzodiazepine receptor antagonist Ro 15-1788 (5 mg/kg) antagonized the behavioral, endocrine, and somatic changes produced by β-CCE, but did not elicit any significant changes in these parameters when administered alone. Thus, administration of β-CCE to primates may be a reliable and reproducible model of human anxiety and, as much, may prove valuable for studying the postulated role of 'stress' or 'anxiety' in a variety of human disorders. In toto, these results strongly suggest that benzodiazepine receptors not only mediate the pharmacologic actions of benzodiazepines, but may also subserve both the affective and physiologic expression of anxiety.

A fifth dimension is the capacity to suffer as a consequence of social deprivation and privation of basic needs due to loss of or separation from a loved one or companion and confinement respectively. Many animals species share this capacity with human beings, and it is another aspect of sentience which can indicate that some animals are as sentient as humans. There is a sixth dimension of sentience: the dimension of fellow feeling or of empathy and altruism. The capacity to suffer with others via empathy is not an exclusively human attribute. There is extensive documentation of altruistic behavior in the more social and continuously evolved mammals such as elephants, chimpanzees, wolves, and dolphins. Evidence of trans-species altruism include well-documented cases of dolphins saving drowning sailors and Koko's, the gorilla's, love for and care of a kitten.

Suffering and Animals in Research

In her analysis and critique of the scientific conscience, Catherine Roberts (1967) has the following to say about the prolonged social deprivation studies to which H. Harlow subjected rhesus monkeys in order to understand the basis of love attachment in man:

Harlow has been criticized recently for transferring concepts from the field of human psychology to the field of animal behavior because in his experiments the "love or affection" of the infant monkeys for the surrogate mothers could be better explained as imprinting. I believe that criticism of the rhesus experiments should rest on a deeper foundation than ethology: to conduct a scientific investigation of the emotional responses of acutely distressed laboratory animals and call it a "contact with the nature of love" reveals a profound unawareness of the limitations of science. And what is more important in the present context, it provides at the same time an admirable illustration of the basic outlook of modern secular and scientific humanism.

She goes on to observe that:

Modern scientists, with the approbation of modern humanists, are subjecting these animals, in highly artificial environments, to extreme mental torture in the proud delusion that they are thereby doing all in their power to help their fellow men. That these experiments are conducted to attain a knowledge of love makes them not only ludicrous but revealing as well. For in the final analysis they reveal a grave lack of understanding of the subject that is believed to be under investigation.

Since the publication of her critique, even more extreme forms of deprivation have been instigated on primates, and, at this time, animal psychologists have developed a new model of human depression dubbed "learned helplessness," which develops in dogs and rodents subjected to inescapable shock, drowning, or other acute psychological stress (Diner 1979).

Roberts questions the values of the humanists who accept such research by stating:

To condemn the rhesus experiments for what they are — odious examples of cruelty to animals that degrade the humanness of those who designed and perpetrated them — obviously does not appeal to modern humanists. Besides opposing their aims, condemnation would constitute a barrier to free inquiry and the attainment of truth. Humanists are, of course, no more insensitive to animal suffering than anyone else and probably much more sensitive than most. They are also awake to the dangers of the misuse of applied science and technology. But they cannot rationally object to an experimental science that depends upon animal suffering for its results when they believe that such results will augment human health, happiness, and survival. For these ends, they maintain, are our supreme ends. Secular and scientific humanists, it must be remembered, have no standard or morality whatsoever except the rational.

A much more stringent ethic is needed to constrain and guide the wholesale use of animals for research, educational, and commercial purposes. Animals should not be subjected to physical or psychological suffering unless the results promise to alleviate a comparable or greater suffering in humans and other animals. To subject animals to suffering for the sake of knowledge when there is no conceivable clinical application or to develop, *post hoc,* an animal model of a human emotional disorder is ethically reprehensible. If the animal is a high fidelity model, then presumably it is suffering much as would a human being. Yet, in spite of the psychologists' claims to the relevance of their animal models, some avoid ethical responsibility by discounting all concerns as being ill-informed and anthropocentric.

DISEASE, PAIN, AND SUFFERING

David Bakan (1967) presents a valuable interdisciplinary review of the nature of disease, pain, and suffering. He cites many studies on both laboratory animals and human patients which demonstrate that separation-estrangement correlates with a higher incidence of several diseases, including mammary cancer in C3H mice, and a higher mortality and morbidity in maternally deprived infants and the elderly during their first year in a home for the aged. In contrast, gentling delays the incidence of induced neoplasia in rats. A traumatic disruption of social relations has been also correlated with asthma, congestive heart failure, diabetes mellitus, disseminated lupus erythematosus, Raynaud's disease, ulcerative colitis, rheumatoid arthritis, and thyrotoxicosis.

ANIMAL MODELS*

Bakan also emphasizes that the incidence of somatic disease among persons with definite psychological disturbance "is substantially greater than normally expected and a relationship between psychological disorder and various forms of sociocultural separation and disintegration has been indicated in a large number of studies."

These findings cast doubt on the *doctrine of specific etiology* — i.e., that for every disease there is a specific cause. In relation to many of the current laboratory animal models of human disease, a similar credibility gap exists between theory and research and the dynamics of disease states that are of such complexity as to be rarely addressed in the laboratory setting. Under natural conditions, the concept of single etiology rarely provides a satisfactory answer to the pathogenesis of diseases, nor can it always in the laboratory. What may appear to be good science on paper, a sophisticated, well-controlled study on laboratory animal subjects,

---

*For a detailed critique of animal models and routine test procedures, see Rowan (1984).

may be of little or no relevance to real life. For example, modeling human drug addiction in animals and making sophisticated biochemical and neurophysiological analyses may have little or nothing to do with the social and psychological problems associated with addictive states in man. Physiological, environmental, and socioemotional factors are important determinants in physical and emotional disease. Illness, manifested psychologically and/or somatically, is an expression of *disease*, the pattern of clinical signs being determined partly by the individual's past and present interpersonal relationships and experiences. Many human illnesses have been shown to occur only when a person perceives that his or her life situation is threatened (Bakan 1967).

MALADAPTIVE RESPONSE

As Selye has emphasized, many diseases are diseases of adaptation. Bakan suggests that adaptive defenses may have maladaptive consequences, including death, and that the organism is not only not better adapted but is injured in the same way as the individual who is handicapped by his neurotic defense mechanisms to real or imagined stress. Therefore, just as the doctrine of specific etiology is inadequate, so too is the Darwinian concept of increased fitness through natural selection because it ignores the fact that so-called adaptive mechanisms are often survival negating rather than survival enhancing. An excessive response to somatic or psychological stress is often the main cause of disease symptoms. Thus Cannon's homeostatic system, when stressed, creates dis-ease via activated defense mechanisms rather than from the external pathogen or stressor. This is the sickness of dystasis.

Bakan goes on to illuminate the point that both Selye and Freud recognized the threat of danger as a trigger for self-injurious somatic and psychic mechanisms, which tend to have their own autonomy. Significantly, Selye believed that knowing what hurts has an inherent curative value, and, in order to overcome disease processes, a conscious state of surrender, of encouraging the body not to defend itself because the defense mechanisms are usually more injurious than the stressor, is theoretically desirable. The suffering associated with disease states is a product of somatic *and* psychological responses, the magnitude of which may be enhanced not only by the virulence of the pathogen or intensity of the external stressor but also by the organism's own defense mechanisms. What makes some individuals react more than others and in fact overreact and suffer intensely or even die? What species differences, if any, exist? Kurtsin (1969) has shown significant differences in the reactions of dogs to various pathogens, radiation, and other stressors; those significantly most susceptible have the most unstable or overreactive temperament. Thus, to ignore the animal's psychology — i.e., its emotional needs, and temperament — can mean inferior animal care and bad, if not irrelevant, research. No good physician ignores the patient's psychology unless he or she believes that people are simply automatons with mechanical problems. Yet, laboratory animals are treated in this way if their behavioral needs and sentience per se are not considered in the design and execution of experiments upon them and in the standards adopted for their routine husbandry and pre- and post-operative care.

To know and provide for the generic and species-typical requirements of laboratory animals — i.e., those requirements necessary for their physical and psychological well-being — is a prerequisite to good research. To know and respect each laboratory animal, nongenerically, as an individual with interests and needs is a prerequisite to humane treatment.

Without understanding and respect, concern for the animal's well-being may be misguided (Fox 1984b). In the absence of empathic concern, no amount of objective knowledge of the animals' physical and psychological requirements is sufficient to ensure humane treatment. One of the greatest barriers to empathic concern is the defense mechanism of denial as exemplified by the withdrawal of empathetic concern for the animal, often under the guise of detached scientific objectivity, in order to avoid the burden of its suffering. Rationalization is another instrumental defense, as when suffering is considered "necessary," "unavoidable," or "insignificant" because of some unproven belief that animals that are less sapient than Homo sapiens must also be less sentient.

Postscript

A.P. Silverman (1978), from Imperial Chemical Industries Ltd., England, published a short paper entitled *Rodent's Defense Against Cigarette Smoke*. He reports on a smoke inhalation toxicity study in which various rodents were exposed to standard puffs of cigarette smoke diluted 1:100 in clean air for four hours, five days a week. Unexpectedly, many of the animals responded by placing their feces in the smoke-delivery tubing, repeatedly and in quantity. *Air-inlet blocking* was first seen within 10 seconds of placing a rat in the smoke cylinder after the first day of exposure. Blocking was seen at least once in six of eight rats, 10 of 12 hamsters, 10 of 16 mice, but not in one of eight guinea pigs. One hamster stuffed the air inlet so effectively that it suffocated.

The author was unable to suggest likely stimuli for inlet blocking in the wild and concluded that "Some rueful amusement is due for behavior we might label as Rodents' Revenge on the Toxicologist." Another conclusion is that the rodents, in performing such a high-order behavior, have a greater capacity for insight and reasoning than is generally credited to them.

Chapter 10

Animal Health and Welfare — Toward the One Medicine +

W hat is health? What is entailed in the healing process and in health maintenance? Modern biomedical science, with its Cartesian view of reality that regards mind and body as functionally separate, can only give a mechanistic answer devoid of any appreciation of affective, emotional, and cognitive dimensions.

The World Health Organization's definition of health is as relevant to animal research and laboratory animal care as it is to human medical practice: "Health is a state of complete physical, mental, and social well-being and not merely the absence of disease or infirmity." To this, we must add the essential factor of environmental and ecological well-being and the central element of empathy in the healing process.

In the field of veterinary medicine, such terms as *animal health technology, animal science,* and *animal management* reflect a very mechanistic attitude toward life, health, healing, and normality. Yet, there is reference to the *healing art* as well as the science of veterinary and human medicine and surgery. This art, which has almost been lost to the successes and excesses of mechanistic scientism and medical technology, is an integral part of health, of psychophysiological well-being, and of the healing process and health maintenance.

Though unscientific by mechanistic definition, the healing art is accessible to scholarly, objective study. The beneficial effects of meditation, the relaxation reponse, the placebo drug phenomenon, and the decrease in blood pressure in persons stroking their pets, as well as their pet's decrease in heart rate, are open to scientific study. They may open the doors of human and veterinary medical practice to the subjective, af-

---

+ *Portions of this chapter were published in* New Methods, The Journal of Animal Health Technology, *(March 1983).*

fective, emotional dimensions of health and the healing process. Such subjective elements as the healer's attitude and the temperament or emotional state of the animal or human patient are factors that have a profound influence upon therapeutic success and the healing process. Likewise, empathy or tender loving care is being recognized as much an integral part of farm and laboratory animal husbandry as it is essential in postoperative recovery of the patient and in the medical correction of and recovery from physical diseases. Massage therapy, acupuncture, electrotherapy, homeopathy, herbology, and other therapies, along with proper diet and exercise, are being increasingly recognized as valid components of holistic or mind-body medicine and health care maintenance. Again, these adjunctive therapies to more traditional treatments are as much a part of the art and science of healing — i.e., what we might call the "One Medicine" — as is the traditional allopathic practice of drug-oriented therapy. Until recently, practitioners of allopathic human and animal medicine have maintained a narrow, if not monopolistic, attitude, in part attributable to vested financial interests, as well as to their faith in the allopathic approach. However, there are now recognized iatrogenic limitations to allopathic medicine, as there are various limitations to be found in other therapies, that are leading to an increasing readiness to objectively evaluate alternative therapeutic procedures. This increased interest in honest evaluation is spurred by the many people who are attracted to alternative therapies because they are dissatisfied with the often costly, iatrogenic, and ineffectual traditional procedures.

While endorsing the search for alternative medical therapies, I am fully aware of the problems of quackery and other pitfalls and limitations. In the United States, organized medicine has vigorously opposed most nontraditional alternatives* and the practitioners thereof. Such protectionism in the absence of fully evaluated alternative therapies, is unconscionable. Let us hope that the working party in the United Kingdom that has been established by the British Medical Association (*British Medical Journal* 287 [1983]: 623) to evaluate these new frontiers will be both objective in their appraisal and receptive to the holistic nature of the healing *arts*. These are the very qualities that are so lacking today in mechanistic medical and veterinary *science*. It is encouraging that there is now an American Veterinary Holistic Medical Association, which represents, politically and scientifically, a major breakthrough in the practice of animal medicine.

As, by analogy, the U.S. Department of Agriculture and agribusiness have opposed organic farming methods.

This is a time for exploration, integration, and synthesis that may lead to the adoption of a variety of complementary therapeutic health-care, and maintenance procedures, some of which, until recently, were variously considered as being quackery, primitive, inferior, or based upon folklore and superstition rather than science. Now the narrow Cartesian mechanist's world view that has so limited the scope of scientific exploration and medical progress for decades (Capra 1982) is beginning to give way to a healthier skepticism. It is hoped that this will lead not only to significant advances in human and veterinary medicine but also to a greater understanding and respect for life and a change in attitude toward animals. Animals are not unfeeling machines. As humanitarians have been proclaiming for decades and recent research has shown, animals, like us, have emotions, needs, and environmental requirements that have a profound effect on their physical and mental health and their ability to tolerate stress and related diseases.

It is not simply an ethical question whether or not it is right to keep laboratory rhesus monkeys in 2 by 3 foot cages, four laying hens in a cage 12 by 18 inches, or veal calves and breeding sows confined in narrow stalls in which they can neither walk nor turn around. Such environments are pathogenic (Fox 1983a). Furthermore, these practices are an extremely disturbing reflection, not of deliberate cruelty, but of the ignorance and insensitivity that result from a mechanistic attitude toward life (Fox 1981; Capra 1982).

Psychoneuroimmunosuppression (Ader 1981) can result from such animal treatment, and this is perhaps the most important concept in the One Medicine that is evolving today. New scientific breakthroughs change consensus, but such breakthroughs necessitate an open-minded skepticism and iconoclastic courage in those who dare explore new frontiers and endeavor to integrate nontraditional therapies in their research and practice. As the attitudes of society and the biomedical establishment toward health and disease change, I anticipate a transformation in the way in which farm and laboratory animals are generally perceived and treated. They are not unfeeling machines; their emotional well-being, which can be improved by a quality environment along with empathic, compassionate treatment by their caretakers, profoundly influences their physical health, their ability to cope with stress and disease, and their capacity to recover from sickness or injury (Fox 1983a).

Likewise, a greater attention needs to be given to the emotional well-being of pets in the veterinary hospital during postoperative care and recovery from surgery, trauma, and disease, and also to postoperative care of animals used for teaching and experimental purposes. Mind and body are inseparable, and the physician, veterinarian, and nursing attendant must attend to both the emotional and physical needs of the patient. Such issues as pain, fear, and anxiety are at last being addressed by the veterinary profession, as the recognition that animals have emotional needs and dependencies becomes more widely accepted. Gentleness and love, resulting from empathic and compassionate understanding, are as important as the healer's technical skills and armamentarium of drugs and diagnostic procedures. The concept of specific disease in one organ or body region is giving way to a more holistic perception of illness affecting the entire organism and its dis-ease in relation to its proximate environment.

Sklar and Anisman (1979) have shown a correlation between stress, an animal's ability to cope, and the influence of these two interacting variables on the development of neoplasia. As Ader (1980) emphasizes, "It would appear that, to a greater or lesser extent, all pathologic processes are subject to the influence of psychosocial interventions of one kind or another." Several studies have now clearly demonstrated how various stressors can impair the immune system (Chang and Rasmussen 1965; Hamilton 1974; Rasmussen et al. 1957) while other stressors can have an enhancing or protective effect. See the review by Ader (1980) who also emphasizes that housing animals individually, rather than in groups, can increase susceptibility to a variety of pathologic processes or can decrease susceptibility to other stressors. Ader (op. cit.) notes that all hormones and neurotransmitters are potentially capable of influencing immune responses. In 1981, Ader compiled an excellent book on this subject entitled *Psychoneuroimmunology*.

Stress may also impair the activity and balance of enzymes and cofactors involved in the metabolism of xenobiotic substances — i.e., drugs and environmental contaminants, most of which are lipophilic and are broken down into more easily excreted, water-soluble compounds via xenobiotic metabolism. Stress and impaired xenobiotic metabolism may, therefore, increase the toxicity of environmental contaminants and various drugs, such as barbiturates and those used to immobilize or sedate captive wild and laboratory animals (Stoskopf 1983).

Ader (1980) wryly observes, "The biomedical scientist, operating within the conceptual and technical constraints imposed by the disciplinary boundaries of a reductionistic philosophy, attempts to control or minimize (or ignore) variability. For the psychosomaticist, such variability is the starting point of his research; it defines the operation of variables with which to be concerned."

Individual differences in disease susceptibility have forced the medical and veterinary research paradigm of a single ultimate cause to change, and, instead, the researcher sees the patient's state of being — his illness or health — as an aspect of his way of life (Wolf 1961). "Modern man is inclined to encounter noxious stimuli, or stresses of a symbolic nature, far more frequently than directly damaging assaults. His responses which, . . . may involve his whole being in the direction of health or disease, depend upon his goals and values. Thus they constitute his way of life? . . . In terms of social as well as bodily health, he has often been more unadapted than adapted, more sick than well." (Wolf op. cit).

This holistic paradigm places medical research in a social context, and, as Wolf emphasizes, genetic, experiential developmental, emotional, cognitive, and motivational — i.e., symbolic — variables need be considered. Clearly, when such variables in laboratory animal husbandry and research are not addressed, the scientific validity and medical applicability of animal research is questionable. A further limitation lies in our lack of understanding of the stresses that are of symbolic nature or signal value in animals and their differences compared to man. An alarm call, a pheromone, or the pressure of a predator or dominant conspecific may be more stressful to an animal than intense electrical shock and may be more relevant stimuli to use in stress studies (Miczek et al. 1982). Social deprivation or crowding stress will likewise vary according to the species and its innate social tendencies and social organization. Mason (1975) was one of the first to demonstrate, in his primate research, that the emotional effects and cognitive associations of noxious stimuli — i.e., their symbolic nature to the animal — are usually more significant and have a more profound and prolonged effect on the animal's physiological reactions than the physical intensity of the stimuli per se. A detailed understanding of the animal's *umwelt* — i.e., perceptual world — or characteristic *weltanshauung* necessitates the integration of applied ethology in laboratory animal husbandry and research. As Wolf emphasizes, stressful experience can have bidirectional effect (e.g., increased or decreased gastric activity and sodium retention), depending upon the situation and underlying affect, be it one of anger or helplessness and depression. And while few diseases are purely psychogenic, attitudinal and emotional influences do have profound effect upon the way in which disease is manifested and, in part, may determine the degree of penetrance of those disorders that are influenced by genetic determinants.

People, like animals, react differently when cornered or seriously threatened; some take risks, while others become more cautious; others fight, while others flee and become passive. For example, the shadow-silhouette of a hawk makes some birds freeze, while others flee for cover. The adaptive pattern of responding to threat, injury, or disease is in part determined by cognitive, and affective *sets* that are influenced by heredity and experience. Thus, no individual or species responds identically to stress, which accounts for the great individual differences in response to noxious agents (e.g., pathogens and toxins), adaptability to stress, and resistance to disease. In summation, without applied ethological knowledge of an animal's *umwelt,* social and environmental needs, and predispositions, many animal models of human disease will continue to be Cartesian, of extremely low fidelity, and of limited value and relevance to human health.* To ignore individual and species differences in response to stress when developing animal models of human disease is to limit medical progress by adhering to an archaic paradigm of over-simplification and mechanistic reductionism.

The physical parameters of disease that an animal model may provide are but a narrow band of the etiological spectrum that must be broadened to encompass a holistic paradigm of health and disease. The need for holistic awareness is reflected in the paucity of detail given in scientific articles on the many husbandry and treatment variables that influence the animal's phenotype and dramatype. Without such a broadening of awareness, there can be little societal justification for the continuation of biomedical research on sentient animals.

Subclinical Disease

Diseases that are almost, but not quite, manifested are surely more widespread than is fully appreciated. Gastric hyperacidity or hypoacidity, which can lead to gastric ulcers or stomach cancer when exacerbated respectively by social stress and nitrosamines, are subclinical diseases. The final expression of disease, which may involve some added emotional stressor or physical agent such as a virus or toxic chemical, receives more attention than the subclinical disease state. Yet in order to prevent disease, the subclinical state — physiological and emotional — of the patient needs to be evaluated.

---

*For two recent reviews of animal models, see Marsh, N., and Haywood, S. 1985 Animal Experimentation: Improvements and Alternatives *FRAME. 5B The Poultry, Bank Place, Nottingham, England and* Models for Biomedical Research: A New Perspective *1985 National Academy Press. Washington D.C.*

A dramatic illustration of this is of people dying in an air crash and, on postmortem examination, having a number of chronic diseases that "would have killed them anyway" or, at least, have made them immuno-incompetent and more susceptible to certain diseases.

No less dramatic is the recent finding (*Feedstuffs* (March 19, 1984): 9) that 95 percent of pigs examined after slaughter have subclinical signs of pneumonia. While they were not overtly sick, they would have appeared dull or lacking in vigor to one who knows pigs that don't live in sickening hog factories. Still, they were well enough to eat, put on meat, and reach slaughter weight in an economically acceptable length of time.

Subclinical disease can best be addressed by extensive tests, including postmortems, of apparently healthy populations of humans and wild and domestic animals. Much more research is needed in this area since it is the key to preventive medicine and health-care maintenance. For example, not keeping pigs in social isolation and handling rabbits regularly can reduce a stress and nutrition-related disease such as artherosclerosis. This can only be known by comparing such animals with those housed or fed and handled differently. The basis of subclinical medical diagnosis and prophylaxis is, therefore, comparative medicine in its broadest sense, including comparisons between species and between individuals of the same species under different social and environmental conditions — i.e., epidemiological demographic, socio-economic, and ecological comparisons. Health and normality are relative, not absolute — but relative to what? If the entire population is mentally and physically sick or in a borderline state of health because of subclinical physical and mental disease, we would never know it without comparative studies and some idea of what it is to be healthy and normal. Only then can the right correctives be devised and administered appropriately at the onset of incipient subclinical health problems and the outbreak of disease.

Surely, the proper practice of human and veterinary medicine is not just to treat disease as it comes (*veniente occurite morbo*). However profitable this attitude may be, it does not prevent suffering nor does it alleviate the chronic malaise, physical and psychological, of incipient, subclinical disease syndromes. They are pathognomonic and not necessarily caused by an inherent weakness of body mechanics (only a minority of hereditable and congenital disorders fit this Cartesian category), but, rather, are caused by maladaptive responses to pathogenic environmental factors, including diet and living conditions. I do not err on the side of the environment and nurture or discount nature as being the primary source of disease, but rather recognize that it is the environment and nurture that can be most readily improved. The inherent nature of the patient is relatively uncontrollable unless selective breeding programs are initiated to enhance adaptive fitness. This is possible, to a limited degree, with domesticated animals and, via genetic counseling, in humans. Aside from the morality of human eugenics and the promised medical miracles of genetic engineering to enhance the fitness and overall disease resistance of domesticated animals and plants, the following ethical question remains to be answered: Is it right, be it through genetic, surgical, or pharmacological interventions, to alter the nature of animals in order to help them adapt to stressful and unhealthy conditions, as in the case with factory-farm animals (Fox 1983a)? It is documented that the clinical manifestations of disease may be suppressed, but this is not a valid index of health and well-being when subclinical disease can be demonstrated by post-mortem, when there is psychoneuroimmunosuppression, and when there are overt signs of behavioral anomalies, frustration, and distress (Fox op. cit.).

The mechanistic and reductionistic analysis of animal and human disease states has its virtues in research, but this approach in practice has serious and often iatrogenic consequences (see Illich 1977; McKeown 1976). The realization is beginning to dawn that health and sickness are functions of the mind, body, and environment that interact in a unified field. This realization constitutes a paradigm shift, a revolution in the practice of human and veterinary medicine and in biomedical research on animals. It is the foundation for the One Medicine (Schwabe 1978).

This book has, I hope, opened the way toward a more integrated, holistic biomedical research and practice since it has shown that proper animal care provides for animals' environmental and psychosocial needs and is a prerequisite if research findings are to be applicable to a more realistic (ecological and behavioral) medical* paradigm. The benefits to be derived from continuing animal research will be increasingly limited and the justification for using animals in biomedical research will be subject to increasing public censure and mounting opposition if the medical paradigm continues to be primarily Cartesian, and the psychosocial needs and environmental requirements of laboratory animals continue to be ignored or neglected. While there is a growing anti-science and antivivisection sentiment in the public sector, private industry and academic and government sectors need not assume a defensive posture when the care of laboratory animals and experimental design address

---

*See Holden (1980) for a review of the new paradigm of behavioral medicine.

the significant experimental variables and correlated humane concerns detailed in this book. All concerned would like to see an end to the presumed necessity of having to subject animals to pain and suffering. Improvements in their care and treatment will not only reduce their suffering, it will also help change the biomedical paradigm from Cartesian reductionism to mind-body holism, which in turn, I predict, will lead to a significant reduction in the numbers of animals used in research.

Chapter 11

Animal Rights:
Ethical Issues and Human Obligations

W hile a worm or lobster will quickly move away from something that may kill or injure it, and thus demonstrate sentience, it might be anthropomorphic to say that they are actually afraid. But, clearly, they are programmed to avoid harm. Even plants avoid harm with spines, chemical secretions, and trophic movements that avoid or seek darkness. We can only identify terror in others through analogy — expressive gestures, certain vocal sounds, and a particular look in the eyes that we recognize empathically (not anthropomorphically) as fear. Expressions of emotion can be easily read in the eyes of mammals and some birds, while it is much more difficult to empathize with less expressive and nonvocal reptiles, fish, and invertebrates. Still, we can identify various mechanisms of defense in such creatures; some reptiles will defend their young, and some species of fish will change color when they are threatened.

Thus, while it is difficult to prove or disprove that worms and lobsters actually experience fear, it is easy to recognize that they, like plants and all living things, have evolved adaptive reactions to avoid harm. They have interests and, in their behavior, express a will to survive, what Albert Schweitzer recognized as their *will-to-be*. Therein is our kinship with all life, regardless of how much more (or less) sensitive and intelligent we (or they) may be. The less rational, the more is the fear, the more intelligent, the more is the anxiety. And, in general, the more conscious, sapient and sentient the being, the more is its anxiety of certain death and life's uncertainties.

Animals' Needs and Wants

From the perspective of animal welfare, an animal's needs can be defined as those requirements essential for its physical well-being: an

157

animal needs food, shelter, and water. Its wants, however, may not seem to be as essential. A dog may *want* to chase a rabbit and a pig may *want* to wallow in mud, but, even if the dog is well-exercised and the pig is kept cool in a confinement building, dare we say that they do not *need* to satisfy these wants? From a mechanistic perspective, this interpretation would be correct. But from the animal's perspective, the satisfaction of various wants may be more important psychologically than the satisfaction of basic needs, some of which are probably unconscious. By having the opportunity to satisfy its wants, an animal has a sense of control over its environment and a feeling of fulfillment.

It is also true that, as with an infant, an animal may want what it doesn't need; for example, a cow relishing a field of clover and spring grass and dying from bloat. Other wants, such as the reproductive urge, are curtailed via castration. Thus, out of convenience and expedience on the one hand and a need to protect the animal 'from itself' on the other hand, certain wants are denied. While it is sensible husbandry to provide for an animal's basic needs and prudent to limit certain wants for its overall welfare, the frustration caused by the denial of its wants or conscious desires may adversely affect the animal's psychological well-being. Although this is not widely recognized, it may nonetheless be true since animals' needs and wants are closely related, and it is well-recognized that deprivation or frustration of basic needs can have adverse physical consequences. Some freedom may be sacrificed in order to enhance overall welfare, as when we dehorn crowded cattle and neuter pets. When such steps enhance an animal's well-being without inhibiting and, thus, frustrating its wants, then they may be ethically acceptable since the animals are being treated in their best interests, thus humanely.

In manipulating the animal's *telos** and directing it toward the satisfaction of human ends, we instrumentally objectify it; however, this does not mean that the animal lacks its own subjectivity, intrinsic value, interests, and wants. We are ethically bound to give equal and fair consideration to an animal's subjectivity if we wish to assume the right of dominion over them and wish to direct those aspects of the animal's *telos* that we objectify as being of extrinsic value to us. In other words, we should do to them as we would have them do unto us, not identically, but kind for kind, according to our different needs, wants, and interests — i.e., species-specific requirements.

**its inherent or intrinsic nature or* beingness.

That humans may have greater understanding than animals does not mean that animals lack awareness. While we may often understand what causes us to feel pain, anger, or anxiety, an animal's lack of rational understanding does not mean that it is incapable of such experience and that it is, thus, not emotionally aware. Humans are aware of their emotions, but they do not always know why they feel and react as they do. If they did know, there would be no need for psychotherapy to bring their feelings into the realm of rational understanding.

Regardless of our instrumental roles and extrinsic value to each other (e.g., patient and doctor, prey and predator, and livestock and husbandman), we all have intrinsic value and interests (needs and wants). A pig is more than bacon in the making and a deer is more than a meal for a pack of wolves. This is because animals, like us, seek fulfillment in many ways under the impulse of the libido, which is the will to be. Under our dominion, their will is not ours exclusively since their wills and beings are separate from ours, even if we bred, raised, control, and direct them to satisfy some final human purpose. The dominion of humane and responsible stewardship recognizes and satisfies the animal's basic needs, wants, and intrinsic nature — the expression of which is the freedom to be. A deer is free to be a deer, even if it is destined to become the wolf's dinner. The same ethical principle should hold for domesticated animals. What we take from their lives in order to satisfy our own wants, we should doubly repay with benevolence, proper care, veterinary attention, affection, and humane treatment. The attitude of dominion as power and the purely materialistic, instrumental valuation of animals as useful objects or products has no moral or ethical basis. It is, surely, unjust and often imprudent in terms of animal health to so limit their needs and wants for reasons of custom, convenience, and financial expedience, as to jeopardize their overall physical and psychological well-being. Animals are ends in themselves, and to regard them solely as merely a means to satisfy human ends is ethically reprehensible.

ANIMAL FREEDOM AND WELL-BEING: WANT OR NEED?*

Freedom for humans is the freedom to be: liberty for the pursuit of happiness. Happiness in the fulfillment of one's being or telos. Because it is a living being and therefore has interests, needs, and wants like we

---

*from Applied Animal Ethology *11* (1983/4): 205-209.

Figure 11-1(a)

Figure 11-1(b)

If applied research on farm animals is to be relevant, then the housing systems used by industry should be adopted in the animal science laboratory. Are these systems acceptable? Note the intense overcrowding of (a) fattening pigs; (b) poultry; (c) close confinement of battery hens; (d) brood sows either in narrow crates; (e) or tethered to the ground; and (f) extreme privation of veal calves.

Figure 11-1(c)

Figure 11-1(d)

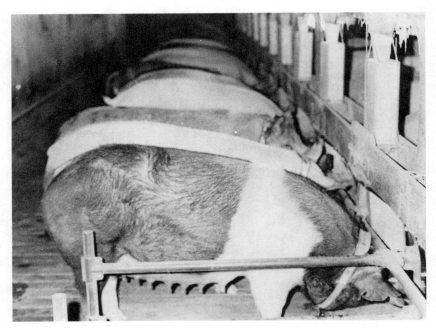

Figure 11-1(e)

Figure 11-1(f)

have an animal also has a *telos*. Must it be able to conceptualize freedom in order to need it? It need not, if its will is unconsciously directed or instinctual. Even if the animal is unconscious and doesn't know, rationally, what it wants, it knows intuitively or instinctively what it needs. Its psyche, or neural organization, directs the will, or motivational system, toward fulfillment of its telos, which includes those external, social, and environmental conditions optimal for its being.

All living things possess will, what Darwin called *the will to survive* and Schweitzer *the will-to-be*. The human will is likewise directed toward survival and being. Through the will, life is directed toward its telic fulfillment, which is toward those conditions optimal for the organism's needs or being and species' continuation.

Thus, while all species of animals may not be able to conceptualize freedom as we humans can, and may not consciously want it, it is reasonable to assume that they all need it because freedom is synonymous with telic purpose and fulfillment.

Conceptually, freedom is not simply the liberty to move toward some goal or ideal situation since it also entails freedom *from* elements that cause stress and distress or frustrate the fulfillment of basic needs and wants. Like us, animals avoid noxious stimuli and stressful circumstances. They show frustration, anxiety, depression, helplessness, and physical sickness when they are unable to cope physiologically and behaviorally. While some of their needs and wants may differ from ours, the basic need for freedom is self-apparent in animals' behavior. Even if they cannot conceptualize freedom or want it, they need it.

However, an animal's need for freedom can be influenced by experiences in early life and by domestication. A highly domesticated dog or pig does not need less freedom than a wolf or wild boar. Such thinking is an anthropomorphic reflection of our own concept of freedom and associated civilized ignorance. Both animals need a kind of freedom that is qualitatively different, but no animal is devoid of the need for freedom. We cannot argue that the more domesticated an animal is, the less freedom it needs because domestication is more of a change in the relationship between the animal and its environment than in the animal itself. If this were not the case, then highly domesticated dogs, pigs, and battery-caged laying hens would not have the capacity to become feral and, when given the opportunity, express the full range of behaviors that their wild counterparts possess. Domesticated animals can differ greatly in size and shape from their wild relatives, but they differ far less in terms of their behavioral needs.

Is it essential that an animal, either captive wild or domesticated, be able to express, for its physical and psychological well-being, its full range of behavior; in other words, to experience its "dogness" or "wolfness"? We accept that it is essential for an animal not to be exposed to, or to have the freedom to avoid, noxious stimuli. However, we do not so readily accept that it is essential for an animal to have the freedom to express its telos, to have such conditions that satisfy species' needs and wants. As we accept that, as civilized beings, we cannot have absolute freedom, we impose this point of view upon domesticated animals. We formulate this point of view as a utilitarian ethic to serve the greater good of society. However, the analogy between civilization and domestication breaks down when we do not do unto animals as we would unto ourselves. We do not offer equal opportunity to animals of the same degree of sentience and intensity of will; we do not give them the same degree of humane treatment and an optimal environment in which to live. Contrast the freedom and care given to a dog kept as a companion and a dog in a laboratory cage kept briefly as part of an LD_{50} test on a new floor polish. There are no moral or scientific grounds for not giving animals, who possess the same degree of sentience and intensity of will and who have the same wants and needs, the same basic freedom and care. If they have limited freedom to avoid distressing elements in their environment, we must provide protective care from noxious and painful stimuli, and we must provide sufficient freedom to enable them to cope with frustration and to satisfy their needs and wants, which, if not satisfied, will be reflected in abnormal behavior, signs of physical stress, psychological distress, disease, and reduced productivity.

Probably the best overt index of an animal's being in a state of freedom — freedom from noxious stimuli such as pain, thirst, and hunger, and from frustration, fear, and anxiety — is when it engages in play behavior. Subjectively, to the human observer, play is an expression of freedom, the freedom to be, to do as one pleases. That animals do play supports the above argument that animals need freedom as much as we do, regardless of whether they can conceptually want to play or to have freedom. The characteristics and forms of freedom will vary according to the individual's and species' needs and wants, which vary rhythmically from hour to season.

Freedom to execute the full range of some categories of behavior, such as comfort activities (e.g., stretching, preening, and rolling), is probably more important physically than the consummation of other activities like the killing of prey in captive predator species that are provided food, and flight from predators in prey species that are protected.

Likewise, freedom to satisfy social, affiliative needs may be more important psychologically in highly social flock and herd animals than the need for a vast amount of empty space. And the freedom to be able to exert some control over the contingent environment in order to minimize stress and frustration, such as being able to avoid cage or penmates, is as important psychologically and physically as a healthful diet, clean air, and water are for physical well-being. Thus, we can speak not only simply of animal freedom but also more specifically of the basic freedoms necessary to satisfy their healthful needs and wants in order that they might be themselves.

It is recognized that an animal raised in an impoverished environment will, if given the opportunity, demonstrate its preference for a more enriched one. But, because of fear or neophobia, it may not want a fully enriched, natural environment although it may well *need* it for its own physical well-being. It may also have a limited ability to make the right choice because of limiting and conflicting influences of prior experience and because we may not have provided the right conditions and contingencies. Such choice tests are of some value in determining the kind of freedom animals need and want, but they are compounded by the above variables and further influenced in some animals by their social attachments to each other and to human caretakers. Thus, a hand-raised bird may choose to stay in one's garden, possibly out of neophobia or out of attachment to place and person. Objectively, such a bird would be judged well and free if it was not showing signs of frustration through abnormal behavior, fear, or husbandry correlated stress and disease. No such judgement can be made, however, when antibiotics and other drugs and treatments, such as reduced illumination, must be given to help the animals adapt.

If, in the absence of such supportive measures, the animal shows signs of stress, distress, and/or disease, are we not correct in assuming that the environment is not conducive to the animal's well-being? What is our yardstick for normalcy and health when such supports are needed to help animals adapt to such pathogenic environments as intensive factory-farm confinement systems when we know that they do not have and probably never will have the biological ability to adapt to such conditions? To be able to reproduce under such conditions is not a valid index of well-being and freedom, or of fulfillment either. The need to reproduce has less to do with physical and psychological well-being than with an instinctive urge to facilitate species' continuation. Some human males will contest this! Animals and humans under considerable stress and distress are still sociobiologically adapted to continue the species, often at the expense of their own well-being. Fertility is one of the erroneous indices of animal well-being often used to assuage the fear that intensively raised farm animals are not suffering. This index of farm animal well-being, like productivity and health, is further invalidated by selective breeding for high sex-drive, fertility, early sexual maturity and the effects of artificial hormones, artificial insemination, and manipulation of light (photoperiod) and diet.

In summation, freedom and well-being are more than intellectual concepts. They are a subjective aspect of being, not exclusive to humanity, but inclusive of all life. This is not an anthropomorphic claim; it is logically probable and empirically verifiable. While it may be anthropomorphic to conclude that all animals want freedom, that they need the freedom to be is an integral part of their existence and a prerequisite of their well-being. Recognition of and respect for animals' need for freedom is an ethical imperative. What kind of freedom is necessary for their well-being is a scientific question and leads to a science of animal welfare.

It can be logically argued that, subjectively, all animals need freedom and that the kind of freedom they require for their well-being can be objectively determined. The subjective side of this issue is one of human responsibility and not one of having to prove that animals consciously desire and conceptualize freedom as we do. This is an anthropocentric projection, a *reverse anthropomorphism,* which is speciesist, illogical, and scientifically invalid. An animal's limited ability to rationalize or conceptualize its needs and to communicate its desire to us does not mean that it does not possess such needs as freedom. Since animals are under our dominion, it is surely our ethical responsibility to understand their needs and, by providing for them, ensure their well-being. That all living things need freedom for their overall well-being is a fundamental principle of good animal husbandry and of animal welfare philosophy. From this perspective, progress in animal welfare science may be enhanced, and its importance more widely recognized. Such freedom may be construed as an animal's right. The philosophic arguments in support of the animal rights construct will now be reviewed.

Animal Rights

A detailed analysis of the question of animal rights is beyond the scope and intent of this book, but it is a subject that is highly relevant to laboratory animal care and experimentation and can no longer be dismissed as anthropomorphic or sentimental idealism.

Animal rights philosophy posits that science animals have interests (Regan 1981), they have rights. These are, of course, not legal rights since animals are not recognized as legal persons. Rather, they are natural or moral rights. If we acknowledge that any sentient creature has an interest in not being harmed and that, in exploiting such creatures, we have a moral obligation to treat them humanely, then we can infer that such treatment is that animal's entitlement: its natural or inherent right under natural law or its moral right in terms of our moral obligation. This ethic is recognized in the anticruelty statutes of many states.

Singer (1975) argues that animals should be given equal and fair consideration, but not equal rights per se since animals don't have the same interests as we do such as the right to the freedom of speech. I have argued (Fox 1983c) that animals of similar sentience should be accorded the right to equal and fair treatment, a necessary consideration in view of the legal and cultural inconsistencies in the ways in which animals in our society are regarded and treated (e.g., a person would be liable to prosecution for burning an animal with a hot iron if it were a dog, but not if it were a calf or a goat).

In recognizing an animal's will to survive (to avoid harm and to continue its species) and its will to be (to seek satisfaction of its interests and fulfillment of its telos), we face the dialectic of human interests and rights versus animals' interests and rights. This dialectic cannot be reconciled simply by assuming that humans are superior and that animals were created primarily for man to exploit. Nor can it be dismissed by the utilitarian belief that it is an historical truth that it is ethically acceptable to sacrifice the rights of a few for the benefit of many since this view leads to biological fascism and scientific imperialism. By recognizing our responsibilities[*] for and indebtedness to the billions of animals we exploit, we are forced to confront the dialectical moral dilemmas and ethical imperatives that undergird our existence. The question of our duty toward animals and of their having rights is, thus, a moral and ethical issue, not some anthropomorphic sentimentality.

WHAT RIGHTS FOR ANIMALS?

The questions about what rights animals should be accorded and why must now be addressed. Opponents have voiced the opinion that

---

[*]*Regardless of the fact that they may be domesticated, man-made, and propagated purely for laboratory research, we have responsibilities toward them even though animals like the hairless mouse would not exist in nature without our involvement.*

animals cannot have rights because they are unable to voice them and that even if they had any rights, all would be subordinate to any human right or claim since we have God-given dominion. Surprising as it may seem, scientists and others having unconditional claims over animals frequently cite the verse from Genesis alluding to man's unquestionable dominion over the rest of creation, a neither objective nor scientifically verifiable reference to say the least. It is to be hoped that such disturbing naivite and self-serving rationalizations among educated and supposedly responsible persons will soon be transcended; courses in bioethics and human and animal rights are now being incorporated into the curriculum of several medical and veterinary schools, as well as at undergraduate college level.

Some excellent reviews in addition to those cited earlier have been published that analyze past and present attitudes towards animals and nature and the influence of philosophers and humanists from Aristotle and Kant, to Descartes and Schweitzer (Clark 1977; Morris and Fox 1978; Fox 1976, 1980; Midgley 1978, 1983; Linzey 1976; Leiss 1972; Paterson and Ryder 1979). It has been, and still is argued, for example, that animals cannot have rights because they are unable to voice or articulate them. Only human beings can have a claim to rights because only we are rational, ethical, and verbal beings. Yet mentally retarded, brain-damaged and comatose people, preverbal infants, and irrational emotionally disturbed mental patients all have some legal rights, and they can have legal representation. Legal standing is also accorded to nonsentient and nonliving entities such as property and corporations. Thus, to deny legal standing to nonhuman animals and natural, nonsentient or nonliving creations, such as trees and lakes, is neither logical nor ethical (Stone 1974). Such a separation between the human and nonhuman has been appropriately dubbed "speciesism" (Singer 1975; Ryder 1975) and is symptomatic of self-serving, humanocentric utilitarianism.

The point is often raised that only those entities that have certain claims or interests can have rights. A comatose patient cannot voice his claims or interests; they can only be assumed by those who have the guardianship role to uphold that person's legal rights. A designated person can also act as the trustee or steward of someone's property or estate. In both cases, the guardian or trustee has the obligation and power to act on behalf of the person or property to protect rights and legal standing.

The obligation is both moral and legal. Similarly, we have a moral as well as some legal obligations to respect and uphold the rights of nonhuman living (sentient and presentient) entities. While we, as guardians or trustees, may not or cannot know what claims or interests such entities have, we have the moral obligation to respect and protect their basic rights, which is their justifiable entitlement. To some extent, we also have a legal obligation to uphold certain rights such as the right to life of endangered species, the right to humane treatment of laboratory and companion or pet animals, and the right to a humane death of all livestock (poultry are excluded from protection under the Humane Slaughter Act).

Just as we assume that a preverbal child or comatose patient has certain interests, so we may assume that other entities have various interests that we, as stewards, guardians, or trustees, have legal and moral obligations to uphold.

Such analogous thinking suffers from one major drawback, apart from being anthropocentric, the implicit assumption of interests. It can be argued pro- and con- till the end of time whether or not trees, lakes, frogs, and dogs have interests. Since we may have certain interests in them (e.g., utilitarian, emotional, esthetic, and economic), the flaw here is that human interests, especially through consensus, can easily take precedence over their interests, especially since the latter may be based upon anthropomorphic projections or intuitive, empathic assumptions which cannot be scientifically verified. Similarly, to base the case for animal rights on the capacity of animals to suffer and to have feelings (Singer 1975) is an anthropocentric view and could lead to speciesism. Somewhere the line must be drawn between those entities that can suffer and those that do not. Even worse is to base the animal rights argument on an interspecies gradient of intelligence rather than suffering, although the question of animal awareness is one that scientist have yet to address (Griffin 1977).

A better case in favor of animal and nature rights, which avoids the traps of anthropocentrism, is made by basing the argument upon the fact that they (nonhuman entities) exist and can be harmed or otherwise adversely affected by human activities. Thus, independent of their degree of sentience or capacity to suffer, of their intelligence, and of their possible interests, we have a moral obligation to respect their natural rights. This does not imply that nonhuman entities have the same rights or moral/legal status as humans or that all rights are absolute and inviolable, but rather that we should at least give them equal consideration.

Before we can speak in support of animal rights, those rights must be defined as objectively and accurately as possible. That animals should be accorded rights is implicit in the fact that we clearly do have obligations towards them. The right to a cage of optimal dimensions, of living with companions, of being provided bedding, a perch, or regular exercise are related to a clearer appreciation of the animal's basic needs. We, as guardians or stewards have the moral and, to some degree, legal obligation to satisfy these basic needs. An animal has a right not to have its basic needs unnecessarily thwarted or frustrated. To what degree we are obligated to provide the best environment in order to optimize their innate potentials is a moot point. Economic considerations notwithstanding, we must at least find a golden mean for captive farm, zoo, and laboratory animals that will minimize such deprivation effects. The ethologist and animal welfare scientist can do much in this regard by defining what the animal's basic needs are and what the costs to the animal are, in terms of physical stress and psychological suffering, if certain needs are not satisfied and by suggesting what husbandry practices can be adopted to eliminate unnecessary stress, frustration, and suffering (Dawkins 1978). With farm animals particularly, the focus has been on shaping the animal genetically and surgically — i.e., by castration, debeaking, and taildocking — to fit the environment. More attention needs to be given to the reverse of this situation because the logical outcome of it could be to remove the legs of animals in order to eliminate their need to walk. The cage sizes recommended by the NIH for primates, dogs, cats, and other laboratory species are approximately half the dimensions stipulated for the same species in the United Kingdom. Clearly, such rudimentary elements of laboratory animal husbandry cannot have been derived from scientific study of the animals' basic needs, and yet we do have the science and technology available to *ask* the animal what environment and/or cage inclusions it prefers. This is an important part of the unfinished agenda in relation to animal rights. Many questions remain to be answered by ethologists and animal welfare scientists, preferably before further legislation and humane reforms are instigated, since, as it has been demonstrated (Dawkins 1978), what may seem intuitively right to us for the animal's well-being may not be what it wants at all. A chicken that preens excessively or a rhesus monkey that self-mutilates may not, respectively, want to get out of a crowded battery cage or have a larger cage or a rope to swing on; the chicken may simply want a perch or a nest box to lay its egg in and the rhesus may want a companion to engage in reciprocal social grooming.

Why should we accord rights to other entities outside of our humanosphere, and what benefits, in a strictly utilitarian sense, may we thereby gain? Since science does not deal with ethical issues and is purportedly an objective and amoral discipline, we must, it would'seem, turn to religion and moral philosophy for some direction and answers.

However, science need not and should not be excluded from ethics and moral responsibility since the consequences of scientific discovery and its technological application can have ecological and social ramifications. It is perhaps because of the assumed sanctity of scientific freedom that the scientific community becomes defensive when the relevance of basic biomedical research is questioned. Social relevance is, however, less germane to the present discussion than is the issue of ethics and moral responsibility. The utilitarian rationalist may see any and all means, including animal suffering, as justifiable if the ends lead to some benefit to man (Fox 1980). These benefits may range from teaching a student some technical skill or acquiring more knowledge for knowledge's sake to discovering a new life-saving drug or surgical procedure. The scientist may design and conduct experiments that minimize animal pain and suffering, or he may seek alternatives such as using organisms of lower sentience or *in vitro* preparations. This is a moral obligation, and only a nominal legal obligation since the Animal Welfare Act allows justifiable or unavoidable pain and suffering. An investigator who questions the value of a particular study and does not follow the Kantian utilitarian doctrine that the ends always justify the means if they lead to some human good is being accountable for his or her actions. Such scientific accountability is surely one of the prime moral obligations of the biomedical scientist towards both human and nonhuman subjects, and the apparent lack of accountability today is a major issue of contention between animal research and antivivisectionist groups. To hide behind the rhetoric and consensus agreement in the sanctity of the freedom of scientific enquiry on the one hand or to demand an unconditional end to all animal experimentation on the other are polemic views that can never be resolved. Understanding and resolution may come when there is better accountability by scientists, a better appreciation of animal rights, and a clearer understanding of the need for animals in biomedical research among antivivisectionists. A common ground must be laid to facilitate a more constructive exchange and reciprocal maturation of attitudes and values by both groups focusing upon the question of animal rights. In other words, the animal rights issue can help establish a common ground. Similarly, the animal scientist, preoccupied with collecting data from farm animals on feed conversion efficiency and growth rates, may benefit from an exchange of views with humanitarians and ethical vegetarians over welfare and rights issues of intensive, confinement raised factory-farmed animals (Harrison 1964; Fox 1983a). Attention to animal rights could, for example, promise significant economic gains since the denial of certain basic rights can cause an increase in disease and a decrease in productivity (Fox op. cit.). Addressing the rights of laboratory animals can lead to better research since the animals will be healthier and more normal once certain rights are satisfied via improvements in general husbandry. Respecting the rights of wild animals and other natural nonsentient entities could mean better protection for the biosphere and a physically and psychologically healthier environment for humans to live in (Fox 1979; Shephard 1978).

Such are some of the utilitarian benefits of supporting animal and nature rights. Another benefit, often emphasized by humanitarians, is that it may help us become better human beings — more empathic, compassionate and responsible (Morris and Fox 1978; Fox 1980). A high incidence of cruelty towards animals in childhood has been correlated with later criminal and sociopathic behavior.

It may seem paradoxical to some that one who may support the rights of animals may at the same time eat them or condone their use in essential biomedical research. There are many such paradoxes in our attitudes toward animals and the uses to which they are put. Objective scrutiny and research is needed to evaluate the possible balances and compromises between the respective rights and welfare of animals and man. We must identify and carefully define empirical, researchable questions that can help us to better understand and that enable us to improve the relations between animals and people. What are the necessary and unnecessary costs in animal lives and suffering that underlie our use of animals? We kill them for food, clothing, and sports; we exploit them as draft animals and circus performers; we use them in biomedical, psychological, and military research. Our demands upon them are ever increasing in number and variety. Do our ends always justify our means? Should animal rights always take second place to any human right, need, or wish? What limits should be placed on the benefits or pleasures humans derive from killing, harming, or utilizing animals? Should economic or scientific values take precedence over the animals' right not to be killed or injured if this is not essential for human health and survival? At what point should an economic or other human-centered reason justify killing or hurting animals?

Many hard choices must at times be made such as inflicting physical suffering or stress on animals in medical experiments, or destroying numbers of wild animals that threaten the ecology of a wildlife refuge. Yet, too often, such choices often lack a sound scientific basis, while the search for economically feasible and humane alternatives is no more than a token endeavor. Close scrutiny of such "scientific" studies frequently reveals rationalizations and traditions of thought and action that are scientifically and ethically untenable. For example, the claim that trapping wildlife helps to prevent rabies outbreaks, which is not scientifically verified, is a common excuse for the continuing use of the steel leghold trap.

Some scientists and educators claim that causing animals to suffer is justifiable if a student is to acquire knowledge or technical skill. Without a humane concern for animals and with minimal scientific research into viable humane alternatives, such utilitarianism can be morally reprehensible. How do students feel when asked to conduct a questionable experiment on a living animal? How do instructors respond? More broadly, what is the public's attitude toward the utilization of and suffering of animals?

Does a laboratory or farm animal have the same rights to life as an animal in a zoo or in the wild? Do the various animals used by humans have one and the same basic right to life and to freedom from human abuse, irrespective of whether they are pets, farm animals, hunted species, or other? What rights does a pet have? Should a veterinarian medicate an unsound horse so that it can race? Should a farm manager raise animals under stressful and inhumane conditions if this reduces the cost of meat? Can humane *and* economic methods be devised?

Examples of other problem areas include the sale and possession of exotic, often rare and endangered, species as pets; various uses of healthy animals for veterinary and medical teaching purposes; genetic engineering; predator control programs; and the adequacy of the housing and care of primates in the light of recent developments in establishing two-way communication with chimpanzees and gorillas. Many additional examples could be cited of questions about man's relations with animals that need to be addressed.

We do have dominion over the earth, and while this has come to be interpreted as domination for utilitarian ends, the Judeo-Christian tradition and the emerging philosophy of animal and nature rights regard dominion as stewardship or trusteeship. Man, giver and upholder of rights, must now face up to this moral imperative for his own good and for the good of all life on earth. We can begin in the classroom, research laboratory, factory farm, and wildlife preserve where the rights issue is our unfinished agenda.

The rights issue thus embraces ecology, ethics, economics, politics, and evolution or the future of all life on earth. It lies at the interface between man, animal, and nature — an interface that has yet to be objectively and rationally addressed. To date, most analyses of this interface have been in terms of cost or risk versus benefits, and, more recently, since the advent of applied ecology, environmental impact assessments must be made. Costs to the environment must now be determined. Similarly, costs to species, particularly those plants and animals that are threatened and endangered by various human activities must also be accounted for. Such hidden costs frustrate many with the bureaucratic red tape of regulatory agencies, but this does represent a first step toward a growing societal awareness of environmental and species' rights. Aldo Leopold's (1966) land ethic is as follows: "A thing is right when it tends to preserve the integrity, stability, and beauty of the biotic community. It is wrong when it tends otherwise."

As LaChapelle (1978) emphasizes, this land ethic "clearly takes ethics out of the miasma of 'human' rights, privileges, and manipulations and puts them where they belong — in the network of relationships between all beings of any particular place."

As ecology has provided a valuable objective basis for the environmental and conservation movements, so applied ethology and the emerging interdisciplinary science of animal welfare will provide a firm foundation for the animal welfare and rights movement.

HUMANE ETHICS AND ANIMAL RIGHTS [+]

The humane ethic of treating animals with compassion has been the principle tenet of the animal welfare movement for many decades. It is based upon the Judeo-Christian doctrine of benevolence to all God's creatures and upon the moral virtue of kindness, inhumanity being regarded as a social evil and a sign of bad character.

This ethic, however valid, is limited because it would seem to accept any form of animal exploitation if it is done humanely. Would an explosive harpoon or instant-kill trap make the slaughter of whales and fur-bearing mammals morally acceptable? Within the narrow tenet of being kind and not cruel toward animals, the answer would be yes.

While the primary goal of the animal welfare movement is to eliminate suffering in those animal species that are exploited by humans, this goal, although exemplary, is narrow sighted. Notwithstanding the practical difficulties of proving animal suffering, especially psychological, suffering could conceivably be eliminated, as in confined farm animals, through the use of tranquilizers, or even brain surgery. A goose being made to eat compulsively, following selective partial destruction or stimulation of its brain to cause hypertrophy of its liver for the liver paté

[+] from Int. J. Stud. Anim. Prob. 4 (1984): 286-289.

trade, may not suffer. But it is being harmed. Likewise, to selective breed a farm animal, like a broiler chicken, that eats to excess so that its rate of growth jeopardizes its health, or to raise a zoo or laboratory animal in a highly restricted environment, may not cause overt suffering, since the animals do "adapt." But they are being harmed, since such treatments can increase their susceptibility to stress and disease. In the parlance of animal rights philosophy, their rights are being violated, regardless of whether or not suffering occurs or can be scientifically proven.

Animal suffering, therefore, is only one aspect of animal exploitation and abuse. Recognizing this, and the fact that the elimination of animal suffering is an extremely limited horizon, the humane movement has greatly expanded its vision and goals by incorporating animal rights philosophy and ecological principles into its educational, legislative, and political activities.

A deeper understanding of what animals do and say, and why, will not only enhance our enjoyment of them as companions or as natural creations for observation and appreciative contemplation; it will also improve the care they receive under humane stewardship and under the dominion of animal researchers, farmers, and others whose livelihoods depend upon the exploitation of animals for the benefit of society. Furthermore, this "animal connection" of understanding is the basis for *informed empathy,* (as distinct from a purely Cartesian, utilitarian anthropomorphic, or esthetic attitude), which leads us inevitably toward what Albert Schweitzer called "a reverence for all life." Once this animal connection of understanding and reverence is established, the societal recognition of the intrinsic worth of animals, and of their rights, will mean a fundamental change in our attitude toward the animal kingdom which will improve our stewardship of planet earth and the lives of all creatures under our dominion. The following synopsis of animal rights philosophy, which relates to the treatment and exploitation of domesticated and wild animals, shows where ethical guidelines and ecological considerations are needed beyond the limited framework of animal suffering per se.

Economic and other social justifications of animal exploitation, particularly the raising of animals for human consumption and their use in biomedical research, should stand the test of moral, as well as utilitarian justification, with reference to the ethics of humane animal exploitation and their intrinsic worth or "rights," which may be articulated as follows:

Animals have an intrinsic nature and interests (needs, wants, etc.) of their own, intentionality or purposiveness, and have intrinsic worth independent of the extrinsic values we may project or impose upon them. These interests may be construed as their rights or entitlement.

Their physical, emotional, and social needs constitute their intrinsic nature, or "animalness" (which has an evolutionary and genetic basis), which entitle them to just treatment and moral concern.

In recognizing that animals have intrinsic worth and interests independent of their extrinsic worth to us, we are ethically enjoined to treat them compassionately. Thus, when they are under our care or stewardship, we are morally and ought legally, to be bound to respect their rights.

Respecting the rights of animals means avoiding unnecessary or unjustifiable death, physical, or psychological suffering, or deprivation or frustration of their basic physical, emotional, and social needs.

Such rights are relative and not absolute (i.e., presumptive). For example, a domestic animal's desire to be free may have to be inhibited for its own good and for the good of society. However, it would be a violation of such an animal's rights (amounting to cruel and unnecessary privation) to keep it continually restrained in a small cage or on a short chain.

To argue that animals have rights is based on more than philosophical presumption or moral reasoning. It is based upon the ecological evidence that they are, as we, an integral part of the biospheric ecological community and also upon the physiological and psychological affinities that many animal species have with us. That we are dominant over them and in control or superior to them are not valid reasons for denying animals equal and fair consideration. The honest reasons for denying them such consideration, and not according them rights, are primarily economic, and also that their exploitation gives us pleasure, and that their interests at times conflict with ours, as overcompetition for resources. An understanding of the intrinsic nature of animals leads to an appreciation of their intrinsic worth and, thus, ultimately to according them rights.

The rights of animals should be given equal consideration with the rights of a human being, but it is important to recognize that this does *not* necessarily imply equal treatment nor that the interests of the animal are accorded the same weight or value as essential human interests.

This provides the ethical basis for determining when the killing or harming of an animal (by causing it to suffer or to be deprived of certain basic needs) is morally justifiable.

In making such ethical determinations, we as moral agents, must consider the animal's intrinsic nature and its rights, and reason informs us that animals are legitimate objects of moral concern.

Thus, the killing of an animal may be ethically acceptable only when there are no reasonable alternatives, as when the animal is: (a) incurably ill and is experiencing great suffering; (b) so deformed or otherwise incapacitated as to be incapable of living without great suffering; (c) endangering the lives of human beings, or causing a severe and unnatural ecological impact, thus endangering the lives of other living creatures; (d) other instances not directly beneficial to the animal arise when its products (meat, fur, etc.) are essential for human well-being and there are no alternatives that are less costly; (e) when we must minimize environmental costs or suffering of other animals; (f) or when the knowledge gained from killing it (as in some biomedical research) is essential for human health or for the benefit of other animals.

Is causing an animal to suffer physically or psychologically ethically acceptable when there are no alternatives and such treatment is essential to human survival and overall health (as distinct from purely economic or other materialistic benefit), or promises to alleviate a significant degree of suffering in man or in other animals (as in medical or veterinary research)?

Subjecting an animal to deprivation or frustration of certain basic needs is only acceptable when such treatment is essential to the welfare of the animal itself, or essential to the fundamental welfare of human beings or other animals, and there are no alternatives to using animals to achieve these goals. Fundamental welfare implies consideration directly relevant to human health, safety and survival, not inessential comforts, economic benefits, or knowledge for its own sake.

The rights of animals vary according to the context of their relationship with human beings. For example, the right to freedom for a house pet has more restraints or qualifications than the right to freedom of a wild animal. Another example concerns the right to life of a parasite that is jeopardizing the life of its host compared to the lives of members of an endangered species.

A major aspect of animal rights philosophy that has been seriously overlooked, because of the instant polarization of this issue into animal versus human rights, is that animals of the same species, or of the same degree of sentience, should be treated with the same degree of humaneness (since they can all suffer similarly). There are no moral or ethical grounds for considering otherwise, and there is certainly no scientific reason why they should be treated differently. The only reasons why similar animals are treated differently are primarily economic and cultural.

In summation, the intrinsic nature of an animal is the basis for rights, from which the above ethical codes may be deduced. Nonhuman beings should be as much a part of our community of moral concern as humans. They are an inseparable part of the ecological community of our planet. The ethical codes are both spiritual and practical, originating from the highest tenets of humane, compassionate, and responsible conduct. They bespeak a reverence for life, cast within the framework of ecologically sound and unselfish planetary stewardship, upon which our survival depends and through which our survival depends and through which the quality and diversity of all life on earth may be protected and enhanced for the "greater good."

While the "greater good" cannot be easily defined for all conditions or circumstances, the concept is framed within the Kantian formulation that no man must be the means to the ends of another. The Talmudic statement: "Whosoever saves a single life is as if he had saved the whole world; whosoever destroys a single life is as if he had destroyed the whole world" is also relevant to resolving the ethical dilemma where the rights and sanctity of the individual must be sacrificed for the "greater," as distinct from some lesser (e.g., ideological or economic) good, for the benefit of all, rather than for the benefit of a select, more powerful few.

The lack of regard and concern for the intrinsic nature, worth, and "rights" of animals is a metaphor for the lack of empathy, care, knowledge, respect and responsibility that humans have for their own kind, be they of the same or opposite sex, or of a different race, socioeconomic class, political, religious or other belief or value system.

It has been argued that since only humans can act as moral agents, it is only they, and not animals, who can have rights. However, to possess rights, one need not be an active moral agent, as in the case of infants and comatose patients. It is logical that since rights constitute a social recognition of other's interests, to deny animals recognition of their rights is to deny the evidence that they, like we, have certain interests, needs, and behavioral requirements. Since we are moral agents, capable of rational, responsible, and compassionate action, it is clearly irrational anthropocentrism to deny other sentient creatures their rights, recognition of which makes us more fully human by broadening and enriching the scope and awareness of our moral community.

The ultimate tragedy, apart from irreversible environmental destruction and extinction of species, is not human and animal suffering so much as the collective atrophy of the human spirit that permits the unethical exploitation and subjugation of animals and humans alike, in the name of economic necessity, political expedience, and other inhumane rationalizations. Social, political and other reforms, although often well intended, as exemplified by the philosophy, actions, and aspirations of animal and human rights groups, will make little progress until it is realized that social transformation is possible only when each individual has become spiritually awakened to act responsibly and has regained the ability to empathize, to have compassionate understanding and respect for the intrinsic worth of other beings, animal and human alike.

ANIMAL RIGHTS, LEGAL OR NATURAL?

Critics of the concept of animals having rights tend to think only in terms of legal rights. However, there is another category of rights termed "natural rights," which, according to *Webster's Third New International Dictionary,* would hold in the absence of organized government and, therefore, of legal rights. Significantly, under the many different meanings of rights listed in Webster's, a right can mean "a power, privilege, or immunity vested in an animal or a group of animals (as by custom: grazing rights of a herd of antelope)."

It is important, therefore, not to condemn the concept of animal rights by perceiving them only in a legalistic framework as legal rights. Animals also have natural rights that we, as a matter of custom, respect and uphold as unwritten law.

Seen this way, animal rights are mainly moral injunctions that constitute a humane and, it is to be hoped, an ecologically sound ethic. So it can be argued that while a pig may have no right (neither legal or natural) not to be eaten, it does have the legal right under the Humane Slaughter Act to be killed humanely. While there is no law that also stipulates that pigs should be raised humanely,* it is as much their natural right to be treated humanely as it is also a tradition or custom of sound animal husbandry. We, therefore, have a moral, rather than legal, obligation to ensure that their right to humane treatment is upheld since it is based upon both custom and natural rights.

Would it be false to claim that those animals that have been bred and raised in captivity for generations have no natural rights? Many of these animals, like mutant strains of mice, could never survive under natural conditions. Though man-made to some degree — and to ever

---

*Although there are state laws that stipulate animals should not be treated cruelly, there are no laws that state how they should be raised and treated.

greater degrees with cloning and genetic engineering — is it not hubris to deny such creatures natural rights, for, by so doing, man is assuming the role of creator, and man has not yet actually created life *de novo* in the laboratory. Domesticated animals are not exclusively our own creations nor are they wholly unnatural creatures. What of the ethics of propagating mutant strains that natural selection would eliminate, but which we selectively propagate for medical and other purposes? During the course of their lives they are subjected to considerable suffering because they are afflicted with such heritable diseases as hemophilia, epilepsy, and impaired disease immunity.

And what of the ethics of keeping animals alive in studies on aging, suffering from chronic degenerative diseases that they would most likely not suffer from in the wild because their average lifespan is much shorter than when they are kept under the more protected conditions of the laboratory?

The ethics of transgenic manipulations — i.e., introducing the genes of one species into another — whereby the integrity of species boundaries is in jeopardy, have yet to be addressed. Is the genetic integrity of species and of individual animals a natural right that we should respect? Or is there no ethical issue in inserting human or rat growth genes into mice to create giant mice, or in creating chimeras like the sheep with a goat's head at the Agricultural Research Centre at Cambridge, England? Does it follow that the more unnatural the creature is, the less claim to natural rights it can have? Or do such unnatural creations, be they genetically engineered, selectively bred mutants, or surgically created chimeras, have a right never to have been created and propagated in the first place?

We have the knowledge and ability to profoundly alter an animal's telos or intrinsic nature and the power to redirect its telos to satisfy our own ends exclusively. How we choose to exercise this knowledge and power depends perhaps in the final analysis, not so much upon how well the morality of natural rights is accepted and legally enforced, but rather to what degree we are able to empathize with animals and treat them with compassion and respect. Is it not perhaps the absence of empathic sensitivity and ethical sensibility that necessitates the fabrication of moral codes and laws?

What Lao Tzu, the sixth century BC philosopher had to say about human relationships is also relevant to human-animal relationships. He wrote: "Stop the teaching of benevolence and get rid of the claim of justice, then the people will love each other once more. . . . Give up kindness, renounce morality, and men will rediscover filial piety and love." Another of his statements clarifies these characteristically paradoxical aphorisms and emphasizes that the essence of humane ethics is compassion and empathy, not law and morality. "When all-embracing reverence is lost, there is righteousness and justice. When these are lost, there is propriety. Propriety is due to lack of trustworthiness [responsibility] and is the beginning of disorder."

Anthropomorphizing*

The above discussion on animal freedom, needs, wants, and rights could be summarily dismissed as being anthropomorphic. However, a number of scientists and philosophers have argued that it is not anthropomorphic to suggest that animals can experience humanlike emotional states such as fear; rather, it is our own anthropocentrism that denies animals such subjective experiences.

Hurnik and Lehman (1982) argue that:

> The evidence that we have that an animal is afraid or in pain does not consist in dubious analogies to human behavior. For example, what grounds are available to support the contention that a sheep which sees or smells a wolf feels afraid? We *do not* say that we know that the sheep is afraid because when human beings are in contact with wolves they feel afraid. Such reasoning would be fallacious and might lead to absurd conclusions. Rather the evidence that the sheep feels fear in the vicinity of the wolf includes observations of physiological and behavioral factors as well as the consideration that fear appears to make a significant contribution to the animal's chance of survival. While it might be suggested that we don't need the hypothesis that the animal feels fear in order to explain the animal's behavior in the presence of the wolf — that such an explanation can be given without reference to the animal's mental state, we believe that this suggestion is superficial. We believe that reference to the animal's fear is warranted because the best available descriptions and explanations of the sheep's observable behavior make reference to its fear. Reasoning in this way is in accord with sound canons of scientific method; it is not anthropomorphic.

Griffin (1982) writes that:

> The possibility that animals have mental experiences is often dismissed as anthropomorphic because it is held to imply that other species have the same mental experiences as man might have under comparable circumstances. But this widespread view itself contains the questionable assumption that human mental experiences are the only kind that con-

*from M.W. Fox. Farm Animals: Husbandry, Behavior and Veterinary Practice. (Baltimore: University Park Press, 1983).

ceivably exist. This belief that mental experiences are a unique attribute of a single species is not only unparsimonious; it is conceited. It seems more likely than not that mental experiences, like many other characters, are widespread, at least among multicellular animals, but differ greatly in nature and complexity.

Without such correlated evidence, we run the risk of projecting our own feelings onto the animal, which may or may not be accurate. Yet there are those who would believe that there are no grounds for such anthropomorphism because they adhere to the Cartesian belief that animals, although they may experience pain, are not aware, in and of themselves as we are, of emotional states. In the light of clear scientific evidence, of analogous neuroanatomical systems and psychophysiological mechanisms and responses to stress in both vertebrate animals and human beings, such parsimony is untenable. There is sufficient documented evidence from stress research, animal psychology, and neurophysiology to support the probability that the subjective, emotional world of animals is more similar to the various subjective states of human consciousness than it is different (Walker 1983; Griffin 1982).

Objective proof of what an animal or human being is subjectively experiencing is impossible, however, and this fact alone demonstrates that the concepts of 'reality,' 'truth,' and 'knowledge' are not the exclusive domain of science. It is clearly unwise, therefore, to rely exclusively upon the scientific method to answer questions of animal consciousness and welfare. The closest approximation is through anthropomorphic — i.e., empathic — correlation of empirically derived observations (e.g., of analogous psychophysiological responses to stress in animals that are seen in humans in association with subjective emotional states such as fear and anxiety). Such anthropomorphic correlation between animals and humans is the basis of comparative medicine, physiology, pathology, and animal models of human disease processes. The stressors and other environmental factors triggering such psychophysiological responses may or may not be similar, significant differences being attributable to species, strain, individual, and age-related variables.

The credibility gap widens when there is a lack of correlation between how the animal responds psychophysiologically to stress, pain, or other environmental stimuli and how a human might respond under similar circumstances; there would then be a greater element of doubt as to what the animal might be actually feeling. Since animals are likely to suffer in a number of different circumstances in which a human being would not suffer, the anthropomorphic identification and/or correlation with the animal should not be limited to investigating analogous contexts, stressors, or other emotion-evoking stimuli. Similarly, looking only at analogous behavioral reactions can be no less misleading since the ethological repertoire of animals is different in many respects from the emotion-correlated behavioral reactions of human beings. Cold temperatures cause a calf or human infant to suffer, but they cause a hamster to simply hibernate. Clearly, therefore, a detailed knowledge of species' characteristics and environmental requirements is essential, otherwise anthropomorphic concern and care would be inaccurate and could jeopardize the animal's welfare. However, when there are significant species differences in behavior and physiology compared to humans, we are even less able to imagine how they might be feeling by "putting ourselves in their place." A lack of correlation between physiological and behavioral changes in the animal and in human beings adds further to the problem of welfare assessment if no such correlations can be made.

PARAMETERS OF WELFARE ASSESSMENT

As philosopher Karl Popper (1972) argues, *falsifiability* — i.e., tests to prove a given hypothesis false or in need of modification — is the hallmark of science, whereas lack of falsifiability leads to pseudoscience, mysticism, and so forth. Yet there is a ghost in the machine when it is hypothesized that animals have emotional experiences. Such a hypothesis, which lacks falsifiability, clearly demonstrates the intrinsic limitations of Popper's philosophy, not of animal science, because the same deficiency applies to the hypothesis that persons other than I have emotional experiences.

The science of animal welfare therefore has serious limitations, which can only be overcome by empathy and recognition that "the currency of the animal welfare debate is the real but largely subjective domain of the individual's (animal's) response to its environment" (Gee and Meischke 1982). This is also the art as distinct from the science of veterinary medicine and animal husbandry. Uninformed sympathy leads to anthropomorphy; informed sympathy leads to empathy and humane stewardship. Purely rational, objective, and instrumental knowledge of animals is, in the final analysis, inadequate since the science of subjective knowledge includes empathy and ethics, as well as good scholarship. Animals' needs and wants cannot be known fully until we attune ourselves to and endeavor to understand the subjective realm of animals — their *umwelts*.

Several variables should be evaluated to determine animal welfare. These include physiological, biochemical, and neuroendocrine indices, behavior, health reproduction and longevity, susceptibility to stress and disease incidence, and productivity such as growth and lactation. This last variable is one of the least reliable indicators of welfare, as emphasized earlier in this book.

Manipulating and measuring a single variable in order to determine the degree of stress or suffering is clearly inadequate research, since the determination of overall well-being, and the science of animal welfare per se, necessitate a multivariable analysis, an interdisciplinary approach in which many interrelated vectors and variables must be identified and studied.

The World Health Organization has defined health as "a state of mental, physical, and social well-being and not merely the absence of disease." As emphasized in Chapter 10, these same criteria need to be established for the husbandry of laboratory and all domesticated and captive wild animals since it is well-recognized that valid research can only be conducted upon healthy animals, unless the intent is to study specifically induced disease states. In most present day laboratory animal research facilities, these criteria are not satisfied, especially for primates, dogs, and cats. At best, their basic physical needs are satisfied. Their mental states and social well-being are generally ignored; a clean cage, clean air, food, water, and the absence of disease being the narrow, mechanistic, and unscientific criteria for laboratory and farm animal health and welfare.

A fourth criterion of human health needs recognition, namely environmental health. Ecological medicine is a relatively new field necessitated to combat new and complex *technogenic* (Hodges and Scofield 1983) and *agricologenic* diseases associated with agricultural and industrial chemicals that contaminate our air, food, and water, and which have complex ecological and molecular (biochemical and cellular) consequences, as well as economic and political ramifications.

Justifying Animal Use in Research

There is one very powerful argument that scientists use to defend and justify their right to use animals for research purposes. This is that the desire for acquiring knowledge — knowledge for knowledge's sake — is a cultural value. It is argued that all knowledge is of potential use to humanity, and its pursuit should not be questioned and obstructed. Such obstruction would be against the best interests of society and also a violation of scientific freedom. This attitude could lead to all knowledge of potential benefit to humanity being placed above such humane concerns as laboratory animal suffering; the means, no matter how much animal suffering is involved, would justify the ends if there was benefit to society.

Yet all knowledge is not of equal value, and it is unscholarly to make such a generalization. Only certain essential knowledge, rather than trivial information, should be justifiably sought at the expense of an animal's suffering.

Animal rights philosopher Regan (1983) makes an important, yet highly controversial, point when he states, "To treat them [animals] *as if* their value were reducible to their utility for human interests, even important human interests, is to treat them unjustly." It is surely unjust to cause animals to suffer for the sake of some hypothetical good for humanity. The ends do not always justify the means. Utilitarian philosopher Singer contends, "If one, or even a dozen animals had to suffer experiments in order to save thousands, I would think it right in accordance with equal consideration of interests that they should do so."

Seligman (1975) states, "Each scientist must ask himself one question before doing any experiment on an animal. Is it likely that the pain and deprivation that this animal is about to endure will be greatly outweighed by the resulting alleviation of human pain and deprivation? If the answer is yes, the experiment is justified." A more rigorous and less anthropocentric principle might be formulated as follows: *If the pain and suffering to the animal would be greater than the amount of pain and suffering that a human might feel under the same experimental conditions, then the experiment should not be permitted.*

However, if we cannot ascertain how much the animal is in pain and suffering, then, ethically, we should not experiment upon them. Scientifically, if we do not know these basic facts, then the value and relevance of the work, aimed at ultimately alleviating pain and suffering in humans, is most probably scientifically invalid and of little relevance clinically. Pain, suffering, and deprivation are intervening variables that affect the animal's behavior, postoperative recovery, drug-responsiveness, immune system, and disease and stress resistance. These variables must be controlled for, their intensity and effect on the animal must be known, otherwise the scientific validity and clinical relevance data derived from animal experimentation will be minimal.

Psychologists Marcuse and Pear (1979) contend that the primary purpose and justification of scientists experimenting upon animals is that the knowledge gained may be of *survival benefit.* How much this belief stems from unconscious anxiety and insecurity, which no amount of animal research is going to help, is worth consideration.

These scientists ask, "Should the good and well-being of humans be placed over that of animals?" The very formulation of such a question is based upon the assumption that the good and well-being of animals and humans are mutually exclusive and that the two are somehow separate. In a more empathic and ecological, rather than anthropocentric, perspective, the good of humans and other animals are mutually inclusive rather than exclusive. Perhaps if scientists like Marcuse and Pear were to examine those human values, motives, and priorities that lead them to make such ill-conceived statements in justification and defense of using sentient animals "for the benefit of humanity," we might benefit far more significantly than from the supposed benefits that might accrue from animal experimentation.

THE RIGHTS OF ANIMALS IN RESEARCH
AND THE VETERINARIAN'S ETHICAL RESPONSIBILITIES [+]

Since the 1970 amendment to the Animal Welfare Act, the veterinarian has considerable jurisdiction over the care of laboratory animals during actual experimentation by the biomedical investigator (see Appendix III). The veterinarian has the authority to intervene on the animal's behalf if he or she believes that the experiment is inhumane — i.e., causes unnecessary pain and suffering. On some university campuses, the veterinarian in charge of laboratory animal care may actually screen proposed experiments from other departments and reject them, even if government funded, if the veterinarian and/or the advisory committee believes that they are inhumane and that the animal suffering is unjustifiable.

Other veterinarians, because of local, social, and political pressures, keep a much lower profile and, rather than evoke the ire of research colleagues, may turn a blind eye to inhumane and often highly unethical and worthless experiments involving animals. To be able to bring in an outside authority to veto such studies might be advantageous, but we must recognize the fact that only the most dedicated veterinarian would risk making waves and creating enemies where he or she works and lives.

Fortunately, there are few veterinarians in laboratory animal care who only service the animal colony in order to provide the researcher with healthy animals and have neither concern nor involvement with how the animals will be used experimentally or cared for afterwards.

[+] *From keynote address to the American Association of Laboratory Animal Science, National Conference, California, 1977.*

Since it is now written into law that the veterinarian has some jurisdiction over how animals will be treated during experimentation, it would
be a serious professional and ethical omission not to assert such authority
where and when appropriate (see Appendixes III and IV).

The Protection of Animals by Law

In 1966, the Animal Welfare Act was passed. The enactment of this
bill (HR 13886) was a landmark decision on the federal level which recognized that animals are abused in this country and that in the absence of
humane sensitivity and ethical responsibility, laws had to be made and
duly enforced in order to protect animals. There have been subsequent
amendments to improve this act, but the division (Animal and Plant
Health Inspection Service) of the USDA responsible for inspection and
enforcement of the act suffers from the inefficiencies of inadequate staff,
slow bureaucratic procedures in bringing about prosecution, and inconsistencies in the evaluations by their staff of reported violations of the
act.

The problems of a growing bureaucracy attempting to monitor and
enforce more and more regulations are indeed complex, and, at times,
seemingly insurmountable. Regulatory agencies such as APHIS not only
need more staff but they also need to take a much stronger posture. As
things are to date, The Humane Society of the United States, for example, if often obliged to "regulate" the federal regulators, to check up
on reported violations that federal agents have either not investigated or
have not taken appropriate action on when there is a clear violation of the
Animal Welfare Act. Cases have included violations by research laboratories, roadside zoos, animal dealers and puppy mill breeders.

The nongovernmental veterinarian, not employed by APHIS, who is
in private practice, working in research, or supervising a university or
commercial laboratory animal facility can do much to help enforce the
Animal Welfare Act. He may choose to work with a local humane group
and report possible violations to a national humane organization such as
the HSUS or directly to APHIS. At the university level, he may effectively
organize an ad hoc interdepartmental committee to evaluate student and
faculty research involving animals in relation to the Animal Welfare Act
and, furthermore, extend the committee's jurisdiction to screen studies
where "justifiable suffering" is claimed by the investigator as necessary
or unavoidable. While the Animal Welfare Act provides the investigator
with such a loophole, institutional pressures should be exerted when
needed. APHIS needs support by virtue of the extent of animal use and

abuse and the financial limitations in providing adequate staff to implement the Animal Welfare Act. An American Universities Federation for Animal Welfare, analogous to the British UFAW would greatly help in these matters, especially in relation to the use of live animals for teaching purposes and honors projects.*

While I have, as a veterinarian, great faith in my profession to further the humane treatment of animals, I am aware of the fact that financial and social concerns may be a cause for one to make compromises. It is clearly a personal decision for a veterinarian to intervene when he or she is confronted with a clear violation of the Animal Welfare Act. One cannot legislate morals or effectively oblige a person to behave ethically, but the Animal Welfare Act does give some power to a veterinarian.

The original Federal Laboratory Animal Welfare Act of 1966 set standards of care and treatment only for animal dealers and certain research facilities. In 1970, the Congress amended the Animal Welfare Act to extend its scope beyond laboratory animals to include animal exhibitions, including zoos and circuses; the wholesale pet trade; research animal and pet auction markets; and previously exempted research facilities. These entities are subject to USDA inspection and are required to register with the USDA. Regulations include minimum standards for adequate housing, sanitation, food, water, cage size, ventilation, separation of different species, shelter from extremes in temperature, veterinary care, humane euthanasia, and humane use of anesthesia and analgesics during experiments (except in cases in which the use of these drugs would interfere with the results). Amendments to the Act passed in 1976, establishing additional standards to cover the transportation of the animals by common carriers. The 1976 amendments also contained anti-dog and -cock fighting provisions.

Legislation was passed in 1970 and strengthened in 1976 to stop the cruel and painful practice of soring the feet of Tennessee walking horses to accentuate their high-stepping gait. Race horses, farm animals (excepting humane slaughter), and the retail pet trade are still exempt from federal animal welfare legislation.

New legislation may come concerning the issue of exercise for dogs. The needs of other laboratory species, including cats and primates,

---

*The recently formed Scientists' Center for Animal Welfare, based in Washington, DC, may soon begin the work in the United States that the Universities Federation for Animal Welfare has so ably undertaken in the United Kingdom.

should also be considered. Exercise may be a subjective anthropomorphism; yet animals, especially those not adapted from an early age to a small cage, may need varied stimulation and space in which to be active, to explore, and to interact socially with each other and/or with a handler. Exercise may not be what they want, but what we might think they want. The drive to exercise is an acquired human need, while the drives to be active, to run, swing, explore, play, and interact socially are basic animal needs that the Animal Welfare Act has virtually neglected and that must be considered in the near future.*

In summary, the protection of animals by the law is to date minimal, but the landmark act of 1966 is a beginning. The British Cruelty to Animals Act, which is much more stringent, was established almost 100 years before U.S. Federal action. Most anticruelty laws are under state jurisdiction, and the inconsistencies among state laws leave much to be desired. Diversity of interests within the various states have led to striking inconsistencies in animal protection laws; what is outlawed in one state is permissible in another. Such extreme relativity in legal ethics necessitates greater federal legislation and enforcement and places an added burden of responsibility onto veterinarians both in laboratories and in the community at large.

Since it is now written into law that the veterinarian has jurisdiction over how animals will be treated during experimentation, it would be a serious professional and ethical omission not to assert such authority where and when appropriate (see Appendix III).

One of the major flaws in enforcing the Animal Welfare regulations in order to ensure the humane treatment of animals in biomedical research, in new product testing, and in teaching is that there are not sufficient veterinarians or inspectors to go around. Although not all PhDs, MDs, or high school teachers are qualified to judge the humaneness of animal experiments, neither are all veterinarians qualified. The point is that more veterinarians, PhDs, MDs, and high school teachers should be educated in the areas of animal behavior and welfare science. In the meantime, committees that consist of a variety of people, representing research, animal care, and perhaps the general public could be used to discuss issues. Then it may be democratically and objectively recognized where and when a given animal experiment is inhumane or unethical. An experiment is unethical (a) when a needless repetition of research already well-documented (a common flaw of high

---

* *The Protection of Animals Act in West Germany stipulates that the animals' behavioral requirements should be provided for.*

school and college science projects); (b) when the degree of physical or psychological suffering of the animal overrides any possible value derived from such a study, either as a learning experience for a student or as a contribution to scientific knowledge; (c) when a more humane alternative is available, or when an organism of lower sentience (e.g., tissue or egg embryo preparation) maybe used as a replacement; (d) when the experiment is poorly designed within adequate hypotheses, controls, and statistical validation; (e) when the researcher cannot justify the use of animals for the betterment of society or of the animals themselves; and (f) when the experiment is conducted purely for profit motives, not for the ultimate benefit of society, as in the development and testing of new, nonessential commercial products.

The above six categories warrant further clarification and the following examples will suffice to illustrate the main thesis of this critique: the rights of animals in research are being violated to such a degree that they virtually have no rights. This is partially due to the fact that the Animal Welfare Act is not being effectively enforced. More significant, however, may be the fact that much of the inhumane and unethical use of animals in research reflects a particular attitude of certain biomedical scientists and students that may be pathological. This psychological dimension will be discussed subsequently. Now, some examples of research studies conducted that respectively fit the above six categories of animal use and abuse.

NEEDLESS REPETITION

High school science fair projects (see Figs. 11-2 and 11-3) that entail injecting rats with weed killer, hamsters with Valium or common household chemicals to see what happens, or inducing acute myocarditis in guinea pigs by injecting a myolytic agent into their hearts. College projects that include the blinding or drugging of rats to determine how their performance in a maze is affected; the study of the effects of electro shock, starvation, and other variables on fighting in rodents; conditioned aversion studies, learned helplessness studies, and studies of maternal deprivation and prolonged social deprivation in primates. All these studies are well-documented, and further repetition is needless as well as in humane. To inflict pain or suffering on an animal purely for educational purposes, and not for the betterment of animal or human health isethically untenable. One may also question "teaching" experiments inveterinary and medical schools such as poisoning dogs with strychnine and other toxicological substances; inducing *Clostridia* infec-

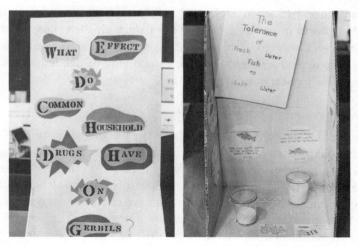

Figure 11-2

High school science fair projects from state class finalists reflect deficiencies in creativity as well as in compassion and basic scientific validity.

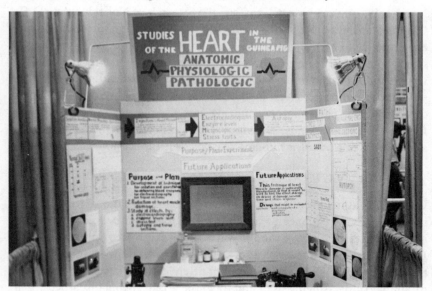

Figure 11-3

High school science fair project — national finalist. A model study of induced heart attacks in guinea pigs (a painful drug was injected into their hearts to destroy the muscle). Such high school science fair projects should be outlawed since they add nothing to scientific knowledge, cause unnecessary pain and suffering in animals, and may well give young people a very detached and uncaring attitude towards life — both animal and human.

tion and other diseases in sheep and guinea pigs; stomach-tubing dogs with chloroform in order to destroy the liver and, then, keeping them alive for several days to do blood studies; repetitive surgery on the same animal over several weeks so that the animal may be debilitated and its postoperative recovery unduly prolonged.

UNJUSTIFIABLE SUFFERING

One class of studies will suffice here: the prolonged restraint of primates in holding chairs for weeks, sometimes months, for a wide range of studies. The ethics of using animals for evaluating the effects of addictive drugs and other self-induced poisons, such as tobacco and alcohol, is also to be questioned. Drug addictions in man are related to emotional and societal ills and may be interpreted as symptoms rather than causes. To mimic such symptoms in animals does little to alleviate the underlying causes in man.

NEED FOR REPLACEMENT AND/OR ALTERNATIVE SPECIES

Again, one example will suffice: the research of Nobel laureate D.C. Gajudsek included the use of reportedly over 120 chimpanzees, a threatened species. The use of this species must be questioned since the researcher himself admitted almost 10 years earlier that more plentiful squirreland rhesus monkeys could have been used instead.

The Ames bacteria test method for rapid screening of potential carcinogens is one particularly promising partial replacement for higher life forms. Other replacement alternatives are needed in biomedical research and testing, not only for humane reasons, but for economics as well.

INADEQUATE EXPERIMENTAL DESIGN

A look at many college honors and higher degree theses will not only reveal the high frequency of needless repetition described in a above but also elements of b above, and it will also reveal inadequacies in design. Lack of originality and genuine creativity may cast doubt on the value of the PhD degree. Weaknesses in design often lead to an excessive number of animal subjects being used and to whole groups being discarded when results don't turn out and everything has to be done over again. It should be emphasized that, in many small colleges, students take care of their own animals. Students may be inexperienced, untrained, or indifferent, and they are generally unaware of the Animal Welfare Act. At one college, a large rat colony was virtually wiped out twice simply because student caretakers did not provide them with water during the summer.

NONRELEVANT BASIC RESEARCH

The category of "basic" research is a politically sensitive area. Suffice it to say that some scientists still sacrifice animals simply to satisfy their intellectual curiosity. The academic pressures to publish or perish are real, and they can result in a number of needlessly repetitive experiments — "parametric tinkering" or "variations on a theme." This should not be interpreted as an indictment of all basic research, but rather as a plea for a more purposive and integrative approach to basic research that today, with excessive reductionism, needless repetition, and replication, can result in an excessive waste of animals and unnecessary and unjustifiable suffering.

The full draft of my letter published in *Science* 194 (1977:862-865) concerns the rights of animals in biomedical research and a growing awareness of our ethical responsibilities toward them:

> These values and attitudes impinge upon biomedical research and especially upon so-called basic research which is the, to quote the director of the New York Museum of Natural History, "freedom to study whatever it (the museum) chooses, without regard to its demonstrable practical value." The scientific community that uses animals and whose basic research is supported wholly, or in part, by the taxpayer must be open to discuss the validity of their work on at least three levels.
>
> (1) Economic — Should the "luxury" of basic research, of seeking knowledge for knowledge's sake (and with no forseeable applied value) be supported by public funds? The creative arts and humanities receive far less support, and they too have little "direct application."
>
> (2) Is it fair? — Ethically speaking, is it right to use animals, to create and destroy life, and to cause suffering (if unavoidably "essential" for the research) for purely intellectual reasons? This objectively amoral and ethically ill-defined conceptual world of academia is ripe for self-scrutiny, but not yet mature enough for outside dialog it would seem, since their reactions to criticism or enquiry are both evasive and defensive.
>
> (3) Is it relevant? — If the relevance of such animal studies to understanding human diseases or other humanocentric problems is claimed, then the basic researcher often creates his own trap. Relevance, after years of reductionism and nonapplied research on esoteric subjects, may be very difficult to demonstrate. To be forced to do this is *contra* to the basic premise of "pure" (nonapplied) research — "we want to know because we want to know, and if that knowledge has any applied value, that is not my concern as a basic researcher" — is a common statement.
>
> It is quite obvious that this complex area of basic biomedical research — including many studies in animal behavior and physiological psychology — needs to be looked at from a new perspective. Beginning

with animal rights is only a start. We will get nowhere if the basic researcher remains locked into his own conceptual world of consensus values and approved standards of animal care. We must all be free to look "objectively" at ourselves and avoid being defensive under the fire of outside criticism by others who do not share the same world view. Basic research, and biomedical research in general, may well benefit once open and constructive dialog is achieved, with ultimate benefit to the well-being of animals themselves.

COMMERCIAL TESTING

This area, above all others, warrants rigorous review; reforms in established procedures and a total reevaluation of standardized methods are urgently needed. Such gross tests as loading the stomachs of dogs with new floor or boot polishes to establish an LD_{50}, which is a wholly unscientific measure agreed upon more by a general consensus than upon sound sequential testing using more sensitive physiological indices other than sickness and death. The Draize eye test is another atrocity, perfumes, deodorants, detergents and other commercial products being placed into rabbits' eyes until the concentration known to cause severe eye inflammation — often leading to panophthalmia and dehiscence of the eye — can be quantified. Analgesics are rarely used because, it is argued, such drugs may interfere with the tests. (This is also a common argument given by biomedical scientists and psychologists.) Many of these tests are not only inhumane, but they are poorly designed and needlessly repetitive. One company is obliged to replicate the tests of another because of federal regulations or because of the company policy not to share or make public their test data. Other tests, no less inhumane, include the instigation of acute pain reactions by a variety of bizarre methods in developing new analgesics.

A newly developed field of occupational hazards and safety testing may well result in the conducting of even more questionable animal tests. The whole area of safety testing new food additives and other new synthetic products, several thousand of which are in our immediate environment,suffers from one major flaw. The possibility of synergism, of coincidental combination of one compound with another, potentiating its carcinogenic, teratogenic, or mutagenic effect cannot ever be adequately evaluated. One can only conclude that much animal testing in this category is anabuse of animal life and a waste of time, talent, and money.

For further examples and fuller details of these and other tests done in the United States and European laboratories, see Pratt (1976) and

Ryder (1975). For a discussion of alternatives in toxicity testing, see Rowan (1984) and Ball et al. (1983).

Against this rather cursory overview of animal use and abuse in research and testing we may well ask if laboratory animals do have any rights at all. I have not selected just a few extreme examples to imply that such animal abuse is widespread in the United States. The fact that such conditions and experiments are still to be found at all demands our immediate concern and concerted action. No rational mind can defend or adequately justify any of the examples cited in the aforementioned six critical areas of concern. That such animal abuses exist at all, irrespective of rationalizations justifying their continuation, must surely be one of the most urgent challenges facing the laboratory research veterinarian. It is primarily in the veterinarian's jurisdiction and realm of ethical responsibility that the ultimate welfare of the laboratory animal now lies. This fact is now established as law under the Animal Welfare Act. The veterinary profession is being looked upon to uphold the law and the rudimentary rights of animals to some degree of humane consideration. Further federal regulations may help bring about a wider recognition of animal rights, although such an externally imposed set of rules is a weak and fragile substitute for an internalized set of humane ethics and responsible compassion towards all life. The latter can only come through educational reforms, which may amount to a radical mutation in societal values and attitudes towards nonhuman life. The former, at best, would, as is the case today, require constant supervisory monitoring and more and more bureaucratic regulations.

Some solutions to the above problems concerning the use and abuse of animals in research are being developed. The National Institutes of Health must set up new guidelines for grant applications that will permit a much more rigorous review of how animals are to be treated in a proposed project. Criteria for objectively evaluating research proposals have been developed by the Institute for the Study of Animal Problems, a division of the Humane Society of the United States.* These criteria, which were decided on the basis of an extensive survey of federally funded research projects, will help enhance the system of peer review of grant applications. If all designated criteria pertinent to a given animal study are not addressed by the applicant, the peer-review board will be more effective in rejecting or querying many proposals. These criteria will cover many questions that are relevant to categories a to e described earlier.

---

*M.W. Fox et al. Evaluation of Awarded Grant/Applications Involving Animal Experimentation *(Washington, DC: Institute for the Study of Animal Problems, 1979)*.

Scientists' accountability is supposedly upheld via the peer-review system for research grant awards and approval, but, unfortunately, this system is inadequate for many reasons, notably (a) professional etiquette (one does not criticize one's peers or superiors, especially since they may some day be reviewing one's own research proposal); (b) the supposed societal value of performing a given experiment is compounded and confounded by other values that in no way justify animal sacrifice or suffering (these include academic status, tenure, scientific recognition, additional income and prestige for the university or research institution); (c) finally, the value of adding further knowledge to a particular discipline is rated high by those within the discipline, but in basic research where there are no clear practical benefits to humanity, can animal suffering be justified if it is unavoidable in the quest for more knowledge?

Silverman (1978) proposes that, "A cost-benefit analysis is necessary at the planning stage of an experiment. How great is the likely benefit to mankind at large? What is the private benefit to the experimenter, in terms of money, prestige, or a PhD? And what is the cost to the animal?"

Another important screening of research studies can and should come at the level of final publication; journal editors should have objective criteria upon which they may appraise a scientific paper on ethical and humane grounds. A special editorial committee may be necessary to hear the pros and cons of a paper rejected on ethical grounds if the author contends that the scientific or medical value of the paper overrides the usual humane and ethical restraints established by the journal.

One group of scientists from the American Animal Behavior Society are considering this editorial policy and have now set up a committee to establish in-house criteria for humane treatment and ethical experimentation of animals.*

A promising system, established by the Canadian Council on Animal Care, entails an ad hoc committee for each university, reviewing *all* experiments involving animal subjects in *all* departments. This committee includes a member at large from the general public such as from

---

*A relevant quandary is worth mentioning. Government guidelines for proper care of animals stipulate daily cage cleaning, stainless steel cages, and a clean white coat for the investigator. Animal behaviorists, whose studies often require seminatural conditions, cannot work under such blanket restrictions. Some species of rodents and other mammals need "dirty" cages and lab coats, otherwise they will spend all their time marking fresh litter and the experimenter's coat!

the local humane society. It is to be hoped that more institutions will follow this system of local monitoring since federal agencies cannot possibly cover all institutions in all states with any reliable degree of efficiency or effectiveness.

Professor Calvin W. Schwabe makes the following poignant statement in this recent book, *Priests, Cattle and Progress in Medicine:** "Laboratory animals have assumed a subordinate role to inanimate 'animals' — machines. It is the laboratory animal-robot culture we now enjoy." These are not the words of an antivivisectionist, but of a respected research veterinarian who reveals in his book several major flaws in comparative biomedical research, which in part account for an increasing use and waste of laboratory animals. He emphasizes that the lack of appreciation of the relevance of spontaneously occurring diseases in animals to human medical research has resulted in (a) suboptimal "cross pollination" between veterinary and medical teaching faculties and research laboratories, (b) inadequate state and federal funding of veterinary education and research, (c) most research in comparative medicine by physicians being focused upon the potentially least rewarding approach to the study of animal diseases, namely artificially induced rather than spontaneous diseases, and in only a few animal species at that, (d) clinical veterinary and epidemiological studies being virtually overlooked as apotential resource for understanding human disease processes.

We must work towards the One Medicine. As Virchow observed, "between animal and human medicine, there is no dividing line — nor should there be. The object is different but the experience obtained constitutes the basis of all medicine." Biomedical researchers, educators, policy makers, and fund-disbursing agencies should read this book, especially the last chapter. Let us hope that Professor Schwabe's dream of collaborative veterinary and medical education and research along the broad, interdisciplinary lines of comparative medicine that he advocates will soon be adopted worldwide. The author's proposal for a model School of Veterinary Medicine includes a Center for Humane Studies, a much needed addition to the curriculum of all veterinary schools. One statement from this important book clearly spells out the veterinarian's responsibilities towards laboratory animals:

> So-called lower animals are not, and never should be treated as, mere laboratory "preparations." They are living, sentient beings which researchers should never regard nor "use" with the abandon one might

---

University of Minnesota Press, 1978.

some *in vitro* solution or tissue culture. One of the veterinary medicine's social responsibilities is to ensure that comparative research never becomes a license to conduct unnecessary or poorly planned experiments of questionable scientific value, or to substitute excessive animal numbers for proper experimental design or an absence of a sufficient degree of standardization of animals. Nor should pursuit of animal studies be permitted by persons who lack adequate knowledge of animal biology and medicine and of available techniques to prevent or reduce fear and pain in these living subjects of research.

Control over the proliferation of laboratory animal tests and research studies is urgently needed. The welfare concerns of keeping them in small, barren cages, and the physical and psychological suffering that often result from invasive experimental procedures, would be mitigated by an overall reduction in the numbers of animals used. Significant reduction could be accomplished once the following recommendations made by the Carpenter* committee are adopted:

   i) A more intensified drive to find alternatives to the use of animals for research.

  ii) More careful thought about experiments before undertaking those involving the use of animals, including consideration of whether the object of the experiment is likely to be achieved by the method used.

 iii) Before embarking on a project entailing the use of animals, a research worker should satisfy himself that no alternative technique (e.g., cell-culture) will meet the need of his investigation.

  iv) Those engaged in experimentation on animals must ask themselves, in considering the ethical justification of a given project, whether the end to be realized is sufficiently significant to warrant such infliction of pain and stress as might be involved. This question, and it is a serious one, cannot be ignored, and a given presupposition for the answering of it must be that the animal should be treated as if it possesses rights.

   v) Where the use of animals, after these safeguards have been taken, is regarded as necessary, careful thought should be given to deciding the number that will be required. Some species may be more appropriate than others in a given instance, either because the nearest approximation to man is a primary consideration, or because of a known specificity of response in a particular species or strain. At this stage economic considerations should not be paramount and scientifically appropriate species should be selected; the use of rare species should be avoided. In planning the number of investigations to be performed, care should be taken to limit the series to the minimum compatible with statistically valid results.

---

*Animals and Ethics *(London: Watkins, 1981)*.

vi) Animals in research-establishments should be under the permanent care of a veterinary surgeon and in particular those having under gone surgery should receive constant care and supervision.

vii) There should be discontinuation of experimentation for trivial purposes, e.g., for luxury goods such as adornment articles (there are already sufficient of these articles available to satisfy any actual need). Experiments designed to prove the obvious should be discontinued. There should also be discontinuation of animal research into products such as tobacco which man continues to take in full consciousness of the hazards of so doing.

Conclusions

I think it has now been clearly established in the foregoing chapters that many animal species used in biomedical research are highly sentient and can suffer not only physically, but also emotionally, and that the psychopathophysiology of disease in animals has emotional and socioenvironmental aspects as it has in humans. With this evidence in mind, the legal, ethical, and moral question of how right it is for us humans to experiment upon animals and cause them to suffer in ways similar to us — physiologically and psychologically — must be faced.

The question and the aforementioned evidence places the animal researcher experimenting upon highly sentient animals, such as baboons, dogs, and rats, in a difficult position. The only justification for experimenting upon such animals and causing them to suffer is based upon utilitarianism beliefs — i.e., serving some greater good — and upon the belief that it would be morally wrong to experiment upon people.

But, can it be less morally wrong to experiment upon highly sentient animals that suffer in many ways like we do? Can a high fidelity animal model — say of AIDS (Acquired Immune Deficiency Syndrome) or neutrino radiation in monkeys — be justified even if it is true that animals suffer *less* from modeling a human disease than we do? And what if they suffer the same or more?

I think that if we look objectively at the available scientific evidence, be it for factory-farmed animals (Fox 1983a) or laboratory-housed experimental animals, we are obliged rationally to accept the fact that such sentient animals are more similar to us than they are different and are, therefore, likely to suffer in ways similar to us when subjected to similar stressors such as a virulent virus, chemical poison, radiation, electrical shock, and water deprivation.

Can there be *any* valid moral or ethical grounds for subjecting animals to suffering similar in kind to that experienced by humans — and possibly even greater in degree because they have limited ability to be rational or to be reasoned with, and because many cannot be comforted by being given emotional support since they are either not sociable or are not socialized to their human caretakers?

If such treatment is judged morally justifiable in order to help humanity then the moral judgement, according to Ryder (1975), is speciesist. It is ethically reprehensible, and its flawed logic is anthropocentric and utilitarian, especially if we agree with Rollin (1982) that there are no morally relevant differences between humans and other sentient animals. Attempting to use differences in species affiliation and intelligence, ability to reason, possession of an immortal soul, etc. as grounds for the presumed right to exploit animals as we choose, is simply defensive rationalization. Our power of dominion (from the Latin *domino,* to rule over) is actually a power that should be used responsibly and compassionately as is implied in the original Hebrew word for dominion, *rahé* (Genesis 1:26). As Rollin (1982) concludes, might does not make right.

However, it can be argued that it is ethically reprehensible to experiment upon one or more humans for the benefit of many. The central provision of the Nuremberg code is that "the voluntary consent of the human subject is absolutely essential . . . . The duty and responsibility for ascertaining the quality of the consent rests upon each individual who initiates . . . the experiment." It is a matter of record that during the Nuremberg war crimes trials of 1945-46, the defense of many doctors was that the prisoners they were experimenting upon were doomed to die anyway. A similar justification is given today for using dogs and cats from animal shelters in research; they too are doomed to die.

While the voluntary consent of an animal to be a subject of experimentation cannot be obtained, it is a fact that some uses of animals (e.g., testing a new drug that may help animals as well as people) are more justifiable than others (e.g., testing new cosmetic products). It is too absolutistic and unrealistic to argue that no animals should ever be subjected to pain, distress, or death for the advancement of *any* human ends, and there is the possibility that some of these advances could also benefit animals. Such utilitarian ends need to be balanced against moral considerations.

Also the long-term consequences of such ends need to be examined. For example, today's organ transplants of animals' hearts and livers into human infants could lead to an industry of animals being bred and raised as organ donors. Is research in this field justified socially and economically since the costs of organ transplants in humans restrict such advances to the more affluent in society? A greater emphasis on public health research and practice might be more prudent and democratic. What of the ethics and long-term ramifications of present research on brain regeneration in rats using rat fetal brain implants? If the rat research proves successful, where is the fetal brain tissue to come from for human patients? Could this lead to a new industry of human fetal tissues and organs with indigent mothers growing and selling their own fetuses? There are no clear answers to the many ethical questions that are now being raised by high-tech advances in medical science, and the animals are caught in the middle.

The more one contemplates the ethics of using animals in research, the more difficult it is to come up with a better yardstick than asking, do the ends justify the means? To this we would add, what alternative means are available to reduce or eliminate animal suffering and death, and what might be the long-term consequences of such presumably valid ends?

Biomedical ethicists might be able to formulate a code or guidelines applicable to using animals in experiments that effectively integrate the above questions and balance moral and utilitarian values without being overly anthropocentric in their approach. Cases such as the Baby Fae scenario, where a human neonate with a congenitally defective heart was given the heart of a baboon in spite of overwhelming evidence that organ transplant rejection would occur raise many new ethical questions. It could be argued that the baby was doomed to die anyway, and that both the patient, relatives, and doctors have a social responsibility to help advance medical knowledge for the benefit of many by using the baby as a guinea pig.

It might be reasoned that since animals naturally exploit each other (e.g., as parasite and host, prey and predator), it is not unnatural for man to exploit animals when necessary.* But, as I have argued elsewhere in detail (Fox 1986), the magnitude of our impact upon the biosphere is actually unnatural since the biological constraints that are naturally imposed upon other animal species are clearly lacking. It is therefore more than ethical sensibility to impose some self-restraint in order to limit our

---

* *Some scientists have even reasoned that there is no ethical or moral issue in genetic engineering of animals because our ability to do is a natural consequence of our own evolution. So are we to conclude that there would be nothing unnatural about such genetically engineered animals?*

impact upon the environment and the degree to which we exploit nonhuman life for our own benefit. It is enlightened self-interest, if not a survival imperative. The following principle of reciprocity is relevant to this issue of self-restraint.

If we adhere to the principle of *reciprocity* (which holds that research on animals and their exploitation for human health and well-being should also benefit animals) then this would eliminate some classes of animal research. These include all forms of military research; cosmetics testing; toxicity testing of food additives, household chemicals, alcohol, tobacco, and other addictive drugs that are nonessential. Likewise, agricultural chemicals such as pesticides and herbicides can be considered nonessential from the perspective of organic or biodynamic farming. Industrial chemicals and pollutants are in a "borderline" category. Their toxicity needs to be known in order to regulate their use and emission for the benefit of humans and animals alike.

Another "borderline" area is animal research done to improve their health and welfare. Ethical vegetarians, who consider farm animal produce as nonessential, would oppose all such research. A more reasonable position is to accept that so long as people consume farm animals and their produce, animal welfare science to improve farm animal health and well-being is ethically acceptable. But such research for fur ranching, and to increase the "harvest" of fur-bearing wildlife should be questioned since furs and skins are as nonessential to human health and well-being (commercial interests notwithstanding) as are wildlife trophies to the status-hunter. However, this is somewhat a borderline area, since without appropriate research and management, exploited species could become extinct.

Research to improve the health and well-being of other exploited animals such as race horses and greyhounds should be questioned since the degree of benefit to the animals is outweighed by the nature of their exploitation which is nonessential to human health and well-being. Zoo animals are in a borderline category because they can benefit their species (as "ambassadors") by their captive presence awakening respect and concern for their conservation in the wild.

Research to improve the health and welfare of companion ("pet") animals crosses the border into acceptability (even though some animal rightists contend the animals should not be kept as pets or bred to become pets). There is increasing evidence that pet-keeping is not some nonessential bourgeois luxury. Companion animals can and do enhance people's health and well-being, thus I would place their exploitation in an "essential" category with the condition that the animals are treated properly with respect and understanding and their needs are provided for.

But respect and understanding, along with protective legislation and more animal-welfare focused research are insufficient to justify all forms of animal exploitation and their continuation. The principle of reciprocity may therefore help us decide which forms of animal exploitation are ethically and socially unacceptable.

From a purely anthropocentric and utilitarian perspective, an animal's life is less important than a human life, and, thus, there is no moral or ethical issue with regard to how they are to be used in biomedical research, teaching, and product safety testing. But in the Indian epic *Mahabbarata* it is written: "Just as life is the most desired object to one, so it is the most desired object to all beings. The seekers after truth, applying the same standard to all as they apply to themselves, show kindness to all creatures." Perhaps we should entertain the possibility that our enculturated anthropocentric and utilitarian world view, which fails in "applying the same [ethical] standard to all," may be a far more serious problem than many of the ills of humanity for which laboratory animals are made to suffer and may, furthermore, be a significant contributing factor in many of these same ills. It can be argued that it is because we do not extend the concept of personhood to animals when we destroy or pollute the ecosystems in which they live that our own personhood suffers from the adverse esthetic, cultural, and physical consequences of a poisoned and desecrated environment.

As for the utilitarian position of justifying the exploitation of a few for the benefit of society — be the few who are exploited, human or nonhuman — this can lead to fascism. Biological fascism is one aspect of scientific imperialism that the animal rights and liberation movement is challenging today.

Some of these people will criticize this book because it seems to be aimed at helping the biomedical research establishment get more out of the laboratory animals they exploit. In part, this is true, simply because humane and judicious use of animals enhances the validity and applicability of the data one obtains from such research. In addition, the book urges a fundamental change in attitudes that underlie animal use practices — a paradigm from Cartesian objectivity and instrumental rationalism to a more emphatic and holistic world view.*

---

* *It should be emphasized that Cartesianism is an extension of Aristotelean philosophy. It was Aristotle who broke away from the Socratic and Platonic schools that recognized the*

Working to make the treatment of animals more humane without endeavoring to change the basic orientation of pratice of contemporary medicine and agriculture* is shortsighted. Likewise, the humane reforms I have recommended may be viewed as an intolerable compromise by some animal rights advocates. My response is that wholesale abolition of animal use in research is simply an unrealistic immediate goal. Animals will, therefore, continue to be exploited and suffer until the science and art of medicine is changed. The most significant and practical benefit (to the animals) of the laboratory animal research documented in this book is to demonstrate the importance of emotional, social, and environmental factors to their health and well-being. As society and the biomedical establishment come to recognize that it is more rational and economical to focus upon the emotional and environmental etiology of human disease — i.e., behavioral and ecological

---

unity of spirit and matter, psyche and soma, and the unity of all life. Aristotle reduced psyche or soul to mind or consciousness devoid of any inherent divinity; his materialistic world view was later incorporated into Roman Catholicism by St. Thomas Aquinas. Consequently, divinity or God was no longer conceived as being innate or co-inherent as soul in all living things, but as a transcendent and omnipotent patriarchal figure. Therefore, only man possesses a spark of divinity.

*Significantly, in Homeric Greek, according to Marilyn Wilhelm** (personal communication), there was no word for body, for body and soul were one. When the spirit departed from the body, the living person became a corpse or soma. Later, soma became the word for body as the dualism of psyche and soma gained acceptance. Modern psychosomatic and holistic (i.e., derived from whole, holy) medicine recognizes the inseparability of mind and body, and organism and environment. As Spinoza observed, "The body is the mind seen from without and the mind is the body felt from within. The body and mind do not work one on the other because they are not other, they are one."*

The separation of psyche and soma, denial of soul or inherent divinity, and of feelings in animals may be thus traced back to Aristotle, whose dualistic and materialistic world view was an integral part of scientific and medical thought until its fallaciousness was revealed by modern theoretical physics (notably by Einstein's theory of relativity) and ecology (which is a living example of Einstein's incomplete unified-field theory). Theologically, Aristotle provided the philosophical basis for a transcendent monotheism, the antithesis of pantheistic monism. The Platonic conception of nous, which included the idea of an innate, divine presence in all living things, was reduced by Aristotle to mean pure theoretical reason in man.

It should also be added that the purportedly amoral objectivity of science may be derived from Aristoteleanism; Aristotle held that virtue is knowledge, thus knowledge for knowledge's sake has its own inherent value, while Socrates held that virtue is knowledge of the good, phronesis being the science of the highest principle — that is a knowledge of values.

*See M.W. Fox, Agricide: The Hidden Crisis that Affects Us All. (New York: Schocken Books, 1985).

**See also Wilhelm M. (1986) Aristotle, Values and Modern Science. In Contemporary Philosophy Vol. II: No. 2 (in press).

medicine — the medical-scientific paradigm will change. This change will lead to a gradual phasing out of much animal research that is considered necessary and unavoidable today. Many animal models of these etiological and causal factors in disease and suffering have been documented in this book, the recognition of which mandates a paradigm shift in the practice of medicine and in the care of laboratory animals, as well as in the kinds of experiments done upon them.

The wholesale and often horrendous ways laboratory animals are made to suffer will rapidly become a thing of the past as the economic and ethical validity of working to end the need to use animals in experiments, tests, and academic exercises is seen to actually parallel medical and social progress. As my former associate, and now Dean of New Programs at Tufts University School of Veterinary Medicine, Dr. Andrew Rowan (1984) has emphasized: "All veterinarians and laboratory animal researchers would like not to have to kill animals and make them suffer in order to advance medical and scientific knowledge, test new drugs, pesticides, and other products and teach students and technicians. We are all antivivisectionists at heart; and we must use our hearts as well as our heads in the care of and experimentation upon sentient animals and in the practice of veterinary and human medicine."

My own thinking has led me to go beyond accepting vivisection as a "necessary evil." Animals were not created for our exclusive use and we abuse our power of dominion over them when we place our burden of fear over suffering, dying, and losing our loved ones upon them. When this power is abused, we forget our humanity and suffer the consequences. The ultimate cost of animal vivisection is a human one: the erosion of compassion which provides constraints that help insure that we use our power of dominion unselfishly and non-destructively.

I am not opposed to all animal research since many non-invasive studies, of their behavioral and environmental needs, can be of great benefit to them. But I am opposed to research that is aimed at making them more productive and profitable for human use, as I am against the deliberate infliction of suffering on animals to advance veterinary and humane medicine. To justify the suffering of a few for the benefit of the many is a contradiction of compassion's ethic of reverence for life, which is an absolute and can never be arbitrary. Far better to progress through treating the already sick and injured. The medical maxim "do no harm," linked with the Golden Rule of treating all living things as we would have them treat us, could provide us with a new paradigm or world view in which our well-being may be better assured.

Appendix I

Humane Attitudes in Animal Care

The following paper by Norman Bleicher* (reprinted by permission) provides a valuable insight into humaneness from the animal care technician's point of view. While this paper deals specifically with the laboratory dog, the humane principles involved are appropriate for all laboratory species. It may be easier, however, to empathize with a more humanoriented, familiar, and expressive species like the dog than with the more distant species such as rodents and lagomorphs. The lack of fellow feeling towards such species can be partially overcome by teaching animal care personnel to understand and appreciate the behavior, emotions, and social needs of these less human-oriented species.

1965. Animal Technicians Associations
Annual Meeting, London
Read in absentia

Humane Considerations
in the Use of the Laboratory Dog

Norman Bleicher
Technical Director
School of Medicine
University of California
Los Angeles, California 90024, U.S.A.

When I first became a technician, my superiors impressed upon me the importance of "good care, and kind and efficient treatment" for our

---

* *paper originally presented at the Animal Technicians Associations, London, England, 1965.*

dogs. There was little at that time (13 years ago) to guide a young and inexperienced technician in a newly formed medical school. The senior technician in our laboratory had begun to compile a notebook containing notes and reprints of available articles on dog care, preoperative and postoperative care, experimental design and technique, and other related topics. Together we started an intensive library search for more information to guide us in the humane care and use of the dogs in our charge. We were at once impressed with the lack of specifically related materials. We found, of course, no simple, concise guide to our definition of humane care of the dog. I now know that there simply is no such thing. The best simple statement I have ever heard defined humane care as "doing the best for and with my animals that I am capable of." It is the development of this capability that should be our goal.

In reflecting on those earlier years, and on a paper on the care of the laboratory dog that I wrote in 1960, I note that the emphasis was on care. The concern at the time, not only in our laboratory, but generally (at least in the United States) was centered about this word, "care." The word was used in a very broad sense, but I think it points out that we were mainly concerned with rather gross problems. We were looking more at the program of the kennel, than at the individual dog. We were concerned with the general conduct of the laboratory rather than the individual experiment. We were concerned with the use of personnel as animal caretakers rather than as animal technicians.

In the past five years we have become very much more sophisticated. I am sure you will agree that there have been significant advances in, and general accord on the basic areas, such as sanitation, nutrition, disease control, anaesthesia, and the value of trained technical personnel. Laboratory instruments and equipment are advanced beyond our expectations. More veterinarians are being employed in animal quarters and on research teams than ever before. Animal technician training is the rule now rather than the exception.

We are now focusing more and more attention on the humane treatment of the individual animal by the individual technician. I believe we have now come to the time when we can more intelligently refer to humane animal care in terms of the relationship between the animal technician and the animal.

We as animal technicians, being immediately responsible for the experimental animal, must each for ourselves develop attitudes of humaneness and guidelines to our personal conduct. The scientists with whom we work may be the recipients of the research funds and of the licenses or permits to perform the experiments they have designed, may be the ones held accountable for the conduct of the experiments and for the quality of the care given the animal; but it is more often than not that we, the animal technicians, have the greater amount of contact with the animal. Our handling and treatment of the animal is a critical factor in the outcome of the research.

We were once called animal caretakers or laboratory technicians, depending upon our major areas of work duties, and usually the caretaker knew little about what went on in the laboratory, and the laboratory technician knew little about what went on in the animal house. Following your lead in England, we in the United States now prefer, and rightly so, to be called animal technicians. This at once infers that we are more than mere mechanical performers of jobs related to the care and use of animals. According to my dictionary, a technician is a person possessing and executing details of procedures essential to the *expert* performance of an art or science. As experts in what is both an art and a science, we must be able to contribute to every phase of the care and use of the dog in the laboratory. It is from the animal technician that I feel continued major contributions toward humaneness will come.

To these ends I had some time ago formulated for my own guidance what I prefer to call considerations of humaneness rather than a definition of humaneness.

To me humaneness is a moral attitude, not a definable set of facts; it is a way of thinking and acting that is adapted by the individual technician to the current animal and act. In dealing with each animal and act in my own daily tasks I therefore keep before me these following considerations of humaneness:

1) Each dog, being a living organism, must have special care consistent with its individual nature and experimental condition.

2) Every consideration before, during, and after the experiment should be given to the dog's bodily comfort and physical state. These include, but are not limited to, kind treatment, proper nutrition and sanitation, prevention of pain during surgical operations, and the minimizing of postoperative pain or painful condition.

3) Consideration must be given to ensure that the animal is in a condition to survive the stresses of the experiment, that the experiment has been properly and thoughtfully designed, and that postoperative care from the moment of completion of surgery is diligently performed to ensure survival of the animal to the completion of the study.

The science of our unique technology can tell us *what* to feed a dog, *how* to clean its quarters, and *why* certain techniques are preferred for the particular experiment. These do not of themselves lead to humaneness. It is in the performance of our technology as an art that we convert scientific fact to humane application.

The development of this art is what I prefer to call the development of "personal humane consciousness."

At first the individual technician must exercise continual deliberate self-appraisal of each practice and procedure. In time this self-appraisal becomes a habit, so that each future act is both subconsciously and overtly evaluated before, during, and after it is performed.

This consciousness must be based on:

1) An understanding of the dog as a complex social animal, with knowledge of its behavior as a species, as composed of many breeds within the species, and of individual differences within the breed;

2) An understanding of the dog as a living organism performing the various life functions which may, in the individual animal under test, be normal or abnormal;

3) A thorough knowledge of dog husbandry; and

4) A proficiency in the technology particular to the course of the investigation.

An indispensable ingredient is a real appreciation, if not affection, for dogs.

Armed thusly, the technician is not only well prepared for his daily encounters with the dogs in his charge, but he can intelligently contribute to the design and execution of the research plan. As a true member of the research team, these technician's expert knowledge of the animal complements the researcher's expert knowledge of his science. This is particularly important when working together with the younger investigator of limited experience.

Had I been able to speak to you in person, I would have followed with illustrations of how I believe we develop personal humane consciousness through the guiding considerations of humaneness. I must leave these to your experience and good judgement.

REFERENCES:

Bleicher, Norman. 1960. Preoperative and postoperative care of the laboratory dog. *Proc. Animal Care Panel,* 10:5-24.

Bleicher, Norman. 1965. *Care of Animals During Surgical Experiments, In: Methods of Animal Experimentation,* ed. W.I. Gay. N.Y.: Academic Press, Inc.

Appendix II*

The Control of the Proximate, Especially Behavioral, Environment

Dramatype Variance and Specific Conditions

So far as the proximate environment is concerned, a simple assumption has been made almost universally until a year or two ago. It is supposed that, provided conditions are kept constant (and are not grossly unhealthy), it does not matter what the conditions are: the physiological responses of the animals will tend to be uniform because they are in a uniform environment. This assumption has now been challenged by Chance (1946, 1956, 1947). + His papers are revolutionary, and we shall devote special attention to them in this section. References are to his 1957 paper unless otherwise specified.

One of the most obvious features of the proximate environment is the current temperature under which animals are maintained and tested. As Chance has observed, the first studies of the effects of temperature on drug responses concerned only such variables as potency, duration and rapidity of action. In 1943, Chen and others examined the effect of temperature on these aspects of the response to a variety of drugs. They incidentally provided figures for the standard errors of their observations, and Chance was to calculate from these that in several responses not only the potency but also the *variance* was affected by the temperature. Sometimes potency and variance were similarly affected; sometimes the two effects were independent.

This Appendix, taken from the text of Russell and Burch's The Principles of Humane Experimental Technique *(1959), is of considerable, practical value to contemporary issues in laboratory animal care and research, as well as being, historically, a landmark to be resurrected.*

+ *see M.R.A. Chance. The contribution of environment to uniformity: Variance control, refinement in pharmacology. Coll. Papers Lab. Animals Bur. 6 (1957): 59-74.*

In 1956 Chance himself published the results of a study of the assay response of immature female rats to serum gonadotrophin. He found that the coefficient of variation in ovary weight (the test response) was affected, independently of the effect on the mean, by a number of different environmental variations. These included changing the animals' cages (this produced different effects according to whether or not littermates were caged together), changes in the social environment (i.e., being caged with stranger rats), variation in the size of the cage, and above all (independent of the last factor) variation in the number of animals caged together. For instance, by caging together a specific number of (female) rats, a predictable coefficient of variation could be obtained, irrespective of the absolute mean response. The optimum condition was found to be that of caging in pairs; the coefficient of variation so obtained was *less than one quarter* of that found when animals were caged in groups of six. Other numbers were tried, and each gave a specific figure for the coefficient of variation.

Under the influence of this discovery, Chance reexamined his own earlier work (1946, 1947) on the toxicity of sympathomimetic amines to mice, and found that there here too temperature differences affected the mean and variance of the response differentially.

Physiological variability can be affected without any effect on the response mean. Thus a cyclical change in the variability of histamine excretion by guinea pigs was demonstrated and shown to be unaccompanied by change in the total amount excreted.

Finally, in the gonadotrophin assay, it was found that change in some environmental factors (such as the number of visits to and disturbances of the rat by the experimenter) had no appreciable effect on the *mean* of this response, while others (such as cage change) did.

It follows from all this that constancy of certain conditions (e.g., caging rats by sixes) may still be associated with an avoidably high variance, while change in other conditions (e.g. visits) causes no variation at all in a particular response. Chance was thus led to the important postulate that *'the size of the variance is related to the exact nature of the conditions'* — his italics — 'and is sometimes unaffected by differences in the conditions'. Hence an environment optimal for uniform response need not be constant (i.e. uniform in time) in all respects, but in certain critical respects it must be not only constant but *right*. To put it in terms we have made familiar by now, in the repetition of experimental conditions *discrimination is more important than fidelity*. (Chance concluded): "science . . . is the art of finding out the relevant facts. This means besides taking advantage of 'lucky breaks' and the opportunities provided by experimental errors, also looking for what is being unconsciously ignored. All awareness is a form of attention and is thus restricted. It is no reflection on any of us, therefore, to find that we wear blinkers half the time."

THE BEHAVIORAL ENVIRONMENT
AND PHYSIOLOGICAL RESPONSES

In 1953, Lane-Petter published a short but important paper about our ignorance of laboratory animal behavior, and the serious consequences this must have in experimentations. There was, as he pointed out, a tendency to disregard this factor altogether. "According to this fallacy, if the animal does not grow the diet is at fault; if it does not breed there is an endocrine disorder; if it will not keep still while it is being inoculated it must be forcibly restrained. Such paralogism is not possible if the animal is regarded — "as having its own innate behavior pattern, representing one of the links between the physical environment and the physical response of the animal."

Lane-Petter gave some arresting examples of animal psychosomatics, especially the responses to behavioural effects of human individuals with whom the animals came into contact. In one guinea-pig colony no deaths had occurred for 5-1/2 months (since it was formed, in fact), until the regular animal technician went on a fortnight's holiday. During the interregnum of another technician, "equally competent and conscientious," four pigs died. Postmortem (including bacteriological) examination gave no clue to the cause of death, and on the return of the original technician the deaths ceased. A less grim and more entertaining observation was that of the surprising slowing of growth of mice at weekends, which could not be correlated with food intake or any fluctuating nonbehavioral factor. It was finally conjectured, plausibly and on the basis of some observation, that the slowing of growth was due to increased activity at week-ends, and hence greater consumption of food intake without growth. This in turn was thought to depend on the habit of humans of not being in the animal house at week-ends. Human presence depresses murine activity, but when the man's away, the mice will play!

No less important for our purposes are homeostatic responses to environmental conditions mediated by the nervous system. Chance remarks that about the only environmental conditions which are taken seriously in bioassay are those of temperature and humidity. Even here, he continues,

One gets the impression. . . that humidity is important to control lest the animal tends to dry up (rather like the crystallization or the deliquescence of a chemical substance), rather than that the alterations in the physiology, which may be made necessary by too humid or too arid an atmosphere, are themselves factors which will distort the animal's response to drugs or various experimental procedures.

Almost all the early work on temperature, for instance, was conceived by its authors as indirect investigation into the action of temperature on enzyme systems in poikilotherms.

Finally, important in their own right and in relation to the other two factors, there remain the responses of animals in various *social* situations, the effects of the social drives of mating, attack, flight, and parental behavior, of dominance hierarchies and group relations, and of all circumstances (such as degree of crowding) which influence them. (The study of psychosomatics in man is almost entirely that of social effects upon individual physiology, via the individual's cerebral and other response mechanisms). . .

. . . Chance himself began a determined approach to the study of social behavior in the laboratory rat, and it was on this basis that he obtained his gonadotrophin assay results. From our summary of these it will be clear that all the effects are behavioral, and such as could only have been detected after sufficient study of normal behavior to pinpoint the likely disturbances. Their other striking feature is the extreme triviality (anthropomorphically speaking) of the variations which could produce such marked effects on this anatomical response. It was in fact found that many subtle environmental nuances were significant for endocrine changes other than that in the response itself. The rapier of mild disturbance is replacing the bludgeon of stress. It is a much more humane instrument in itself, but its effects on *reduction* are likely in the long run to be sensational, when these pioneer studies are extended in scale and scope. The theoretical issues raised are touched on by Chance in this key paper (1957). They will call in due course for profound changes in physiological thought. But the tapping of this rich vein lies in the future, and here we need only point to the importance of such work for reduction by control of variance.

Towards A New Bioassay

In the second part of his (1957) paper, Chance adumbrates a New Deal for bioassay as a whole. The implications of the gonadotrophin assay results are far-reaching. Such factors as cage cleaning, cage changing, introduction of food troughs — in short, any intrusions on the rat's familiar territory are now seen to be substantially important for assay variance (and the rat is to some extent a bioassay animal). Chance writes:

> Procedures of this kind are different from laboratory to laboratory, and the days on which they occur also vary. In the same laboratory the timing of these changes may vary from test to test, but what is perhaps less apparent is that in the same laboratory these same factors may interfere differently in supposedly repeat tests, or accidental circumstances may affect one part of a test and not another. A water bottle knocked off and replaced is sufficient interference. A cage found to be defective and replaced will have a profound effect. Procedures which would normally go unchallenged must now be carefully controlled and their effects sought after.

As Chance also points out,

> Our lack of knowledge as to what details are important is emphasized by the fact that additional care is taken of particular factors such as light intensity in estrogen assays, for example, when the relevance of these factors is discovered. It should, therefore, be clear that a systematic study should be made of the environmental factors affecting any one procedure.

As a starting-point for such a study, Chance provides a systematic classification of environmental factors, and discussion of several of these, such as heat loss in relation to behavior. He notes that rats are tested in conditions which are in many ways not optimal for them. Thus they are always used (in bioassay) in what is effectively the middle of the night for these nocturnal animals, although their diurnal activity cycle can easily be reversed by suitable environmental control, to make it fit temperatures substantially below their optimum, and this must have manifold behavioral and physiological repercussions. Chance is careful to point out that a correlation between optimum conditions and low variance has yet to be shown in this context, and cannot be assumed *a priori*. However, most of his suggestions would be likely considerably to reduce distress, apart from their advantages for variance control.

Four other general points made by Chance deserve notice before we close this chapter. All of them relate to increased control of the experimental animal's physiology and behavior for test purposes.

First, he notes a special possibility — the use of stocks of animals which are free of specific pathogens. Such stocks are now available for laboratory use. Besides removing an obvious source of variance, this is clearly one answer to the problem of contingent mortality.

Second and more general, Chance directs attention to the importance of the *metameter* of a response, a term introduced by Hogben for the variable which is measured as the actual assay response. Many pharmacological papers do not fully specify the nature of a response, the way in which it was measured, and the units in which the measurement was made. Such specification would ideally include complete description of the conditions of testing, but we have seen this to be a goal for the future. Meanwhile, by careful study of the animal used, metameters can be chosen which are standardized, and which minimize variance due to interactions on a short time base between animal and procedure. A very simple improvement of this kind enabled local anaesthetics to be assayed at the same level of precision in single tests, instead of in several repeated tests, and by a relatively humane method. This considerably reduced the number of animals needed for the assay.

In connection with metameters, we may cite an important comment by Hume:

> A great many assays depend on the determination of an ED_{50} or an LD_{50} — that is, on a quantal response which entails the counting of all-or-nothing events (deaths and survivals). That quantal methods are statistically inferior to those which use a continuous variate is recognized by statisticians (Emmens 1948). It is technically preferable, therefore, to use wherever possible a continuous variate such as body temperature, a reaction-time, the weight of body or organs, the pulse rate, or an analysis of blood or urine, rather than a discontinuous variate such as a count of deaths or survivals; and meanwhile, from a humane point of view, it is desirable to avoid using death as the endpoint if some pleasanter technique can be found. One cannot help wondering how far the extensive use of the 50 percent survival test is a hangover due to habit and custom, and whether suitable continuous variates have been sought as diligently as could be desired. Even for testing toxicity with an LD_{50}, death might not be the only possible endpoint that could be chosen if the phenomena of the moribund state were to be adequately analysed. . . .

Third, Chance observes that one way of counteracting phenotypic variations is to make animals uniform in particular ways by *training* procedures, thus employing what was normally sources of variance as modes of reducing it.* He cites a particularly humane example, the development of tests for mild analgesics by Bonnycastle and Leonard. These workers

---

* *This principle may have been "discovered" by natural selection itself. It is possible that some degree of genetic heterogeneity may be countered in the development of behavior by the uniform experiences commonly undergone by members of one species in a circumscribed ecological niche. . .*

trained rats to lift their tail away from the source of heat used as a painful stimulus. Chance remarks,

> By so doing, [they] obliterated the instinctive variability of response which accounts for one rat squealing, another crouching to a painful stimulus, and a third lifting the tail away from the same painful stimulus. At the same time [they] ensured that the rat was able to behave in such a way that the amount of pain it received was reduced to a minimum. Positive training, therefore, appears to be a possible way of influencing the behavior of animals towards uniformity as well as towards the provision of humane procedures.

Finally, Chance himself has noted that variability in innate behavior may include the case of a population which is diethic or polyethic in just the same way as we speak of dimorphism or polymorphism. "We shall undoubtedly have to envisage, therefore, selection of animals from a variable stock, as well as breeding for uniformity, at a later stage of our work" (Chance 1957). Selection of this sort is clearly yet another way of controlling variance.

All these brilliant suggestions depend entirely upon the study of laboratory animal behavior, which will provide a new dimension of experimental control. As most of them indicate, this control will bring great rewards in the *refinement* of procedures; here we may conclude that in the study of laboratory animal behavior lie the richest prospects of *reduction*.

Appendix III

Section of Animal Welfare Act Relevant to the Veterinarian's Role and Judicial Authority*

3.10 Veterinary care.

(a) Programs of disease control and prevention, euthanasia, and adequate veterinary care shall be established and maintained under the supervision and assistance of a doctor of veterinary medicine.

(b) Each dog and cat shall be observed daily by the animal caretaker in charge, or by someone under this direct supervision. Sick or diseased, injured, lame, or blind dogs or cats shall be provided with veterinary care or humanely disposed of unless such action is inconsistent with the research purposes for which such animals was obtained and is being held: *PROVIDED HOWEVER,* that the provision shall not effect compliance with any State or local law requiring the holding, for a specified period, of animals suspected of being diseased.

(c) (1) In the case of a research facility, the program of adequate veterinary care shall include the appropriate use of anesthetic, analgesic, or tranquilizing drugs, when such use would be proper in the opinion of the attending veterinarian at the research facility. The use of these three classes of drugs shall be in accordance with the currently accepted veterinary medical practice as cited in appropriate professional journals or reference guides which shall produce in the individual subject animal a high level of tranquilization, anesthesia, or analgesia consistent with the protocol or design of the experiment.

(2) It shall be incumbent upon each research facility through its animal care committee and/or attending veterinarian to provide

*32 F.R. 3273, Feb. 24, 1967, as amended at 36 F.R. 24925, Dec. 24, 1971.

guidelines and consultation to research personnel with respect to the type and amount of tranquilizers, anesthetics, or analgesics recommended as being appropriate for each species of animal used by that institution.

(3) The use of these three classes of drugs shall effectively minimize the pain and discomfort of the animals while under experimentation.

Appendix IV

Toward a Philosophy of Veterinary Medicine+ and Animal Care

There is as yet no philosophy of veterinary medicine. Is the practice of veterinary medicine based upon a value-neutral (i.e., objective) scientific approach to animal health and disease? Rollin (1981) observes, "Until very recently, virtually no emphasis has been placed in the veterinary curricula on the moral and social dimensions of veterinary medicine. . . . The practice of veterinary medicine is taught as though it were value neutral." But the practice of the "art" and science of veterinary medicine is not devoid of values, notably those economic and emotional values that people place upon animals and thus upon the veterinarian. The veterinarian has not only these factors to influence his or her value-neutral, clinical-scientific objectivity, but also such personal values as self-esteem, competence, financial costs and needs, professional ethics, etc. And now the veterinary profession is being confronted by a wholly new value dimension: the notion that animals have intrinsic worth, interests, rights, and possibly souls.

As the industrialized exploitation of animals has intensified — notably "factory" farming, horse racing, animal research and product testing, along with habitat destruction, environmental pollution, and extinction of species — the question of animal rights and veterinarians' responsibilities to animals has arisen.

Veterinarians and laboratory animal care "technicians" may feel they have a duty toward animals, but are bound to some degree (financially and otherwise) to serve society first. For economic reasons, or reasons of fashion, animal sickness, suffering, destruction, deformities, and surgical mutilations are accepted by certain segments of society. Does this mean that veterinarians and their assistants and animal care at-

+ *from* The Veterinary Record *115:(1984.a):12-13.*

tendants should accept such treatment to animals regardless of the costs to animals in terms of their well-being? The veterinary profession is caught in the middle and we have no ethical principles clearly defined with regard to our responsibilities, as healers, toward our animal patients as distinct from our clients, whose interests may conflict with those of the animals.

The veterinarian is cast in a dual role, being perceived as belonging to a caring profession and yet is employed as an animal health and production-maintenance technician for the animal industries. Are these dual roles mutually exclusive? They are if we believe that ethics, philosophy, and moral argument are not an integral part of our profession and that scientific criteria alone are an adequate enough contribution to improve the care and treatment of animals in our industrial society. What price is our professional integrity if organized veterinary medicine cannot take a strong advocacy stance on behalf of animals and *lead* society toward a more compassionate stewardship of all creatures? Such an initiative necessitates far more than providing scientific expertise to enhance animal production and treat or prevent disease.

While veterinary and other scientific animal welfare committees may compile scientific criteria for animal well-being and also define standards for "optimal" care, the acceptance and adoption of such criteria and standards are determined primarily by the economic interests and constraints of clients and industries (biomedicine, agribusiness, wildlife and pet industries, and horse and dog racing) and not by a broader societal recognition of animals' intrinsic value, interests, and right to equal treatment and fair consideration.

Furthermore, "expert" scientific animal welfare committees might well reflect upon Schweitzer's (1947) insight that "In ethical conflicts, a person can only make subjective decisions." And that means not using scientific criteria only, such as animal productivity and health (regardless of the drugs given preventatively), to formulate an ethical position in response to the ethical issue of animal welfare. To rely exclusively on production figures, health and fertility records as indices of farm animal welfare, is scientifically invalid (for references, see Fox 1983).

Pout (1983) has recently stated, ". . . veterinarians cannot use science as a rational basis for moral decisions because if we talk as technicians we are merely using Cartesian values, 'for those who paid more attention to Descartes' science than his theory of knowledge, it was not difficult to extend the theory that animals were mere automata: why not say the same of man?' " (Russell 1979).

A purely scientific, economic, or other objective response is inappropriate since the issue of animal welfare is primarily subjective. This is why it is often dismissed as an "emotional" issue due to the anthropomorphizing misperceptions of animals by people. But the issue is not one of human subjectivity: it concerns the animal's subjective state. To demand equal and fair treatment for all animals of similar sentience is *not* anthropomorphic: it is objective, "scientific," and logically sound.

Ethical Inconsistencies in Animal Treatment

A major aspect of animal rights philosophy which has been seriously overlooked, because of the instant polarization of this issue into animal versus human rights, is the following: animals of the same species or of a similar degree of sentience should be treated with the same degree of humaneness (since they can all suffer similarly). There are no moral or ethical grounds for considering otherwise, and there is certainly no scientific reason why they should be treated differently. The only reasons why similar animals are treated differently are primarily economic. How much the animal is valued, ignorance and insensitivity aside, determines how well the animal is treated. The veterinarian, whose skills in enhancing animal well-being are called upon and paid for, is caught in the middle.

Thus, rather than the veterinarian being a significant arbiter and interlocutor for animal well-being and animals' rights to equal and fair treatment, economics is the prime determinant of how well animals are cared for. Contrast the care of a prize dairy cow and a "factory" one that is spent in four years, or a companion dog and one being used in an LD_{50} test of a new floor wax.

As we recognize the human right to equal opportunity, so we should recognize that regardless of their financial or other extrinsic worth, animals of similar sentience should be given the right to equal and fair treatment. If this is unacceptable, then we must accept a societal consensus that is purely utilitarian, materialistic, mechanistic and dominionistic. A philosophy of veterinary ethics that embraces a genuine concern for the highest standards of animal care, health, and overall well-being has no place in such a society. Thus if we are to preserve the dignity and integrity of our profession, the societal consensus needs to be challenged and transformed.

A pet owner keeping a dog permanently tethered or crated like a sow, or parrots crowded into a cage like battery hens, could be prosecuted under the Animal Welfare Act, yet farmers and fur ranchers are immune. This is ethical inconsistency and is biologically absurd since these species are of similar sentience and should therefore be entitled to equal and fair consideration and treatment.

Without challenging those societal values that lead to animals not being given equal and fair treatment, and by not working toward such equality, it will continue to be cheaper and more expedient for society to cut back on veterinary treatment for those animals that are of little value as individuals, as has happened with farm animals.

To defer to custom, expediency, or "economic progress" and to condone the inequitous treatment of animals in society today is surely not in the veterinary profession's best interests (as witness the gradual extinction of the farm veterinarian, especially in the United States). And by so doing, do we not demean our own moral obligations as a caring and healing profession? Standing for animals' right to equal and fair treatment is enlightened self-interest. Is it also an ethical imperative?

The veterinary profession can help broaden society's perception of animals to facilitate respect for and empathy with the subjective (emotional) realm of animals. Such appreciation of animals in their own light and right is what philosopher Buber (1970) termed the "I-Thou" relationship, which he eloquently described in his experiences with animals and nature. The objectifying I-It relationship of sheer utility (i.e., man's need to exploit animals) is not exclusive, but rather is inclusive within this "I-Thou" dimension. Empathy as subjective concern and objective knowledge is the essence of right relationship; of sensible planetary stewardship and humane animal husbandry (Fox 1984b). And is it not also the hallmark of good veterinary practice, embracing both the science and *art* of veterinary medicine?

As we come to understand the significance of empathy, we will be in a better position, I believe, to develop a veterinary philosophy. Caring without objective knowledge is impotent and often inappropriate sympathy. Objective knowledge without sympathy is mechanistic, dehumanizing and "deanimalizing." Empathy is also a sign of what Gilligan (1983) terms moral maturity, as for instance when, in her terms, both intellect and empathy are combined in our thinking, "it joins the heart and the eye in an ethic that ties the activity of thought to the activity of care." Without such an integration, purely intellectual, rational thinking is alienating and object-ifying, and purely sympathetic responding is subjective and potentially inappropriate. Rational empathy is the only basis for ethically responsible behavior.

The following statements by Albert Schweitzer (1961, 1982) contain the essential ethical ingredients of a veterinary philosophy, which do not prohibit the exploitation of animals but rather provide the moral framework within which such exploitation can be objectively evaluated:

> A person is only ethical when life, as such, is sacred to him, that of plants and animals as well as that of his fellow men, and when one denotes oneself helpfully to all life that is in need of help.
>
> In the past we have tried to make a distinction between animals which we acknowledge have some value and others which, having none, can be liquidated when and as we wish. This standard must be abandoned. Everything that lives has value simply as a living thing, as one manifestation of the mystery that is life.

In conclusion, not all veterinarians may feel it incumbent upon them to consider their ethical responsibilities towards animals since animals are the property and primary responsibility of clients. They may choose to limit their responsibilities to providing the best possible technical expertise within the economic constraints of reality. However, there is an ethical inconsistency since these constraints can mean that animals of similar sentience are not accorded the right to equal and fair veterinary treatment. This places the veterinary profession in a double bind and represents an impasse that will, it is to be hoped, be resolved as a philosophy of veterinary medicine is developed. Changing societal attitudes towards animals and the growing animal rights movement necessitate that we must begin to address several aspects of veterinary practice and of the profession's involvement with such animal-related industries as intensive farming, biomedical research, and wildlife resource exploitation, from an ethical perspective.

It would be useful to know at this stage, what consensus exists amongst veterinarians: Are we merely a service profession, or do we have an ethical obligation, as animal doctors, to lead society toward a greater respect for animals and to giving equal and fair treatment to those of the same sentience? From my perspective, this would be enlightened self-interest for our profession, and for society also.

In sum, as I have emphasized earlier (Fox 1983c) how we treat animals cannot solely be based upon what we know about them scientifically with respect to their sentience and mental states. There are other factors that may constrain or condone their exploitation and the extent to which we may harm them, cause them to suffer, kill them, or deprive them physically and psychologically. These factors are religious, moral, ethical, esthetic, emotional, legal, sociocultural, political, economic, and ecological. There is also a spiritual factor, which may be regarded as a refined synthesis of religious, moral, ethical, esthetic, and emotional values and perceptions. Expressed philosophically as a respect for the intrinsic nature and worth of all cretures, it may be interpreted as reverence for the inherent divinity within all of creation.

References

Ackerman, S.H., Hofer, M.A., and Weiner, H. 1975. Age at maternal separation and gastric erosion susceptibility in the rat. *Psychosom. Med.* 37:180-84.

_____. 1979. Sleep and temperature regulation during restraint stress in rats is affected by prior maternal separation. *Psychosom. Med.* 41:311-19.

Adams, H.R. 1976. Antibiotic-induced alterations of cardiovascular reactivity. *Fed. Proc.* 35:1148-51.

Ader, R. 1965. Behavioral and physiological rhythms and the development of gastric erosions in the rat. *Psychosom. Med.* 29:345-53.

_____. 1967. The influence of psychological factors on disease susceptibility in animals. *In: Husbandry of laboratory animals,* ed. M.L. Conalty. New York: Academic Press.

_____. 1968. Effects of early experiences on emotional and physiological reactivity of the rat. *J. Comp. Physiol. Psychol.* 66(2):264-8.

_____. 1980. Psychosomatic and psychoimmunologic research. *Psychosom. Med.* 42:307-21.

Ader, R., ed. 1981. *Psychoneuroimmunology.* New York: Academic Press.

Ader, R. 1983. Developmental psychoneuroimmunology. *Develop. Psychobiol.* 16:251-67.

Ader, R.A., and Cohen, N. 1975. Behaviorally conditioned immunosuppression. *Psychosom. Med.* 37:332-40.

Ader, R., and Conklin, P. 1963. Handling of pregnant rats: effects on emotionality of their offspring. *Science* 142:411-2.

229

Ader, R., and Friedman, S.B. 1965. Differential early experience and susceptibility to transplanted tumor in the rat. *J. Comp. Physiol. Psychol.* 59:361-4.

Ader, R., and Hahn, E.W. 1963. The effects of social environment on mortality to whole body X-irradiation in the rat. *Psychol. Rep.* 13:211-5.

Ader, R., Kreuter, A., Jr., and Jacobs, H.L. 1963. Social environment, emotionality, and alloxan diabetes in the rat. *Psychosom. Med.* 25:60-68.

Ader, R., and Plaut, S.M. 1968. Effects of prenatal maternal handling and differential housing on offspring emotionality, plasma corticosterone levels, and susceptibility to gastric erosions. *Psychosom. Med.* 30:277-86.

Albert, Z. 1967. Effect of number of animals per cage on the development of spontaneous tumors. *In: Husbandry of laboratory animals,* ed. M.L. Conalty. New York: Academic Press.

Alumets, J., Hakanson, R., Sundler, F., and Thorell, J. 1979. Neuronal localization of immunoreactive enkephalin and B-endorphin in the earthworm. *Nature* 279:805-6.

Amkraut, A.A., Solomon, G.F., and Kraemer, H.C. Stress, early experience and adjuvant induced arthritis in the rat. *Psychosom. Med.* 33:203-44.

Anderson, J.D., and Cox, C.S. 1967. Microbial survival. *In: Airborne microbes,* eds. P.H. Gregory and Monteith, 203-26. 17th Symposium of the Society of General Microbiology, Cambridge University Press.

Andervont, H.B. 1944. Influence of environment on mammary cancer in mice. *J.Nat. Cancer Inst.* 4:579-81.

Anton, A.H. 1969. Effect of group size, sex and time on organ weights, catecholamines and behavior in mice. *Physiol. Behav.* 4:483-7.

Anton, A.H., Schwartz, R.P., and Kramer, S. 1968. Catecholamines and behavior in isolated and grouped mice. *J. Psychiatr. Res.* 6:211-20.

Archer, J. 1970. Effects of population density on behavior in rodents. *In: Social Behaviour in Birds and Mammals,* ed. J.H. Crook, 169-210. New York: Academic Press.

Arling, G.L., and Harlow, H.F. 1967. Effects of social deprivation on maternal behavior of rhesus monkeys. *J. Comp. Physiol. Psychol.* 64(3):317-7.

Ashoub, M.R., Biggers, J.D., McLaren, A., and Michie, D. 1958. The effect of the environment on phenotypic variability. *Proc. Roy. Soc. B.* 149:192-203.

Baer, H. 1971. Long-term isolation stress and its effects on drug response in rodents. *Lab. Anim. Sci.* 21:341-9.

Bakan, D. 1967. *Disease, pain and suffering.* Boston:Beacon Press.

Balls, M., Riddell, R.J., and Worden, A.M. eds. 1983. *Animals and Alternatives in Toxicity Testing.* New York: Academic Press.

Banerjee, B.N., and Woodward, G. 1970. A comparison of outdoor and indoor housing of Rhesus monkeys. *Lab. Anim. Care* 20:80-84.

Barbenhenn, K.R. 1961. Some effects of litter size on social behavior in laboratory rats. *Transactions of the N.Y. Academy of Sci.,* 2d Ser. 23:443-6.

Barfield, J., and Geyer, L.A. 1972. Sexual behavior: ultrasonic postejaculatory song of the male rat. *Science* 176:1349-50.

Barnes, T.C. 1959. Isolation stress in rats and mice as a neuropharmacological test. *Fed. Proc.* 12:365.

Barnete, S.A., and Burns, J. 1967. Early stimulation and maternal behavior. *Nature* 213:150.

Baumel, I., De Feo, J.J., and Lal, H. 1969. Decreased potency of CNS depressants after prolonged social isolation in mice. *Psychopharmacologia* 15:153-8.

Beecher, H.K. 1957. The measurement of pain. *Pharmacol. Rev.* 9:59-209.

Beecher, H.K., ed. 1960. *Disease and the advancement of basic science.* London: Harvard University Press.

Bell, R.W., Reisner, G., and Linn, T. 1961. Recovery from electroconvulsive shock as a function of infantile stimulation. *Science,* 133, 1:428.

Bellhorn, R.W. 1980. Lighting in the animal environment. *Lab. Anim. Sci.* 30:440-50.

Berkson, G. 1967. Abnormal and stereotyped motor acts. *In: Comparative Psychopathology,* eds. J. Zubin and H.F. Hunt. New York: Grune and Statton, Inc.

_____. 1968. Development of abnormal stereotyped behaviors. *Dev. Psychobiol.* 1(2):118-32.

Berkson, G., Mason, A.W., and Saxon, S.V. 1963. Situation and stimulus effects on stereotyped behaviors of chimpanzees. *J. Comp. Physiol. Psychol.* 56:786-92.

Bernardis, L.L., and Skelton, F.R. 1963. Effect of crowding on hypertension and growth in rats bearing regenerating adrenals. *Proc. Soc. Exp. Biol. Med.* 113:952-4.

Bernstein, I.S., and Gordon, T.C. 1977. Behavioral research in breeding colonies of Old World monkeys. *Lab. Anim. Sci.* 27:532-40.

Bickhardt, K., Buttner, D., Muschen, U., and Plonait, H. 1983. Influence of bleeding procedure and some environmental conditions on stress-dependent blood constituents of laboratory rats. *Lab. Animals* 17:161-6.

Biggers, J.D., McLaren, A., and Michie, D. 1958. Variance control in the animal house. *Nature* 182:77-88.

Blizzard, D.A. 1971. Individual differences in automatic responsivity in the adult rat. *Psychosom. Med.* 33:445-57.

Bogden, A.E. 1974. The effects of environmental stress on immunological responses. *In: Environmental variables in animal experimentation,* ed. H. Magalhaes. Lewisburg: Bucknell University Press.

Boice, R. 1973. Domestication. *Psych. Bull.* 80:215-30.

Bowsher, D. 1981. *In: Self-awareness in domesticated animals,* eds. D.G.M. Wood-Gush, M. Dawkins, and R. Ewbank. Potters Bar, Hertfordshire, England: The Universities Federation for Animal Welfare.

Bowsher, D., and Albe-Fessard, D. 1962. *In: The assessment of pain in man and animals,* eds. C.A. Keele, and D. Bowsher. London: Universities Federation for Animal Welfare.

Brain, R. 1965. *The Report of the Technical Committee to Enquire into the Welfare of Animals Kept Under Intensive Livestock Husbandry Systems.* London: Her Majesty's Stationery Office.

Breazile, J.E., and Kitchell, R.L. 1969. Pain perception in animals. *Fed. Proc.* 28:1379-82.

Brian, P., and Benton, D. 1979. The interpretation of physiological correlates of differential housing in laboratory rats. *Life Sci.* 24:99-116.

Broderson, J.R., Lindsey, J.R., and Crawford, J.E. 1976. The role of environmental ammonia in respiratory mycoplasmosis of rats. *Am. J. of Path.* 85:115-30.

Bronson, F.H. 1967. Pheromonal influences on mammalian reproduction. *In: Husbandry of laboratory animals,* ed. M.L. Conalty. New York: Academic Press.

_____. 1979. Light intensity and reproduction in wild and domestic house mice. *Bio. Repro.* 21:235-9.

Bronson, F.H., and Chapman, V.M. 1968. Adrenal-oestrous relationships on grouped or isolated female mice. *Nature* 218:483-4.

Brown, A.M. 1970. ed. *The effects of environment.* Symposium Proceedings. Carworth Europe Collected Papers, no. 4. Huntingdon, England: Carworth Europe.

Brown, G.M., and Martin, J.B. 1974. Corticosterone, prolactin and growth hormone responses to handling and new environment of the rat. *Psychosom. Med.* 36:241-7.

Buber, M. 1970. *I and thou.* translated by W. Kaufman, New York: Scribners.

Bush, M., Custer, R., Smeller, J., and Bush, L.M. 1977. Physiological measures of non-human primates during physical restraint and chemical immobilization. *J. Amer. Vet. Med.* 171:866-70.

Butler, R.G. 1980. Population size, social behaviour and dispersal in house mice: A quantitative investigation. *Anim. Behav.* 28:78-85.

Canland, D.K., Bryan, D.C., Nazar, B.L., Kopf, K.J., and Sendor, M. 1970. Squirrel monkey heart rate during formation of status orders. *J. Comp. Physiol. Psychol.* 70:417-3.

Capra, F. 1982. *The turning point.* New York: Scribners.

Carpenter, E. 1980. *Animals and Ethics.* London: Watkins.

Carr, W.J., Roth, P., and Amore, M. 1971. Responses of male mice to odors from stressed vs. nonstressed males and females. *Psychon. Sci.* 25:275-6.

Cass, J.S. 1970. Chemical factors in laboratory animal surroundings. *Bio-Science* 20(11):658-9.

Chamove, A.S., Anderson, J.R., Mongan-Jones, S.C., and Jones, S.P. 1982. Deep woodchip litter: hygiene, feeding, and behavioral enhancement in eight primate species. *Int. J. Stud. Anim. Prob.* 3:308-18.

Chance, M.R.A. 1946. Aggregation as a factor influencing the toxicity of sympathomimetic amines in mice. *J. Pharmacol. Exp. Therap.* 87:214-22.

_____. 1947. Factors influencing the toxicity of sympathomimetic amines in solitary mice. *J. Pharmacol. Exp. Therap.* 89:289-96.

_____. 1956. Environmental factors influencing Gonadotrophin assay in the rat. *Nature* 177:228-9.

Chany, S., and Rasmussen, A.J., Jr. 1965. Stress-induced suppression of interferon production in virus-injected mice. *Nature* 205:623-4.

Chignell, C.F., Sik, R.H., Gladen, B.C., and Feldman, D.B. 1981. The effect of different types of flourescent lighting on reproduction and tumor development in the C3H mouse. *Photochem. Photobiol.* 34:617-21.

Christian, J.J., and Davis, D.E. 1964. Endocrines, Behavior, and population. *Science* 146(3651):1550-60.

Christian, J.J., and Williamson, H.O. 1958. Effect of crowding on experimental granuloma formation in mice. *Proc. Soc. Exp. Biol. Med.* 99:385-7.

Cisar, C.F., and Jayson, G. 1967. Effects of frequency of caged cleaning on rat litters prior to weaning. *Lab. Anim. Care.* 17:215-18.

Clark, M.M., and Galef, G., Jr. 1977. The role of the physical rearing environment in the domestication of the Mongolian gerbil (*Meriones unguiculatus*). *Anim. Behav.* 25:298-316.

_____. 1980. Effects of rearing environment on adrenal weights, sexual development, and behavior in gerbils: An examination of Richter's domestication hypothesis. *J. Comp. Physiol. Psychol.* 94:857-63.

_____. 1981. Environmental influence on development, behavior, and endocrine morphology of gerbils. *Physiol. Behav.* 27:761-5.

Clark, S.R.L. 1977. *The moral status of animals.* Oxford: Clarendon Press.

Clough, G. 1982. Environmental effects on animals used in biomedical research. *Biol. Rev.* 57:487-523.

Conalty, M.L., ed. 1967. Husbandry of Laboratory Animals. *Proceedings of the 3rd International Symposium of the International Committee on Laboratory Animals.* New York and London: Academic Press.

Connor, J.L. 1975. Genetic mechanisms controlling the domestication of a wild house mouse population *(Mus musculus* L.*). J. Comp. Physiol. Psychol.* 89:118-30.

Cosnier, J. 1967. The role of certain early environmental conditions on the psychophysiological development of animals. *In: Husbandry of laboratory animals,* ed. M.L. Conalty, 493-511. New York: Academic Press.

Dantzer, R., and Mormede, P. 1983. Stress in farm animals: A need for re-evaluation. *J. Anim. Sci.* 57(1):6-18.

Darwin, C. 1915. *The descent of man,* 2nd ed. Chicago: Rand McNally.

Davis, D.E. 1971. Physiological effects of continued crowding. *In: Behavior and environment,* ed. A.H. Essex, 133-47. New York: Plenum Press.

_____. 1973. *Committee Report for Laboratory Animal Ethology.* Institute of Laboratory Animal Resources. National Research Council: National Academy of Sciences. Washington, D.C.

Dawkins, M. 1976. Toward an objective method of assessing welfare in domestic fowl. *Appl. Anim. Ethol.* 2:245-54.

_____. 1978. *New Scientist* 80:118.

_____. 1980. *Animal Suffering: The Science of Animal Welfare.* New York: Chapman Hall

Denenberg, V.H., and Rosenberg, K.M. 1967. Nongenetic transmission of information. *Nature* 216 (5115):549-50.

Denenberg, V.H., Wehmer, F., Werboff, J., and Zarrow, M.X. 1969. Effects of post-weaning enrichment and isolation upon emotionality and brain weight in the mouse. *Physiology and Behavior* 4:403-6.

Denenberg, V.H., and Whimbey, A.E. 1963a. Behavior of adult rats is modified by the experiences their mothers had as infants. *Science* 142(3596): 1192-93.

_____. 1963b. Infantile stimulation and animal husbandry: a methodological study. *J. Comp. Physiol. Psychol.* 56:877-8.

Diner, J. 1979. *Physical and mental suffering of experimental animals.* Washington, DC: Animal Welfare Institute.

Doolittle, D.P., Wilson, S.P., and Geisking, D. 1976. Effect of caging variables on body weight and weight gain in mice. *Lab. Anim. Sci.* 26:556-9.

Drickamer, L.C. 1974. Day length and sexual maturation in female house mice. *Develop. Psychobiol.* 8:561-70.

Drickamer, L.C., and Hover, J.E. 1979. Effects of urine from pregnant and lactating female house mice on sexual maturation of juvenile females. *Develop. Psychobiol.* 12:545-51.

Dubner, R. 1983. Pain research in animals. *In: Role of Animals in Biomedical Research. Annals N.Y. Acad. Sci.* 406:128-32.

Duncan, I.J.H. 1978. The interpretation of preference tests in animal behavior. *Appl. Anim. Ethol.* 4:197-200.

Einon, D.F., Humphreys, A.D., and Chivers, S.M. 1981. Isolation has permanent effects upon the behavior of the rat but not the mouse, gerbil or guinea pig. *Develop. Psychobiol.* 14:343-55.

Eisen, E.J. 1966. Comparison of two cage-rearing regimes on reproductive performance and body weight of the laboratory mouse. *Lab. Anim. Care* 16:447-53.

_____. 1975. Influence of the male's presence on maturation, growth and feed efficiency of female mice. *J. Anim. Sci.* 40:816-20.

Eisenberg, John F., and Kleiman, Devra G. 1972. Olfactory communication in mammals. *Annual Review of Ecology and Systematics* 3:1-32.

Ellis, T.M. 1967. Environmental influences on drug responses in laboratory animals. *In: Husbandry of laboratory animals,* ed. M.L. Conalty, 561-88. New York: Academic Press.

Enna, S.J. 1984. Role of gamma-aminobutyric acid in anxiety. *Psychopathology* 17 (Suppl. 1):15-24.

Erwin, J. 1977. Factors influencing aggressive behavior and risk of trauma in Pigtail macaques *(Macaca nemestrina). Lab. Anim. Sci.* 27:541-7.

Erwin, J., and Anderson, B. 1975. Agnostic behavior of pregnant female monkeys *(Macaca nemestrina):* possible influence of total gonadal hormones. *Psychol. Rep.* 36:699-702.

Estola, T., Makela, P., and Tapani, H. 1979. The effect of air ionization on the air-borne transmission of experimental new disease virus infection in chickens. *J. Hyg. (Cambridge)* 83:59-67.

Ferchmin, P.A., Bennet, E.L. and Rosenweig, M.R. 1975. Direct contact with enriched environment is required to alter cerebral weights in rats. *J. Comp. Physiol. Psychol.* 88:360-702.

Ferguson, W., Herbert, W.J., and McNeillage, D.J.C. 1970. Infectivity and virulence of *Trypanosoma (tripnosoon) brucii* in mice. *Trop. Animal Health and Prod.* 2:59-64.

Festing, M. 1977. Bad animals mean bad science. *New Scientist* 73:130-1.

Flecknell, P.A. 1983. Pain relief in experimental animals. *Letters Vet. Rec.* Nov. 5th:453.

Flecknell, P.A. 1985. The relief of pain in animals. *In* (eds): M.W. Fox and Mickley *Advances in Animal Welfare Science.* Martinus Nijhoff Boston in press.

Fletcher, J.L. 1976. Influence of noise on animals. *In: Control of the Animal House Environment,* 51-62. Laboratory Animal Handbooks, vol. 7. London: Laboratory Animals Ltd.

Floeter, M.K., and Greenough, W.T. 1979. Cerebellar plasticity: Modification of Purkinje cell structure by differential rearing in monkeys. *Science* 206:227-9.

Forgays, D.G., and Forgays, J.W. 1952. The nature of the effect of free-environmental experience in the rat. *J. Comp. Physiol. Psychol.* 55:816-8.

Fouts, J.R. 1976. Overview of the field: environmental factors affecting chemical or drug effects on animals. *Fed. Proc.* 35:1162-65.

Fox, J.G., Thiebert, P., Arnold, D.L., Krewski, D.R., and Grice, H.C. 1979. Toxicology Studies. II. The Laboratory Animal. *Food and Cosmetics Toxicology* 17:661-75.

Fox, M.W. 1965. Environmental factors influencing stereotyped and allelomimetic behavior in animals. *Lab. Anim. Care* 15:363-70.

_____. 1966. Natural environment: theoretical and practical aspects for breeding and rearing laboratory animals. *Lab. Anim. Care* 16:316-20.

_____. 1970. Environmental influences on behavior of domestic and laboratory animals. *Adv. in Vet. Sci. and Comp. Med.* 15:47-67.

_____. 1971. Effects of rearing conditions on the behavior of laboratory animals. *In: Defining the laboratory animal.* Washington, DC: National Academy of Sciences.

_____. 1971b. *Integrative development of brain and behavior in the dog.* Chicago: University of Chicago Press.

_____. 1974. *Concepts of ethology.* Minneapolis, MN: Univ. Minnesota Press.

_____. 1976. *Between animal and man.* New York: Coward, McCann, and Geoghegan.

_____. 1977. *The dog: its domestication and behavior.* New York: Garland Press.

_____. 1980. *Returning to eden: animal rights and human responsibility.* New York: Viking Press

_____. 1983a. *Farm animals: Husbandry, behavior and veterinary practice: Viewpoints of a critic.* Baltimore: University Park Press.

_____. 1983b. *The healing touch.* New York: Newmarket Press.

_____. 1983c. Philosophy, ecology, animal welfare, and the 'rights' question. *In: Ethics and Animals,* eds. H.B. Miller and W.H. Williams, 307-315. Clifton, NJ: Humana Press.

_____. 1984a. Toward a Veterinary Ethic. *Vet. Rec.* 115:12-13.

_____. 1984b. Empathy, humaneness and animal welfare. *In: Advances in Animal Welfare Science,* eds. M.W. Fox and L.D. Mickley, 61-74. Holland: Martinus Nijhoff.

_____. 1986. *The Holocaust of the Animals.* manuscript in preparation.

Fox, M.W., and Spencer, J. 1969. Exploratory behavior in the dog: experiential or age dependent? *Develop. Psychobiol.* 2:68-74.

Fraser, D., and Waddell, M.D. 1974. The importance of social and self-grooming for the control of ectoparasitic mites on normal and dystrophic laboratory mice. *Lab. Practice* February:12-14.

Freedman, D.G. 1958. Constitutional and environmental interactions in the rearing of four breeds of dogs. *Science* 127:585-6.

Friedman, S.B., Glasgow, L.A., and Ader, R. 1969. Psychosocial factors modifying host resistance to experimental infection. *New York Acad. Science* 164:381-93.

Frolich, M., Walma, S.T., and Souverijn, J.H.M. 1981. Probable influence of cage design on muscle metabolism of rats. *Lab. Anim. Sci.* 31:510-12.

Fuller, C.A., Sulzman, F.M., and Moore-Ede, M.C. 1978. Thermoregulation is impaired in an environment without circadian time cues. *Science* 199:794-6.

Fuller, J.L. 1967. Experimental deprivation and later. *Behavior Science* 158:1645-52.

Fullerton, C., and Cowley, J.J. 1971. The differential effect of the presence of adult male and female mice on the growth and development of the young. *J. of Genetic Psychology* 119:89-98.

Gamble, M.R. 1982. Sound and its significance for laboratory animals. *Bio. Rev.* 57:395-421.

Gantt, W.H., Newton, J.E.O., Royer, E.L., and Stephens, J.H. 1966. Effect of person. *Conditioned Reflex* 1:18-35.

Gartner, K., Buttner, D., Dohler, K., Friedel, R., Lindena, J., and Trautschold, I. 1980. Stress response of rats to handling and experimental procedures. *Lab. Anim.* 14:267-74.

Gee, R.W., and Meishke, H.R.C. 1982. The veterinarian and animal welfare. *Vet. Rec.* 110(4):86.

Gellhorn, E. 1967. The tuning of the nervous system: Physiological formulations and implications for behavior. *Perspect. Biol. Med.* 10:591-9.

Georgiev, J. 1978. Influence of environmental conditions and handling on the temperature rhythm of the rat. *Biotelemetry and Patient Monitoring* 5:229-34.

Gilligan, C. 1983. *In a different voice.* Boston: Harvard University Press.

Godlovitch, S.R., and Harris, J., eds. 1972. *Animals, men and morals: An inquiry into the mal-treatment of non-humans.* New York: Taplinger.

Goldfoot, D.A. 1977. Rearing conditions which support or inhibit later sexual potential of laboratory-born rhesus monkeys: hypotheses and diagnostic behavior. *Lab. Anim. Sci.* 27:548-56.

Gould, D. 1977. In place of lab animals. *New Scientist* 73:210-11.

Gray, J.A. 1982. *The Neuropsychology of Anxiety.* New York: Oxford University Press.

Greenman, D.L., Bryant, P., Kodell, R.L., and Sheldon, W. 1983. Relationship of mouse body weight and food consumption/wastage to cage shelf level. *Lab. Anim. Sci.* 33:555-8.

Griffin, D. 1977. *The question of animal awareness.* New York: Rockefeller University Press.

Griffin, D.R. 1982. *The question of animal awareness.* (2nd edition) New York: Rockefeller University Press.

Gross, W. 1972. Effect of social stress on occurrence of Marek's disease in chickens. *Amer. J. Vet. Res.* 33:2275-79.

Gross, W.B. 1984. The well-being of poultry. *In: The behavior and welfare of farm animals;* W.F. Hall. Proceedings of the Conference on the Human-Animal Bond, Minneapolis, MN. June 13-14, 1983.

Hahn, E.W., and Howland, J.W. 1962. Modification of irradiation response of female rats by population density. *Radiat. Res.* 19:676-81.

Hamilton, D.R. 1974. Immunosuppressive effects of predator induced stress with acquired immunity to *Hymenolepis nana. J. Psychosom. Res.* 18:143-53.

Harlow, H.F. 1959. Love in infant monkeys. *Sci. Am.* 200: 68-74.

Harlow, H.F. 1962. Development of affection in primates. *In: Roots of behavior,* ed. E.L. Bliss. New York: Hafner.

Harlow, H.F., and Harlow, M.K. 1962. The effects of rearing conditions on behavior. *Bull. Menninger Clin.* 26(5):213-24.

Harlow, H.F. and Harlow, M.K. 1966. Learning to love. *Amer. Scientist* 54:244-72.

Harlow, H.F., and Suomi, S.J. 1971. Production of depressive behaviors in young monkeys. *J. of Autism and Childhood Schizophrenia.* 1:246-55.

Harrison, R. 1964. *Animal Machines.* London:Stuart.

Hatch, A.M., Wibert, G.S., and Zawidzka, Z. 1965. Isolation syndrome in the rat. *Toxical Appl. Pharmacol.* 7:737-45.

Hediger, H. 1950. *Wild animals in captivity.* London: Butterworth.

Henderson, N. 1970. Genetic influences on the behavior of mice can be obscured by laboratory rearing. *J. Comp. Physiol. Psychol.* 72:505-11.

Henderson, N.D. 1976. Short exposures to enriched environments can increase genetic variability in mice. *Develop. Psychobiol.* 9:459-553.

Henry, J.P., Meehan, J.P., and Stephans, P. 1967. The use of psychosocial stimuli to induce prolonged systolic hypertension in mice. *Psychosom. Med.* 29:408-32.

Henry, J.P., and Stephens, P. 1969. The use of psychosocial stimuli to induce renal and cardiovascular pathology in mice. *Psychosom. Med.* 31:454-5.

Henry, J.P., Stephens, P.M., Axelrod, J., and Mueller, R.A. 1971. Effects of psychosocial stimulation on the enzymes involved in the biosynthesis and metabolism of noradrenaline. *Psychosom. Med.* 33:227-37.

Herman, B.H., and Panksepp, J. 1980. Ascending endorphin inhibition of distress vocalizations. *Science* 211:1060-62.

Hill, C.A. 1966. Coprophagy in apes. *Int. Zoo Yearb.* 6:251-7.

Hinde, R.A., Spencer-Booth, Y., and Bruce, M. 1966. Effects of 6-day maternal deprivation on rhesus monkey infants. *Nature* 210(5040):1021-3.

_____. 1971. Effects of brief separation from mother on rhesus monkeys. *Science* 173:111-8.

Hoffman, J.C, 1973. The influence of photoperiods on reproductive functions in female mammals. *In: Endocrinology. II. Handbook of Physiology,* section 7, 57-77. Washington, DC: American Physiological Society.

Hoffman, R.A., and Stowell, R.E. 1973. Outdoor housing of nonhuman primates. *Lab. Anim. Sci.* 23:74-79.

Hodges, R.D., and Scofield, M. 1983. Effects of agricultural practices on the health of plants and animals produced: a review. *In: Environmentally Sound Agriculture,* ed. W. Lockerelz, 3-34. New York: Praeger.

Holden, C. 1980. Behavioral medicine. *Science* 204:479-81.

Huck, U.W., and Price, E.O. 1975. Differential effects of environmental enrichment of the open-field behavior of wild and domestic Norway rats. *J. Comp. Physiol. Psychol.* 89:892-8.

Hurnik, F., and Lehman, H. 1982. Unnecessary suffering: Definition and evidence. *Intl. J. Stud. Anim. Prob.* 3(2):131-7.

Hutteunen, M.O. 1971. Persistent alteration of turnover of brain nonadrenaline in the offspring of rats subjected to stress during pregnancy. *Nature* 230:53-55.

ICLA 1971. International Committee on Laboratory Animals. *Defining the laboratory animal.* IVth International Symposium. Washington: National Academy of Sciences.

Illich, I. 1977. *Medical nemesi.* New York: Bantam Books.

_____. 1968. Effect of noise in the animal house on seizure susceptibility. and growth of mice. *Laboratory Animal Care Journal* 18(5):557-60.

Iturrian, W.B., and Fink, G.B. 1968. Effect of noise in the animal house on seizure susceptibility and growth of mice. *Laboratory Animal Care Journal* 18(5):557-60.

_____. 1969. Effects of age and condition-test interval (days) on an audio-conditioned convulsive response in CF#1 mice. *Develop. Psychobiol.* 3:1-5.

Jacques, L.B., and Hiebert, L.M. 1972. Relation of stress to hemorrhage in laboratory animals. *In:* Paper presented at Canadian Association Laboratory Animal Science, 37-52. Edmonton: Animal Care Technology Proceedings.

James, W.T. 1951. Social organization among dogs of different temperaments, Terriers and Beagles, reared together. *J. Comp. Physiol. Psychol.* 44:71-77.

_____. 1953. Social facilitation of eating behavior in puppies after satiation. *J. Comp. Physiol. Psychol.* 46:427-8.

Jensen, G.D., and Bobbitt 1968. Implication of primate research for understanding infant development. *In: Animal and human,* ed. J.H. Masserman. New York: Grune and Stratton.

Joffe, J.M. 1965. Genotype and prenatal and premating stress interact to affect adult behavior in rats. *Science* 150(30705):1844-5.

Joffe, J.M., Rawson, R.A., and Mulick, J.A. 1973. Control of their environment reduces emotionality in rats. *Science* 180:1383-4.

Joy, V., and Latane, B. 1971. Autonomic arousal and affiliation in rats. *Psychon. Sci.* 25:299-300.

Kane, N.L., and Knutson, J.F. 1976. Influence of colony lighting conditions on home-cage spontaneous aggression. *J. Comp. Physiol. Psychol.* 9:899-7.

Kaplan, J.R., Adams, M.R., and Bumsted, P. 1983. Heart rate changes associated with tethering of cynomologus monkeys. Abstract *Lab. Anim. Sci.* 33:493.

Kaplan, J.R., Manuck, S.B., Clarkson, T.B., Lusso, F.M., Taub, D.M., and Miller, E.W. 1983. Social stress and atherosclerosis in normocholesterolemic monkeys. *Science* 220:733-5.

Kaufman, I.C., and Rosenblum, L.A. 1966. The reaction of separation in infant monkeys: Anaclictic depression and conservation-withdrawal. *Psychosom. Med.* 29:648-76.

_____. 1967. Depression in infant monkeys separated from their mothers. *Science* 155:1030.

Kavanau, L. 1967. Behavior: confinement, adaptation and compulsory regimes in laboratory studies. *Science* 143:490.

_____. 1976. How much light do animals like? *New Scientist* 74:530-2.

Keeley, K. 1962. Prenatal influence on behavior of offspring of crowded mice. *Science* 135:44-45.

Keiper, R.R. 1969. Causal factors of stereotypes in caged birds. *Anim. Behav.* 17:114-9.

Keller, S.E., Weiss, J.M., Schleifer, S.J., Miller, N.E., and Stein, M. 1981. Suppression of immunity by stress: effect of a guided series of stressors on lymphocytic stimulation in the rat. *Science* 213:1397-4.

Kendrick, D.C. 1972. The effects of stimulation and intermittent fasting and feeding on life span in the black-hooded rat. *Develop. Psychobiol.* 6:225-34.

Keverne, E.B., Bowman, L., and Dilley, S. 1978. Suppression of oestrogen-induced LH surges by social subordination in talapoin monkeys. *Nature* 275:56.

King, J.A. Closed social groups among domestic dogs. *Proc. Am. Phil. Soc.* 98:327-36.

King, J.T., Lee, Y., and Visscher, M.B. 1955. Single versus multiple cage occupancy and convulsion frequency in C2H mice. *Proc. Soc. Exp. Biol. Med.* 88:661-3.

Kitchell, R.L., and Erickson, H.H. 1983. *Animal pain perception and alleviation.* Bethesda, MD: American Physiological Society.

Korn, J.H., and Moyer, K.E. 1968. Behavioral effects of isolation in the rat: the role of sex and time of isolation. *J. Genetic Psych.* 113:263-13.

Kosman, M.E. 1965. The effect of grouping on the rat's response to a psychomimetic agent. *Int. J. Neuropsychiatr.* 1:90-94.

Krueger, A.P., Kotaka, S., and Reed, E.J. 1971. The course of experimental influenza in mice maintained in high concentrations of small negative ions. *Int. J. Biometero.* 15:5-10.

Krueger, A.P., and Reed, E.J. 1972. Effect of the air ion environment on influenza in the mouse. *Int. J. Biometero.* 16:209-32.

Krueger, A.P., Reed, E.H., Day, M.B., and Brook, K.A. 1974. Further observations on the effect of air ions on influenza in the mouse. *Int. J. Biometero.* 18:46-56.

Krushinski, I.V. 1962. *Animal Behavior.* New York Consultant Bureau.

Kurtsin, I.P. 1968. *In: Abnormal Behavior in animals,* ed. M.W. Fox. Philadelphia: W.B. Saunders.

LASA 1965. The experimental animal in research. Symposium No. 1. *Food and Cosmetics Toxicology* 3:5-63, 165-228.

LaBarba, R.C., and White, J.L. 1971. Litter size variations and emotional reactivity in BALB/c mice. *Journal of Comparative and Physiological Psychology* 75:254-7.

LaChapelle, D. 1978. *Earth wisdom*. Los Angeles, CA: The Guild of Tutors Press.

Landi, M.S., Kreider, J.W., Lang, M., and Bullock, L.P. 1982. Effects of shipping on the immune function of mice. *Am. J. Vet. Res.* 43:1654-7.

Lang, C.M., and Vesell, E.S. 1976. Environmental and genetic factors affecting laboratory animals: impact on biomedical research. *Fed. Proc.* 35:1123-4.

LaTorre, J.C. 1968. Effect of differential environmental enrichment on brain weight and on acetylcholinesterase and cholinesterase activities in mice. *Exper. Neur.* 22:493-503.

Lawlor, M. 1984. Behavioral approaches to rodent management. *In: Standards in Laboratory Animal Management,* 40-49. Potters Bar, Hertfordshire, England: Universities Federation for Animal Welfare.

Lay, Y.L., Jacoby, R.O., and Jonas, A.M. 1978. Age-related and light-associated retinal changes in Fischer rats. *Invest. Opthalmol. Visual Sci.* 17:634-8.

Leiss, W. 1972. *The domination of nature.* New York: Braziller.

Lemonde, P. 1959. Influence of fighting on leukemia in mice. *Proc. Soc. Exp. Biol. Med.* 102:292-5.

_____. 1967. Influence of various environmental factors on neoplastic diseases. *In: Husbandry of laboratory animals,* ed. M.L. Conalty. New York: Academic Press.

Leopold, A. 1966. *A Sand County almanac.* London: Oxford University Press.

Les, E.P. 1968. Cage population density and efficiency of feed utilization in inbred mice. *Lab. Anim. Care* 18:305-7.

_____. 1972. A disease related to cage population density: tail lesions of C3H/HeJ mice. *Lab. Anim. Sci.* 22:56-60.

Levine, S. 1957. Maternal and environmental influences on the adrenocortical response to stress in weanling rats. *Science* 156:258-60.

Levine, S., and Cohen, C. 1959. Differential survival to leukemia as a function of infantile stimulation in DBA/2 mice. *Proc. Soc. Exp. Biol. Med. N.Y.* 102:53-54.

Levine, S., and Mullins, R.F. 1966. Hormone influences on brain organization in infant rats. *Science* 152:1585-92.

Linzey, W. 1976. *Animal rights.* London; SCM Press.

Lockard, R.B. 1968. The albino rat: a defensible choice or a bad habit? *Amer. Psychologist* 23:734-42.

Lombardi, J.R., and Vandengerg, J.G. 1977. Pheromonally induced sexual maturation in females regulation by the social environment in the male. *Science* 196:545-6.

Lore, R.K. 1969. Pain avoidance of rats reared in restricted and enriched environments. *Developmental Psychology* 1:482-4.

Lynch, J.J. 1970. Psychophysiology and development of social attachment. *J. Nerv. and Mental Disease* 151:231-44.

Lynch, J.J., and Gantt, W. 1968. The heart rate component of the social reflex in dogs: The conditional effects of petting and person. *Conditional Reflex* 3(2):69-80.

Lyons, D.M., and Banks, E.M. 1982. Ultrasounds in neonatal rats: novel, predator and conspecific odor cues. *Develop. Psycholbiol.* 15:455-60.

McCall, R.B., Lester, M.C., and Carter, C.M. 1969. Caretaker effect on rats. *Develop. Psychol.* 1(6):771.

McKeown, T. 1976. *The role of medicine: mirage or nemesis.* London: Nuffield Provincial Hospital Trust.

Mackintosh, J.H., and Grant, E.C. 1966. The effect of olfactory stimuli on the agonistic behavior of laboratory mice. *J. Tierpsychol.* 23(5):584-7.

MacLennan, A.J., and Maier, S.F. 1983. Coping and the stress-induced potentiation of stimulant stereotypy in the rat. *Science* 219:1091-2.

McNamee, G.A., Jr., Wannemac, R.W., Dinterma, R.E., Rozmiare, H., and Montrey, R.D. 1983. A system for chronic blood sampling infusion and temperature monitoring in the caged monkey. (Abstract) *Lab. Anim. Sci.* 33:492.

McSheehy, T. 1976. *Control of the Animal House Environment.* Laboratory Animal Handbooks, no. 7. London, England: Laboratory Animals Ltd.

Manuck, S.B., Kaplan, J.P., and Clarkson, T.B. 1983. Behaviorally induced heart rate reactivity and atherosclerosi in Cynomolgus monkeys. *Psycho. Som. Med.* 45:95-108.

Manosevitz, M., and Pryor, J.B. 1975. Cage size as a factor in environmental enrichment. *J. Comp. Physiol. Psychol.* 89:648- 54.

Marcuse, F.L., and Pear, J.J. 1979. Ethics and Animal Experimentation: personal views. *In: Psychopathology in Animals,* ed. J.D. Keehn. New York: Academic Press.

Markowitz, H. 1982. *Behavioral enrichment in zoo animals.* New York: Van Nostrand Reinhold.

Markowitz, H., and Stevens, V.J., eds. 1978. *Behavior of captive wild animals.* Chicago: Nelson Hall.

Marsden, H.M., and Bronson, F.H. 1964. Strange male block to pregnancy: its absence in inbred mouse strains. *Nature* 207:878.

_____. 1965. The synchrony of oestrus in mice: relative roles of the male and female environments. *J. Endocrin.* 32:313-9.

Mason, J.W. 1975. *In: Emotions: their parameters and measurement,* ed. L. Levi. New York: Raven Press.

Mason, W.A. 1968. Early social deprivation in the nonhuman primates: implications for human behavior. *In: Environmental influences,* ed. D.C. Glass, 70-100. New York: Rockefeller University.

_____. 1984. Monkeys show two types of stress. *Research Resources Reporter* February: 6-8.

Mather, J.G. 1981. Wheel-running activity: a new interpretation. *Mammal Review* 11:41-3.

Mendoza, S.P., and Mason, W.A. 1983. Animal models. *Calif. Vet.* 37:91-2.

Meier, G.W., and Stuart, J.L. 1959. Effects of handling on the physical and behavioral development of Siamese kittens. *Psych. Reports* 5:497-501.

Melzack, R. 1972. *The puzzle of pain.* New York: Penguin Books.

Melzack, R., and Scott, T.H. 1957. The effect of early experience on response to pain. *J. Comp. Physiol. Psychol.* 50:155-61.

Menaker, M. 1969. Biological clocks. *BioScience.* 19(8):681-9.

Meskin, L.H., and Shapiro, B.L. 1971. Teratogenic effect of air shipment on A/JAX mice. *J. Dent. Res.* 50:169.

Meyer, H.M. 1968. Abnormal behavior in zoo animals. *Abnormal behavior in animals,* ed. M.W. Fox. Philadelphia: Saunders.

Michael, Richard P., Keverne, E.B., and Bonsall, R.W. 1971. Pheromones: Isolation of male sex attractants from female primate. *Science* 172:964-6.

Midgley, M. 1978. *Beast and Man: The Roots of Human Nature.* Ithaca, New York: Cornell University Press.

_____. 1983. *Animals and Why They Matter.* Athens: University of Georgia Press.

Milkovic, K., Paunovic, J.A., and Joffe, J.M. 1975. Effects of pre- and postnatal litter size on development and behavior of rat offspring. *Develop. Psychobiol.* 9:365-75.

Miller, R.E., Mirsky, I.A., Caul, W.F., and Sakata, T. 1969. Hyperphagia and polydipsia in socially isolated Rhesus Monkeys. *Science* 165:1027-8.

Mitchell, G.D. 1969. Paternalistic behavior in primates *Psychological Bulletin* 71(6):399-417.

Mitchell, G. 1970. Abnormal behavior in primates. *In: Primate Behavior,* ed. L.A. Rosenblum, 195-249. New York: Academic Press.

Monjan, A.M., and Collector, M.I. 1977. Stress induced modulation of the immune response. *Science* 196:307-8.

Moore, R.R., and Stuttart, S. 1979. Dr. Guthrie and *Felis domesticus* or tripping over the cat. *Science* 205:1031-3.

Morgan, D.J., and Upton, P.K. 1975. The effect of sampling techniques on acid-base flame and other blood parameters in sheep. *Lab. Anim.* 9:93-98.

Morris, D. 1966. Abnormal rituals in stress situations: the rigidification of behavior. *Philosophical Transactions of the Royal Society of London* 251(B):327-30.

Morris, R.K., and Fox, M.W., eds. 1978. *On the fifth day: Animal rights and human ethics.* Washington, DC: Acropolis Press.

Morrison, R.R., Ludvigson, H.W. 1970. Discrimination by rats of conspecific odors of reward and nonreward. *Science* 167:904-5.

Morton, D.B., and Griffiths, P.H.M. 1985. Guidelines on the recognition of pain, distress and discomfort in experimental animals and an hypothesis for assessment. *Vet. Rec.,* 116:431-436.

Morton, J.R. 1968. Effects of early experience, "handling and gentling" in laboratory animals. *In: Abnormal behavior in animals,* ed. M.W. Fox. Philadelphia: Saunders.

Morton, J.R.C., Denenberg, V.H., and Zarrow, M.X. 1963. Modification of sexual development through stimulation in infancy. *Endocrinology* 72(3):439-42.

Mugford, R.A., and Nowell, N.W. 1971. The preputial glands as a source of aggression promoting odors in mice. *Physiology and Behavior* 6:247-9.

Muhlbock, O. 1951. Influence of environment on the incidence of mammary tumours in mice. *Acta Un. Int. Cancr.* 7:251-3.

Mulder, J.B. 1971. Animal behavior and electromagnetic energy waves. *Lab. Anim. Sci.* 21:389-93.

Murphree, O.D., Peters, J.E., and Dykman, R.A. 1967. Effect of person on nervous, stable, and crossbred pointer dogs. *Conditioned Reflex* 2(4):273-6.

National Research Council. 1971. *A Guide to Environmental Research on Animals.* Washington, DC: National Academy of Sciences.

National Research Council. 1978. *Laboratory Animal Housing.* Washington: National Academy of Sciences.

Neamand, J., Sweeney, W.T., Creamer, A.A., and Conti, P.A. 1975. Cage activity in the laboratory beagle: a preliminary study to evaluate a method of comparing cage size to physical activity. *Lab. Anim. Sci.* 25:180-3.

Nebert, D.W., and Felton, J.S. 1976. Importance of genetic factors influencing the metabolism of foreign compounds. *Federation Proc.* 35:1133-41.

Neilsen, M., Braestrup, C., and Squires, R.F. 1978. Evidence for a late evolutionary appearance of brain/specific benzodiazepine receptor. *Brain Res.* 141:342-6.

Nerem, R.M.L., Levisque, M.J., and Cornhill, J.F. 1980. Social environment as a factor in diet-induced atherosclerosis. *Science* 208:1475-6.

Newberne, P.M. 1975. Influence of pharmacological experiments of chemicals and other factors on diets of laboratory animals. *Fed. Proc. Fed. Am. Soc. Exp. Biol.* 34(2):209-18.

Newton, G., and Heimstra, N.W. 1960. Effects of early experience on the response to whole-body X-irradiation. *Can. J. Psychol.* 14:111-20.

Newton, W.M. 1972. An evaluation of the effects of various degrees of long-term confinement on adult beagle dogs. *Lab. Anim. Sci.* 22:860-4.

_____. 1978. Environmental impact on Laboratory Animals. *Adv. in Vet. Sci. and Comp. Med.* 22:1-28.

Nikoletseas, M., and Lore, R.K. 1981. Aggression in domesticated rats reared in a burrow-digging environment. *Aggressive Behav.* 7:245-52.

Ninan, P.T., Insel, T.M., Cohen, R.M., Cook, J.M., Skolnick, P., and Paul, S.M. 1982. Benzodiazepine receptor-mediated experimented 'anxiety' in primates. *Science* 18:1332-4.

Nissen, H.W. 1930. A study of exploratory behavior in the whole rat by means of the obstruction method. *J. Genet. Psychol.* 37:361-76.

Novakova, V. 1966. Weaning of young rats: effects of time on behavior. *Science* 151(3709):475-6.

Obeck, D.K. 1978. Galvanized caging as a potential factor in the development of the 'fading infant' or 'white monkey' syndrome. *Lab. Anim. Sci.* 28:698-704.

Olivereau, J.M., and Lambert, J.F. 1981. Effects of air ions on some aspects of learning and memory of rats and mice. *Int. J. Biometero.* 25:53-62.

One or many animals in a cage? *Nut. Rev.* 24(1966):116-9.

Oswalt, R.M., Herrick, S., and Hale, A. 1973. Preference of rats given early temporal auditory patterns. *Percep. and Motor Skills* 36:907-10.

Ott, J.N. 1974. The importance of laboratory lighting as an experimental variable. *In: Environmental variables in animal experimentation,* ed. H. Magahlaes, 31-57. Lewisburg: Bucknell University Press.

Overmeier, J.B. 1981. Interference with coping: an animal model. *Acad. Psychol. Bull.* 3:105-18.

Parkes, A.S., and Bruce, H.M. 1961. Olfactory stimuli in mammalian reproduction. *Science.* 134:1049-54.

Paterson, D.A., and Ryder, R., eds. 1979. *Animal Rights: A symposium.* London: Centaur.

Peterson, E.A. 1980. Noise in the animal environment. *Lab. Anim. Sci.* 30:422-39.

Pettigrew, J.D., and Freedman, R.D. 1973. Visual experience without lines: effect on developing cortical neurons. *Science* 182:599-600.

Pfaff, J. 1974. Noise as an environmental problem in the animal house. *Lab. Ani.* 8:347-54.

Pfaffenberger, C.J., and Scott, J.P. 1959. The relationship between delayed socialization and trainability in guide dogs. *Jr. of Genetic Psychology* 95:145-55.

Porter, G., Lane-Petter, W., and Horne, M. 1963. Effects of strong light on breeding mice. *J. Ani. Tech. Assoc.* 14:117-9.

Pout, D.D. 1983. *Towards a philosophy of veterinary medicine.* (unpublished manuscript).

Pratt, C.L., and Sackett, G.P. 1967. Selection of social partners as a function of peer contact during rearing. *Science* 155:1133-5.

Price, E.O. 1984. Behavioral aspects of animal domestication. *Quart. Rev. Biol.* 59:1-32.

Raab, W., Bajusz, E., and Kimura, H. 1968. Isolation stress, myocardial electrolytes and epinephrine cardiotoxicity in rats. *Proc. Soc. Exp. Biol. Med.* 127:142-7.

Ranyor, T.H., Steinhagen, W.H., and Hamm, T.E., Jr. 1983. Differences in the macroenvironment of a polycarbonate caging system: bedding vs. raised wire floors. *Lab. Anim.* 17:85-89.

Rao, D.S., and Glick, B. 1977. Effect of cold exposure on the immune response of the chicken. *Poultry Science* 56(3):992-6.

Rasmussen, A.F., Jr., Marsh, J.T., and Brill, N.Q. 1957. Increased susceptibility to herpes simplex in mice subjected to avoidance learning stress or restraint. *Proc. Soc. Exp. Biol. Med.* 96:183-9.

_____. 1983. *The case for animal rights.* Berkeley: University of California Press.

Reece, W.O., and Wahlstom, J.D. 1970. Effect of feeding and excitement on the packed cell volume of dogs. *Lab. Anim. Care* 20:1114-8.

Regan, T. 1981. *All that dwell therein.* Berkeley: University of California Press.

Regan, T., and Singer, P., eds. 1976. *Animal rights and human obligations.* Englewood, NJ: Prentice-Hall.

Reite, M., Kaufman, I.C., and Pauley, J.D. 1974. Depression in infant monkeys: Physiological correlates. *Psychosomatic Medicine* 36(4):363-7.

Richter, C.P. 1957. On the phenomenon of sudden death in animals and man. *Psychosom. Med.* 19:191-8.

_____. 1971. Inborn nature of the rat's 24-hour clock. *J. Comp. and Physiol. Psychol.* 75:1-4.

_____. 1976. Artifactual seven-day cycles in spontaneous activity in wild rodents and squirrel monkeys. *J. Comp. Physiol. Psychol.* 90:572-82.

Riley, V. 1974. Biological contaminants and scientific misinterpretations. *Cancer Res.* 34:1752-4.

_____. 1975. Mouse mammary tumours: alteration of incidence as apparent function of stress. *Science* 189:465-7.

_____. 1981. Psychoneuroendocrine influence on immunocompetence and neoplasia. *Science* 212(4489):1100-9.

Riley, V., and Spackman, D. 1976. Melanoma enhancement by viral-induced stress. *Pigment Cell* 2:163-73.

_____. D. 1977. Housing stress. *Lab. Anim.* 6:16-21.

Roberts, C. 1967. *The scientific conscience.* New York: George Braziller.

Robinson, W.G., Jr., and Kuwabara, T. 1976. Light induced alterations of retinal pigment epithelium in black, albino and beige mice. *Exp. Eve. Res.* 22:549-57.

Rollin, B. 1981. *Animal rights and human morality.* New York: Prometheus.

Rollin, B. 1985. Animal pain. In: eds. M.W. Fox and L. Mickley. *Advances in Annual Welfare Science* Martinus Nijhoff. Boston.

Romero, J.A. 1976. Influence of diurnal cycles on biochemical parameters of drug sensitivity: the pineal gland as a model. *Federation Proc.* 35:1157-61.

Rose, R.M., Bernstein, I.S., and Gordon, T.P. 1975. Consequences of social conflict on plasma testosterone levels in rhesus monkeys. *Psychosom. Med.* 37:62-73.

Rose, R.M., Holaday, J.W., and Bernstein, I.S. 1971. Plasma testosterone, dominance rank and aggressive behaviour in male rhesus monkeys. *Nature* 231:366-8.

Rosellini, R.A., Binik, Y.M., and Seligman, E.P. 1976. Sudden death in the laboratory rat. *Psychosom. Med.* 38:55-8.

Rosenzweig, M.R. 1971. Effects of environment on the development of brain and behaviour. *In: The biopsychology of development,* eds. E. Toback, L. Aronson, and E. Shaw, 303-342. New York: Academic Press.

_____. 1984. Experience, memory and the brain. *Amer. Psychol.* 39:365-76.

Rosenzweig, M.R., Bennett, E.L., and Diamond, M.C. 1972. Brain changes in response to experience. *Scientific Amer.* February: 22-29.

Rosenzweig, M.R., Bennett E.L., Alberti, M., Morimoto, H., and Renner, M. 1982. Effects of differential environments and liberation on ground squirrel brain measures. *Soc. for Neurosciences Abstracts* 8:669.

Ross S., and Ross, J.G. 1949. Social facilitation of feeding of dogs. *J. Genet. Psychol.* 74:97-108.

Rowan, A. 1984. *Of mice, models and men*. Albany: State University of New York Press.

Rowell, T.E. 1967. A quantitative comparison of the behavior of a wild and caged baboon group. *Anim. Behav.* 11:235-43.

_____. 1970. Baboon menstrual cycles affected by social environment. *J. Reprod. Fert.* 21:133-41.

Russell, B. 1979. *History of western philosophy*. London: Unwin.

Russell, W.M.S., and Burch, R.L. 1959. *The principles of humane experimental technique*. London: Methuen.

Ryan, V., and Wehmer, F. 1974. Effect of postnatal litter size on adult aggression in the laboratory mouse. *Develop. Psychobiol.* 8:363-70.

Ryder, R. 1975. *Victims of science*. London: Davis-Poynter.

Sackett, G.P. 1966. Development of preference for differentially complex patterns by infant monkeys. *Psychon. Sci.* 9(6):441-2.

_____. 1968. Abnormal behavior in laboratory-reared rhesus monkeys. *In: Abnormal behavior in animals*, ed. M.W. Fox. Philadelphia: Saunders.

Sackett, G.P., Porter, M., and Holmes, H. 1965. Choice behavior in rhesus monkeys: effects of stimulation during the first months of life. *Science* 147:304-6.

Sade, D.S. 1965. Some aspects of parent-offspring and sibling relations in a group of rhesus monkeys, with a discussion of grooming. *Am. Jr. of Physical. Anthrop.* 23(1):1-17.

Saltarelli, C.G., and Coppola, C.P. 1979. Influence of visible light on organ weights of mice. *Lab. Anim. Sci.* 29:319-22.

Salzen, E.A. 1967. Imprinting in birds and primates. *Behavior* 28(3-4):232-54.

Scheline, R.R. 1973. Metabolism of foreign compounds by gastrointestinal microorganisms. *Pharmacol. Rev.* 25(Dec.):451-523.

Schumacher, S.K., and Moltz, H. 1982. The maternal pheromone of the rat as an innate stimulus for pre-weaning young. *Physiol. Behav.* 38:67-71.

Schwabe, C. 1978. *Cattle, priests and progress in medicine.* Minneapolis: University of Minnesota Press.

Schweitzer, A. 1947. *In: Albert Schweitzer, An Anthology,* ed. C.R. Joy. Boston: Beacon Press.

_____. 1961. *Out of my life and thought.* Translated by C.T. Campion. New York: Holt Rinehart and Winston.

_____. 1982. *Animals, nature and Albert Schweitzer.* ed. A.C. Free. Great Barrington: The Albert Schweitzer Center.

Scott, J.P. 1962. Critical periods in behavioral development *Science* 138(3544):949-58.

Scott, J.P., and Fuller, J.L. 1965. *Genetics and social behavior of the dog.* Chicago, Il.: University of Chicago Press.

Seligman, M.E.P. 1975. *Helplessness: On depression, development and death.* San Francisco: W.H. Freeman.

Serrano, L.J. 1971. Carbon dioxide and ammonia in mouse cages: effects of cage covers, population and activity. *Lab. Anim. Sci.* 21:75-79.

Shaefer, G.J. 1971. The effects of preweaning handling and postweaning housing on behavior and resistance to deprivation induced stress in the rat. *Develop. Psychobiol.* 5:231-8.

Shephard, P. 1978. *Thinking animals.* New York: Viking Press.

Sharpe, R.M., Choudhurg, S.A.R., and Brown, P.S. 1973. The effect of handling weanling rats on their usefulness in subsequent assays of follicle-stimulating hormone. *Lab. Anim.* 7:311-4.

Silverman, A.P. 1978. *Animal behavior in the laboratory.* New York: Pica.

_____. 1978. Rodents' defense against cigarette smoke. *Anim. Behav.* 26:1279-80.

Singer, P. 1975. *Animal liberation.* New York: Random House.

_____. 1979. *Practical ethics.* Cambridge: Cambridge University Press.

Sklar, L.S., and Anisman, H. 1979. Stress and coping factors influence tumor growth. *Science* 205:513-5.

Skolnick, P., et al. 1984. A novel chemically induced animal model of human anxiety. *Psychopathology* 17 (suppl.): 25-36.

Sloan, L.R., and Latane, B. 1974. Social deprivation and stimulus satiation in the albino rat. *J. Comp. Physiol. Psychol.* 87:1148-56.

Smotherman, W.P., Brown, C.P., and Levine, S. 1977. Maternal responsiveness following differential pup treatment and mother-pup interaction. *Horm. Behav.* 8:242-53.

Smotherman, W.P., Wiener, S.G., Mendoza, S.P., and Levine, S. 1977. Maternal pituitary-adrenal responsiveness as a function of differential treatment in pups. *Dev. Psycho biol.* 10:113-22.

Soave, O.A. 1974. Mortality of cats in research institutions: a five-year study. *Lab. Anim. Sci.* 24:99-103.

Soloman, G.F., Levine, S., and Kraft, J.H. 1968. Early experience and immunity. *Nature* 220:821-2.

Southwick, C.H. 1959. Eosinophil response of C57BR mice to behavioral disturbance. *Ecology* 40:156-7.

Spalding, J.F., Archuleta, R.F., and Holland, L.M. 1969. Influence of the visible colour spectrum on activity in mice. *Lab. Anim. Care* 19:50-4.

Spalding, J.F., Holland L.M., and Tietjen, G.L. 1969. Influence of the visible colour spectrum on activity in mice. II. Influence of sex, colour and age on activity. *Lab. Anim. Care* 19:209-13.

Stanislaw, H., and Brain, P.F. 1983. The systematic response of male mice to differential housing: a path-analytical approach. *Behavioral Process* 8:165-75.

Stara, J.F., and Berman, E. 1967. Development of an out-door feline colony for long-term studies in radiology. *Lab. Anim. Care* 17:81-4.

Stein, D.G. 1971. The effects of saline or blank injections during development of maze learning of maturity. *Devel. Psychobiol.* 5:319-22.

Steyn, D.G. 1975. The effects of captivity stress on the blood chemical values of the Chacma baboon *(Papio Ursinus)*. *Lab. Anim.* 9:111-20.

Stone, C.D. 1974. *Should trees have standing? Towards legal rights for natural objects.* Los Altos, CA: William Kaufman, Inc.

Stoskopf, M.A. 1983. The physiological effects of psychological stress. *Zoo Biol.* 2:179-190.

Stroebel, C.F. 1969. Biologic rhythm correlates of disturbed behavior in rhesus monkeys. *Bibliotheca Primatologica* 9:91-105.

Suckler, A.M., and Welfman, A.S. 1967. Effects of isolation stress on peripheral leukocytes of female albino mice. *Nature* 214:1142-3.

Taylor, G.T. 1982. Urinary odors and size protect juvenile laboratory mice from adult male attack. *Develop. Psychobiol.* 15:171-86.

Taylor, G.T. and Moore, S. 1975. Social position and competition in laboratory rats. *J. Comp. Physiol. Psychol.* 88:424-30.

Teelman, K., and Wellie, W.H. 1974. Microorganism counts and distribution patterns in air conditioned animal laboratories *Lab. Anim.* 8:109-18.

Terman, G.W., Sharit, Y., Lewis, J.W., Cannon, J.T., and Liebeskind, J.C. 1984. Intrinsic mechanisms of pain inhibition: activation by stress. *Science* 226:1270-1277.

Terry, R.L. 1970. Primate grooming as a tension reduction mechanism. *Journal of Psychology* 76:129-36.

Thompson, N.S. 1967. Primate infanticide. *Lab. Primate Newsletter* 6(3):18.

Thompson, W.R., and Heron, W. 1954. The effects of early restriction on activity in dogs. *J. Comp. Physiol. Psychol.* 47(1):77-82.

Tinklepaugh, O.L. 1928. The self-mutilation of a male Macacus rhesus monkey. *J. Mammal* 9:293-300.

Tobach, E., and Bloch, H. 1956. Effect of stress by crowding prior to and following tuberculosis infection. *Am. J. Physiol.* 187:399-402.

Tolman, C.W. 1968. The varieties of social stimulation in the feeding behavior of domestic chicks. *Behavior* 30(4):275-86.

Treadwell, P.E., and Rasmussen, A.F. 1961. Role of the adrenal in stress-induced resistance to anaphylactic shock. *J. Immun.* 87:492-7.

Tucker, M.J. 1984. Nutrition — an important factor. In: *Standards in Laboratory Animal Management,* 51-54. Potters Bar, Hertfordshire, England: Universities Federation for Animal Welfare.

Turnquist, J.E. 1983. Influence of age, sex, and caging on joint mobility in the Patus monkey *(Erythrocebus patas)*. *Am. J. Phys. Anthrop.*61:211-20.

Turpin, B. 1977. Variation of early social experience and environmental preference in rats. *J. Comp. Psychol.* 91:29-32.

Valenta, J.G., and Rigby, M.K. 1968. Discrimination of the odor of stressed rats. *Science* 161:599-601.

Vandenbergh, J.G. 1969. Male odor accelerates female sexual maturation in mice. *Endocrinology* 84(3):658-60.

Vessell, E.S., and Lang, C.M. 1976. Environmental and genetic factors affecting laboratory animals: impact on biomedical research. *Federal Proceedings* 35:1123-65.

Vessell, E.S., Lang, C.M., White, W.J., Passananti, G.T., and Tripp, S.L. 1973. Hepatic drug metabolism in rats: Impairment in a dirty environment. *Science* 179:896-7.

Visintainer, M.A., Volpicelli, J.R., and Seligman, M.E. 1982. Tumor rejection in rats after inescapable or escapable shock. *Science* 212:437-9.

Wade, N. 1976. Animal Rights: NIH sex study brings grief to New York museum. *Science* 194:162.

Wade, N. 1978. India bans monkey export: U.S. may have breached accord. *Science* 199:280.

Wagner, M.W. 1971. Laboratory living produces a different animal. *Psychologische Beitrage* 13:79-88.

Wallace, M.E. 1976. Effects of stress due to deprivation and transport in different genotypes of house mouse. *Lab. Anim.* 10:335-47.

_____. 1982. Some thoughts on the laboratory cage design process. *Int. J. Stud. Anim. Prob.* 3:234-42.

Walker, S. 1983. *Animal thought*. Boston: Routledge and Kegan Paul.

Wecker, S.C. 1963. The role of early experience in habitat selection by the prairie deer mouse *Peromyscus Manicultatus bairdi*. *Ecological Monograph* 33(4):307-25.

Weihe, W.H. 1973. The effect of temperature on the action of drugs. *In: The pharmacology of thermoregulation;* eds. P. Lomax and E. Schonbaum. Karger Basel.

_____. 1976. The effect of light on animals. *In: Control of the animal house environment,* ed. T. McSheehy. Laboratory Handbooks, no. 7. London: Laboratory Animals Ltd.

Weisbroth, S.H. 1979. Chemical contamination of beddings: problems and recommendations. *Lab. Anim.* 8:24-34.

Weiss, J., and Taylor, G.T. 1984. A new cage type for individually housed laboratory rats. *In: Standards in Laboratory Management,* 85-89. Potters Bar, Hertfordshire, England: The Universities Federation for Animal Welfare.

Weiss, J.M. 1971. Effects of coping behavior in different warning signal conditions on stress pathology. *J. Comp. Physiol. Psychol.* 77:1013.

Weiss, S.M., ed. 1971. *Perspectives in behavioral medicine.* New York: Academic Press.

Weisse, I., Stotzer, H., and Seitz, R. 1974. Age and light-dependent changes in the rat eye. *Virchows Archiv fur pathologische Anatomie und Physiologie und fur klinische Medizin* 362:145-56.

Welch, B.L., and Welch, A.S. 1966. Differential effect of chronic grouping and isolation on the metabolism of brain biogenic amines. *Fed. Proc.* 25:623.

Weltman, A.S., Sackler, A.M., and Schwartz, R. 1970. Maternal effects on behavior and white blood cells of isolated mice. *Life Science* 9(pt. 1):291-300.

Weltman, A.S., Sackler, A.M., Schwartz, R., and Owens, H. 1968. Effects of isolation stress on female albino mice. *Lab Anim. Care* 18(4):426-35.

Weltman, A.S., Sackler, A.M., and Sparber, S.B. 1962. Endocrine aspects of isolation stress on female mice. *Fed. Proc.* 21:184.

Wemelsfelder, F. 1984. Boredom in animals. *In: Advances in Animal Welfare Science,* eds. M.W. Fox and L. Mickley, 115-154. The Netherlands: Martinus Nijhoff.

Whimbey, A.E., and Denenberg, V.H. 1967. Experimental programming of life histories: the factor structure underlying experimentally created individual differences. *Behavior* 29:296-314.

Wilberg, G.S., Grice, H.C. 1965. Effect of prolonged individual caging on toxicity parameters in rats. *Food Cosmet. Toxicol.* 3:597-603.

Wilson, E.O. 1975. *Sociobiology.* Cambridge, MA: Belknap Press.

Wolfle, T. 1978. Paper presented at Amer. Assoc. *Lab. Animal Care.* Anaheim, California.

Yerkes, R.M. 1925. *Almost human.* London: Jonathan Cape.

Zimbardo, P.G., and Montgomery, K.C. 1957. Effects of 'free environment' rearing upon exploratory behavior. *Psychol. Rep.* 3:589-94.

Index

261